Confessions Diary of a Narcissist

3rd EDITION

Sam Vaknin, Ph.D.

The Author is NOT a Mental Health Professional.
The Author is certified in Counselling Techniques by Brainbench.

Editing and Design:
Lidija Rangelovska

*A Narcissus Publications Imprint
Prague & Skopje 2005*

© 1999-2013 Copyright Lidija Rangelovska

All rights reserved. This book, or any part thereof, may not be used or reproduced in any manner without written permission from:

Lidija Rangelovska – write to: malignantselflove@gmail.com

> To get FREE updates of this book JOIN the Narcissism Study List.
> To JOIN, visit our Web sites:
> http://www.narcissistic-abuse.com/narclist.html or
> http://groups.yahoo.com/group/narcissisticabuse

Visit the Author's Web site   http://samvak.tripod.com
Facebook   http://www.facebook.com/samvaknin
YouTube channel   http://www.youtube.com/samvaknin

Buy other books and video lectures about pathological narcissism and relationships with abusive narcissists and psychopaths here:

http://www.narcissistic-abuse.com/thebook.html

Created by:

Lidija Rangelovska, Skopje
REPUBLIC OF MACEDONIA

CONTENTS

Foreword

Prologue

Introduction - The Habit of Identity

The Narcissistic Personality Disorder
A Primer on Narcissism
Bibliography

The Journal of a Narcissist
How I "Became" a Narcissist
My Woman and I
Narcissist, the Machine
Looking for a Family
The Magic of My Thinking
The Music of My Emotions
I Love to be Hated
Grandiosity Deconstructed
The Entitlement of Routine
Wasted Lives
The Split Narcissist
The Anxiety of Boredom
A Great Admiration
The Narcissist in Love
Why Do I Write Poetry?

The Sad Dreams of the Narcissist

The Lonely Narcissist

The Green Eyed Narcissist

The Discontinuous Narcissist

Dr. Jackal and Mr. Hide

Portrait of the Narcissist as a Young Man

Pseudologica Fantastica

I Cannot Forgive

The Ghost in the Machine

That Thing Between a Man and a Woman...

The Malignant Optimism of the Abused

No One Counts to Ten

The Ubiquitous Narcissist

The Disappearance of the Witnesses

Physique Dysmorphique

Being There

Other People's Pain

The Weapon of Language

Studying My Death

Beware the Children

It is My World

Conspicuous Existence

The Self-Deprecating Narcissist

A Holiday Grudge

Ideas of Reference

The Delusional Way Out

The Selfish Gene - The Genetic Underpinnings of Narcissism

The Silver Pieces of the Narcissist

For the Love of God

The Opaque Mirror

Narcissistic Routines

Pathological Narcissism – A Dysfunction or a Blessing?

The Losses of the Narcissist

Transformations of Aggression

Chronos and Narcissus

The Labours of the Narcissist

The Objects of the Narcissist

To Age with Grace

Discussing Narcissism

Grandiosity Hangover and Narcissistic Baiting

The Energy of Self

Whistling in the Dark

The Embarrassing Narcissist

Grandiosity and Intimacy – The Roots of Paranoia

Losing for Granted

Facilitating Narcissism

Telling Them Apart

The Adrenaline Junkie

Narcissism and Evil

Narcissism, Substance Abuse, and Reckless Behaviours

The Cyber Narcissist

Abusing the Gullible Narcissist

The Two Loves of the Narcissist

The Professions of the Narcissist

Misdiagnosing Narcissism – The Bipolar I Disorder

Misdiagnosing Narcissism – Asperger's Disorder

Misdiagnosing Narcissism – Generalised Anxiety Disorder (GAD)

Acquired Situational Narcissism

The Narcissist's Reality Substitutes

The Narcissist's Confabulated Life

The Narcissist - From Abuse to Suicide

The Narcissist's Object Constancy

Back to La-la Land

The Cult of the Narcissist

The Pathological Charmer

The Misanthropic Altruist

Grandiosity Bubbles

The Depressive Narcissist

The Narcissist and His Friends

The Enigma of Normal People

The Intermittent Explosive Narcissist

The Narcissism of Differences Big and Small

Inner Dialog, Cognitive Deficits, and Introjects in Narcissism

The Prodigy as Narcissistic Injury

Indifference and Decompensation in Pathological Narcissism

Pathological Narcissism, Psychosis, and Delusions

The Narcissist as Eternal Child

Idealisation, Grandiosity, Cathexis, and Narcissistic Progress

The Narcissist's Inner Judge

The Author

Online Bibliography

Online index
Go here: http://samvak.tripod.com/siteindex.html

FOREWORD

Hello. Recognise me? No? Well, you see me all the time. You read my books, watch me on the big screen, feast on my art, cheer at my games, use my inventions, vote me into office, follow me into battle, take notes at my lectures, laugh at my jokes, marvel at my successes, admire my appearance, listen to my stories, discuss my politics, enjoy my music, excuse my faults, envy me my blessings. No? Still doesn't ring a bell? Well, you have seen me. Of that I am positive. In fact, if there is one thing I am absolutely sure of, it is that. You have seen me.

Perhaps our paths crossed more privately. Perhaps I am the one who came along and built you up when you were down, employed you when you needed a job, showed the way when you were lost, offered confidence when you were doubting, made you laugh when you were blue, sparked your interest when you were bored, listened to you and understood, saw you for what you really are, felt your pain and found the answers, made you want to be alive. Of course you recognise me. I am your inspiration, your role model, your saviour, your leader, your best friend, the one you aspire to emulate, the one whose favour makes you glow.

But I can also be your worst nightmare. First I build you up because that's what you need. Your skies are blue. Then, out of the blue, I start tearing you down. You let me do it because that's what you are used to. You are dumfounded. But I was wrong to take pity on you. You really ARE incompetent, disrespectful, untrustworthy, immoral, ignorant, inept, egotistical, constrained, disgusting. You are a social embarrassment, an unappreciative partner, an inadequate parent, a disappointment, a sexual flop, a financial liability.

I tell you this to your face. I must. It is my right, because it is. I behave, at home and away, in any way I want to, with total disregard for conventions, mores, or the feelings of others. It is my right, because it is. I lie to your face, without a twitch or a twitter, and there is absolutely nothing you can do about it. In fact, my lies are not lies at all. They are the truth, my truth. And you believe them, because you do, because they do not sound or feel like lies, because to do otherwise would make you question your own sanity, which you have a tendency to do anyway, because from the very beginning of our relationship you placed your trust and hopes in me, derived your energy, direction, stability, and confidence from me and from your association with me. So what's the problem if the safe haven I provide comes with a price? Surely I am worth it and then some.

Run to our friends. Go. See what that will get you. Ridicule. People believe what they see and what they see is the same wonderful me that you also saw and still do. What they also see is the very mixed up person that you have obviously become. The more you plead for understanding, the more convinced they are that the crazy one is you, the more isolated you feel, and the harder you try to make things right again, not by changing me but by accepting my criticisms and by striving to improve yourself. Could it be that you were wrong about me in the beginning? So wrong as that? How do you think our friends will react if you insist that they are also wrong about me? After all, they know that it really is you who have thwarted my progress, tainted my reputation, and thrown me off course.

I disappoint you? Outrageous! You are the one who have disappointed me. Look at all the frustrations you cause me. Lucky for you, I have an escape from all this, and fortunately my reputation provides enough insulation from the outside world so I can indulge in this escape with impunity. What escape? Why, those eruptions of rage you dread and fear. Ah, it feels so good to rage. It is the expression of and the confirmation of my power over you, my absolute superiority. Lying feels good too, for the same reason, but nothing compares to the pleasure of exploding for no material reason and venting my anger with total abandon, all the time a spectator at my own show and at your helplessness, pain, fear, frustration, and dependence.

In fact my raging is precisely what allows me to stay with you. Go ahead. Tell our friends about it. See if they can imagine what it's like, let alone believe it. The more outrageous the things you say about me, the more convinced they are that it is you who have taken a turn for the worse. And don't expect much more from your therapist either. You may tell him this or that, but what he sees when I visit him is something quite different. So what's the therapist to believe? After all, it was you who came for help. No! That's what this is all about. No! That simple two-letter word that, regardless of how bad I am, you simply cannot say. Who knows? You might even acquire some of my behaviour yourself.

But you know what? This may come as a shock, but I can also be my own worst nightmare. I can and I am. You see, at heart my life is nothing more than illusion-clad confusion. I have no idea why I do what I do, nor do I care to find out. In fact, the mere notion of asking the question is so repulsive to me that I employ all of my resources to repel it. I reconstruct facts, fabricate illusions, act them out, and thus create my own reality. It is a precarious state of existence indeed, so I am careful to include enough demonstrable truth in my illusions to ensure their credibility. And I am forever testing that credibility on you and on the reactions of others.

Fortunately my real attributes and accomplishments are in sufficient abundance to fuel my illusions seemingly forever. And modern society, blessed/cursed modern society, values most what I do best and thus serves as my accomplice. Even I get lost in my own illusions, swept away by my own magic.

So, not to worry if you still do not recognise me. I don't recognise me either. In fact, I am not really sure who I am. That's probably a question you never ask of yourself. Yet I wonder about it all the time. Perhaps I am not too different from everyone else, just better. After all, that's the feedback I get. My admirers certainly wish they were me. They just don't have the gifts I have, nor the courage I have to express them. That's what the universe is telling me.

Then again THE universe or MY universe? As long as the magic of my illusions works on me too, there really is no need for distinction. All I need is an abundant fan club to stay on top of it all. So I am constantly taking fan club inventory, testing the loyalty of present members with challenges of abuse, writing off defectors with total indifference, and scouting the landscape for new recruits. Do you see my dilemma? I use people who are dependent on me to keep my illusions alive. So really it is I who am dependent on them.

Even the rage, that orgasmic release of pain and anger, works better with an audience. On some level I am aware of my illusions, but to admit that would spoil the magic. And that I couldn't bear. So I proclaim that what I do is of no consequence and no different from what others do, and thus I create an illusion about my creating illusions.

So, no, I don't recognise me any better than you do. I wouldn't dare. Like my fans, I marvel at my own being. Then again, sometimes I wish that I were not the person I am. You find that confusing? How do you think it makes me feel? I need my own magic to stay afloat. Sometimes others like me recruit me into their magic. But that's ok. As long as we feed off of each other, who's the worse for wear? It only confirms my illusion about my illusions: that I am no different from most other people, just a bit better.

But I AM different and we both know it, although neither one of us dares to admit it. Therein lies the root of my hostility. I tear you down because in reality I am envious of you BECAUSE I am different. At some haunting level I see my magic for what it is and realise that people around me function just fine WITHOUT any "magic".

This terrifies me. Panic stricken, I try all my old tricks: displays of my talents, unnecessary deceptions, self-serving distortions, skilful seductions, ludicrous projections, frightening rages, whatever. Normally, that works. But if it fails, watch out. Like a solar-powered battery in darkness, my fire goes out and I cease to exist. Destitution sets in.

That is the key to understanding me. Most people strive for goals and feel good when they approach them. They move toward something positive. I move in the same direction but my movement is away from something negative. That's why I never stop, am never content, no matter what I achieve. That negative thing seems to follow me around like a shadow. I dowse myself in light and it fades, but that's all it does. Exhausted, I ultimately succumb to it, again and again.

Where did it come from, this negativity? Probably from before I learned to talk. When you were exploring your world for the first time, with the usual little toddler mishaps, your mother kept a careful eye on you, intervened when she saw you heading for danger, and comforted you when you made a mistake, even if you cried.

Well, that's not how it was for me. My mother's expectations of me were much higher. Mistakes were mistakes and crying was not the way to get her approval. That required being perfect, so that's exactly what I became. Not the little awkward toddler that I was, but my mother's model child. Not the brave and curious little person that I really was, but the fearful personification of my mother's ideal.

What you were experiencing through your little mishaps and mistakes were small doses of shame. What you were learning from your quick recoveries was shame repair. At first your mother did most of the repairing. Through repetition, you gradually learned how to do it by yourself. Shame repair brain circuitry was being laid down that would carry you for the rest of your life. I had no such luck. I simply did not acquire that skill when nature had intended my brain to acquire it. No one enjoys shame. But most people can deal with it. Not me. I fear it the way most people fear snakes.

How many others like me are there? More than you might think, and our numbers are increasing. Take twenty people off the street and you will find one whose mind ticks so much like mine that you could consider us clones. Impossible, you say. It is simply not possible for that many people – highly accomplished, respected, and visible people – to be out there replacing reality with illusions, each in the same way and for reasons they know not. It is simply not possible for so many shame-phobic robots of havoc and chaos, as I describe myself, to function daily midst other educated, intelligent, and experienced individuals, and pass for normal. It is simply not possible for such an aberration of human cognition and behaviour to infiltrate and infect the population in such numbers, virtually undetected by the radar of mental health professionals. It is simply not possible for so much visible positive to contain so much concealed negative. It is simply not possible.

But it is. That is the enlightenment of "Narcissism Revisited" by Sam Vaknin. Sam is himself one such clone. What distinguishes him is his uncharacteristic courage to confront, and his uncanny understanding of, that which makes us tick, himself included. Not only does Sam dare ask and then answer the question we clones avoid like the plague, he does so with relentless, laser-like precision. Read his book. Take your seat at the double-headed microscope and let Sam guide you through the dissection.

Like a brain surgeon operating on himself, Sam explores and exposes the alien among us, hoping beyond hope for a resectable tumour but finding instead each and every cell teaming with the same resistant virus. The operation is long and tedious, and at times frightening and hard to believe. Read on. The parts exposed are as they are, despite what may seem hyperbolic or farfetched. Their validity might not hit home until later, when coupled with memories of past events and experiences.

I am, as I said, my own worst nightmare. True, the world is replete with my contributions, and I am lots of fun to be around. And true, most contributions like mine are not the result of troubled souls. But many more than you might want to believe are. And if by chance you get caught in my web, I can make your life a living hell. But remember this. I am in that web too. The difference between you and me is that you can get out.

**Ken Heilbrunn, M.D.
Seattle, Washington, USA
ksbrunn@aol.com**

Return

PROLOGUE

I met Sam on an Internet list about 5 years ago. I'd been studying personality disorders and narcissism at the time, looking at it from Jungian, spiritual, and literary points of view as well as psychological, and I was just not too terribly impressed with the psychological state of the art on those topics.

Sam invited me to visit his site, and without knowing him from Adam, I just wrongly assumed that he was one more run-of-the-mill shrink writing standard stuff about narcissism. I replied something like, "No, that won't be necessary, I am the only person in the whole world who truly understands narcissism" – a supremely narcissistic reply, in other words.

I went ahead and visited his site anyway, and was most impressed. I e-mailed him back then, and told him of my mistake, and said I thought his work was way ahead of the standard psychological writings on the subject. You just can't understand something as complex and subtle as narcissism without integrating your feelings, your soul and your heart with it, and the supposedly "objective" stuff written by professionals was just missing key dimensions that made it flat and cold "dead information" instead of "living knowledge".

Sam's writing on the subject pulsated with heat, it ran red with blood, it crackled with flames of passion, it cried out in agony. Sam KNEW narcissism like the fish knows the water and the eagle knows the air, because he had lived it. He described it's small insignificant currents, he knew what it does when the weather changes, he knew exactly what happens to little frogs, snakes and crickets whenever they fall into the stream. Most psychologists only know ABOUT narcissism – Sam UNDERSTANDS it.

Paul Shirley, MSW

Return

INTRODUCTION

The Habit of Identity

Warning and Disclaimer
The contents of this book are not meant to substitute for professional help and counselling. The readers are discouraged from using it for diagnostic or therapeutic ends. The diagnosis and treatment of the Narcissistic Personality Disorder can only be done by professionals specifically trained and qualified to do so – which the author is not. The author is NOT a mental health professional, though he is certified in Mental Health Counselling Techniques.

In a famous experiment, students were asked to take a lemon home and to get used to it. Three days later, they were able to single out "their" lemon from a pile of rather similar ones. They seemed to have bonded. Is this the true meaning of love, bonding, coupling? Do we simply get used to other human beings, pets, or objects?

Habit forming in humans is reflexive. We change ourselves and our environment in order to attain maximum comfort and well being. It is the effort that goes into these adaptive processes that forms a habit. The habit is intended to prevent us from constant experimenting and risk taking. The greater our well being, the better we function and the longer we survive.

Actually, when we get used to something or to someone – we get used to ourselves. In the object of the habit we see a part of our history, all the time and effort we had put into it. It is an encapsulated version of our acts, intentions, emotions and reactions. It is a mirror reflecting that part in us which formed the habit in the first place. Hence, the feeling of comfort: we really feel comfortable with our own selves through the agency of our habitual objects.

Because of this, we tend to confuse habits with identity. When asked WHO they are, most people resort to communicating their habits. They describe their work, their loved ones, their pets, their hobbies, or their material possessions. Yet, surely, all of these do not constitute identity! Removing them does not change it. They are habits and they make people comfortable and relaxed. But they are not part of one's identity in the truest, deepest sense.

Still, it is this simple mechanism of deception that binds people together. A mother feels that her offspring are part of her identity because she is so used to them that her well being depends on their existence and availability. Thus, any threat to her children is perceived by her as a threat to her own Self. Her reaction is, therefore, strong and enduring and can be recurrently elicited.

The truth, of course, is that her children ARE a part of her identity in a superficial manner. Removing them will make her a different person, but only in the shallow, phenomenological sense of the word. Her deep-set, true identity will not change as a result. Children do die at times and the mother does go on living, essentially unchanged.

But what is this kernel of identity that I am referring to? This immutable entity which is who we are and what we are and which, ostensibly, is not influenced by the death of our loved ones? What can resist the breakdown of habits that die hard?

It is our personality. This elusive, loosely interconnected, interacting, pattern of reactions to our changing environment. Like the Brain, it is difficult to define or to capture. Like the Soul, many believe that it does not exist, that it is a fictitious convention.

Yet, we know that we do have a personality. We feel it, we experience it. It sometimes encourages us to do things – at other times, it prevents us from doing them. It can be supple or rigid, benign or malignant, open or closed. Its power lies in its looseness. It is able to combine, recombine and permute in hundreds of unforeseeable ways. It metamorphoses and the constancy of these changes is what gives us a sense of identity.

Actually, when the personality is rigid to the point of being unable to change in reaction to shifting circumstances – we say that it is disordered. One has a personality disorder when one's habits substitute for one's identity. Such a person identifies himself with his environment, taking behavioural, emotional, and cognitive cues exclusively from it. His inner world is, so to speak, vacated, his True Self merely an apparition.

Such a person is incapable of loving and of living. He is incapable of loving because to love another one must first love oneself. And, in the absence of a Self that is impossible. And, in the long-term, he is incapable of living because life is a struggle towards multiple goals, a striving, a drive at something. In other words: life is change. He who cannot change, cannot live.

Sam Vaknin

Return

Diary of a Narcissist

The Narcissistic Personality Disorder

A Primer on Narcissism

What is Narcissism?

A pattern of traits and behaviours which signify infatuation and obsession with one's self to the exclusion of all others and the egotistic and ruthless pursuit of one's gratification, dominance and ambition.

- Most narcissists (50-75%, according to the DSM-IV-TR) are men.
- The *Narcissistic Personality Disorder (NPD)* is one of a "family" of personality disorders (known as "Cluster B"). Other members of Cluster B are Borderline PD, Antisocial PD and Histrionic PD.
- NPD is often diagnosed with other mental health disorders ("co-morbidity") – or with substance abuse and impulsive and reckless behaviours ("dual diagnosis").
- NPD is new (1980) mental health category in the Diagnostic and Statistics Manual (DSM).
- There is only scant research regarding narcissism. But what there is has not demonstrated any ethnic, social, cultural, economic, genetic, or professional predilection to NPD.
- It is estimated that 0.7-1% of the general population suffer from NPD.
- Pathological narcissism was first described in detail by Freud. Other major contributors are: Klein, Horney, Kohut, Kernberg, Millon, Roningstam, Gunderson, Hare.
- The onset of narcissism is in infancy, childhood and early adolescence. It is commonly attributed to childhood abuse and trauma inflicted by parents, authority figures, or even peers.
- There is a whole range of narcissistic reactions – from the mild, reactive and transient to the permanent personality disorder.
- Narcissistic Supply is outside attention – usually positive (adulation, affirmation, fame, celebrity) – used by the narcissist to regulate his labile sense of self-worth.
- Narcissists are either "cerebral" (derive their Narcissistic Supply from their intelligence or academic achievements) or

- "somatic" (derive their Narcissistic Supply from their physique, exercise, physical or sexual prowess and romantic or physical "conquests").
- Narcissists are either "classic" [see definition below] or they are "compensatory", or "inverted" [see definitions here: "The Inverted Narcissist"].
- The classic narcissist is self-confident, the compensatory narcissist covers up in his haughty behaviour for a deep-seated deficit in self-esteem, and the inverted type is a co-dependent who caters to the emotional needs of a classic narcissist.
- NPD is treated in talk therapy (psychodynamic or cognitive-behavioural). The prognosis for an adult narcissist is poor, though his adaptation to life and to others can improve with treatment. Medication is applied to side-effects and behaviours (such as mood or affect disorders and obsession-compulsion) – usually with some success.

The ICD-10, the International Classification of Mental and Behavioural Disorders, published by the World Health Organisation in Geneva [1992] regards Narcissistic Personality Disorder (NPD) as *"a personality disorder that fits none of the specific rubrics"*. It relegates it to the category "Other Specific Personality Disorders" together with the eccentric, "haltlose", immature, passive-aggressive, and psychoneurotic personality disorders and types.

The American Psychiatric Association, based in Washington D.C., USA, publishes the Diagnostic and Statistical Manual of Mental Disorders, fourth edition, Text Revision (DSM-IV-TR) [2000] where it provides the diagnostic criteria for the Narcissistic Personality Disorder.

The DSM defines NPD as *"an all-pervasive pattern of grandiosity (in fantasy or behaviour), need for admiration or adulation and lack of empathy, usually beginning by early adulthood and present in various contexts."*

The DSM specifies nine diagnostic criteria. For NPD to be diagnosed, five (or more) of these criteria must be met.

[In the text below, I have proposed modifications to the language of these criteria to incorporate current knowledge about this disorder. My modifications appear in *italics*.]

[My amendments do not constitute a part of the text of the DSM-IV-TR, nor is the American Psychiatric Association (APA) associated with them in any way.]

[Click here to download a bibliography of the studies and research regarding the Narcissistic Personality Disorder (NPD) on which I based my proposed revisions.]

**Proposed Amended Criteria for
the Narcissistic Personality Disorder**

- Feels grandiose and self-important (e.g., exaggerates accomplishments, talents, *skills, contacts, and personality traits to the point of lying,* demands to be recognised as superior without commensurate achievements);
- Is *obsessed* with fantasies of unlimited success, *fame, fearsome* power or *omnipotence, unequalled* brilliance (*the cerebral narcissist*), *bodily* beauty *or sexual performance* (*the somatic narcissist*), or ideal, *everlasting, all-conquering* love *or passion*;
- Firmly convinced that he or she is unique and, being special, can only be understood by, *should only be treated by*, or associate with, other special or unique, or high-status people (or institutions);
- Requires excessive admiration, *adulation, attention and affirmation – or, failing that, wishes to be feared and to be notorious* (Narcissistic Supply);
- Feels entitled. *Demands automatic and full compliance* with his or her unreasonable expectations for special and *favourable priority* treatment;
- Is "interpersonally exploitative", i.e., *uses* others to achieve his or her own ends;
- *Devoid* of empathy. Is *unable* or unwilling to identify with, *acknowledge, or accept* the feelings, needs, *preferences, priorities, and choices* of others;
- Constantly envious of others *and seeks to hurt or destroy the objects of his or her frustration. Suffers from persecutory (paranoid) delusions as he or she* believes that they feel the same about him or her *and are likely to act similarly*;
- Behaves arrogantly and haughtily. *Feels superior, omnipotent, omniscient, invincible, immune, "above the law", and omnipresent (magical thinking). Rages when frustrated, contradicted, or confronted* by people he or she considers inferior to him or her and unworthy.

Return

Bibliography

1. Alford, C. Fred. Narcissism: Socrates, the Frankfurt School and Psychoanalytic Theory. New Haven and London, Yale University Press, 1988
2. Devereux, George. Basic Problems of Ethno-Psychiatry. University of Chicago Press, 1980
3. Fairbairn, W. R. D. An Object Relations Theory of the Personality. New York, Basic Books, 1954
4. Freud S. Three Essays on the Theory of Sexuality [1905]. Standard Edition of the Complete Psychological Works of Sigmund Freud. Vol. 7. London, Hogarth Press, 1964
5. Freud, S. On Narcissism. Standard Ed. Vol. 14, pp. 73-107
6. Goldman, Howard H. (Ed.). Review of General Psychiatry. 4th Ed. London, Prentice Hall International, 1995
7. Golomb, Elan. Trapped in the Mirror: Adult Children of Narcissists in Their Struggle for Self. Quill, 1995
8. Greenberg, Jay R. and Mitchell, Stephen A. Object Relations in Psychoanalytic Theory. Cambridge, Mass., Harvard University Press, 1983
9. Grunberger, Bela. Narcissism: Psychoanalytic Essays. New York, International Universities Press, 1979
10. Guntrip, Harry. Personality Structure and Human Interaction. New York, International Universities Press, 1961
11. Horowitz M. J. Sliding Meanings: A Defence against Threat in Narcissistic Personalities. International Journal of Psychoanalytic Psychotherapy, 1975; 4:167
12. Horowitz M. J. Stress Response Syndromes: PTSD, Grief and Adjustment Disorders. 3rd Ed. New York, NY University Press, 1998
13. Jacobson, Edith. The Self and the Object World. New York, International Universities Press, 1964
14. Jung, C.G. Collected Works. G. Adler, M. Fordham and H. Read (Eds.). 21 volumes. Princeton University Press, 1960-1983

15. Kernberg O. Borderline Conditions and Pathological Narcissism. New York, Jason Aronson, 1975
16. Klein, Melanie. The Writings of Melanie Klein. Roger Money-Kyrle (Ed.). 4 Vols. New York, Free Press, 1964-75
17. Kohut H. The Chicago Institute Lectures 1972-1976. Marian and Paul Tolpin (Eds.). Analytic Press, 1998
18. Kohut M. The Analysis of the Self. New York, International Universities Press, 1971
19. Lasch, Christopher. The Culture of Narcissism. New York, Warner Books, 1979
20. Levine, J. D., and Weiss, Rona H. The Dynamics and Treatment of Alcoholism. Jason Aronson, 1994
21. Lowen, Alexander. Narcissism: Denial of the True Self. Touchstone Books, 1997
22. Millon, Theodore (and Roger D. Davis, contributor). Disorders of Personality: DSM-IV and Beyond. 2nd ed. New York, John Wiley and Sons, 1995
23. Millon, Theodore. Personality Disorders in Modern Life. New York, John Wiley and Sons, 2000
24. Riso, Don Richard. Personality Types: Using the Enneagram for Self-Discovery. Boston: Houghton Mifflin 1987
25. Roningstam, Elsa F. (Ed.). Disorders of Narcissism: Diagnostic, Clinical, and Empirical Implications. American Psychiatric Press, 1998
26. Rothstein, Arnold. The Narcissistic Pursuit of Reflection. 2nd revised Ed. New York, International Universities Press, 1984
27. Schwartz, Lester. Narcissistic Personality Disorders – A Clinical Discussion. Journal of American Psychoanalytic Association – 22 [1974]: 292-305
28. Salant-Schwartz, Nathan. Narcissism and Character Transformation. Inner City Books, 1985 – pp. 90-91
29. Stern, Daniel. The Interpersonal World of the Infant: A View from Psychoanalysis and Developmental Psychology. New York, Basic Books, 1985
30. Vaknin, Sam. Malignant Self Love – Narcissism Revisited. Skopje and Prague, Narcissus Publications, 2003
31. Zweig, Paul. The Heresy of Self-Love: A Study of Subversive Individualism. New York, Basic Books, 1968

Return

Diary of a Narcissist

The Journal of a Narcissist

How I "Became" a Narcissist

I remember the day I died. Almost did. We were in a tour of Jerusalem. Our guide was the Deputy Chief Warden. We wore our Sunday best suits – stained dark blue, abrasive jeans shirts tucked in tattered trousers. I could think of nothing but Nomi. She left me two months after my incarceration. She said that my brain did not excite her as it used to. We were sitting on what passed as a grassy knoll in prison and she was marble cold and firm. This is why, during the trip to Jerusalem, I planned to grab the Warden's gun and kill myself.

Death has an asphyxiating, all-pervasive presence and I could hardly breathe. It passed and I knew that I had to find out real quick what was wrong with me – or else.

How I obtained access to psychology books and to Internet from the inside of one of Israel's more notorious jails, is a story unto itself. In this film noire, this search of my dark self, I had very little to go on, no clues and no Della Street by my side. I had to let go – yet I never did and did not know how.

I forced myself to remember, threatened by the immanent presence of the Grim Reaper. I fluctuated between shattering flashbacks and despair. I wrote cathartic short fiction. I published it. I remember holding myself, white knuckles clasping an aluminium sink, about to throw up as I am flooded with images of violence between my parents, images that I repressed to oblivion. I cried a lot, uncontrollably, convulsively, gazing through tearful veils at the monochrome screen.

The exact moment I found a description of the Narcissistic Personality Disorder is etched in my mind. I felt engulfed in word-amber, encapsulated and frozen. It was suddenly very quiet and very still. I met myself. I saw the enemy and it was I.

The article was long winded and full of references to scholars I never heard of before: Kernberg, Kohut, Klein. It was a foreign language that resounded, like a forgotten childhood memory. It was I to the last repellent details, described in uncanny accuracy:

grandiose fantasies of brilliance and perfection, sense of entitlement without commensurate achievements, rage, exploitation of others, lack of empathy.

I had to learn more. I knew I had the answer. All I had to do was find the right questions.

That day was miraculous. Many strange and wonderful things happened. I saw people – I SAW them. And I had a glimmer of understanding regarding my self – this disturbed, sad, neglected, insecure and ludicrous things that passed for me.

It was the first important realisation – there were two of us. I was not alone inside my body.

One was an extrovert, facile, gregarious, attention-consuming, adulation-dependent, charming, ruthless and manic-depressive being. The other was schizoid, shy, dependent, phobic, suspicious, pessimistic, dysphoric and helpless creature – a kid, really.

I began to observe these two alternating. The first (whom I called Ninko Leumas – an anagram of the Hebrew spelling of my name) would invariably appear to interact with people. It didn't feel like putting a mask on or like I had another personality. It was just like I am MORE me. It was a caricature of the TRUE me, of Shmuel.

Shmuel hated people. He felt inferior, physically repulsive and socially incompetent. Ninko also hated people. He held them in contempt. THEY were inferior to his superior qualities and skills. He needed their admiration but he resented this fact and he accepted their offerings condescendingly.

As I pieced my fragmented and immature self together I began to see that Shmuel and Ninko were flip sides of the SAME coin. Ninko seemed to be trying to compensate Shmuel, to protect him, to isolate him from hurt and to exact revenge whenever he failed. At this stage I was not sure who was manipulating who and I did not have the most rudimentary acquaintance with this vastly rich continent I discovered inside me.

But that was only the beginning.

Return

My Woman and I

No woman has ever wanted to have a child with me. It is very telling. Women have children even with incarcerated murderers. I know because I have been to jail with these people. But no woman has ever felt the urge to perpetuate US - the we-ness of she and I.

I was married once and almost married twice but women are very hesitant with me. They definitely do not want anything binding. It is as though they want to maintain all routes of escape clear and available. It is a reversal of the prevailing myth about non-committal males and women huntresses.

But no one wants to hunt a predator.

It is an arduous and eroding task to live with me. I am atrabilious, infinitely pessimistic, bad-tempered, paranoid and sadistic in an absent-minded and indifferent manner. My daily routine is a rigmarole of threats, complaints, hurts, eruptions, moodiness and rage. I rail against slights true and imagined. I alienate people. I humiliate them because this is my only weapon against the humiliation of their indifference to me.

Gradually, wherever I am, my social circle dwindles and then vanishes. Every narcissist is also a schizoid, to some extent. A schizoid is not a misanthrope. He does not necessarily hate people – he simply does not need them. He regards social interactions as a nuisance to be minimised.

I am torn between my need to obtain Narcissistic Supply (the monopoly on which is held by human beings) - and my fervent wish to be left alone. This wish, in my case, is peppered with contempt and feelings of superiority.

There are fundamental conflicts between dependence and contempt, neediness and devaluation, seeking and avoiding, turning on the charm to attract adulation and being engulfed by wrathful reactions to the most minuscule "provocations". These conflicts lead to rapid cycling between gregariousness and self-imposed ascetic seclusion.

Such an unpredictable but always bilious and festering atmosphere is hardly conducive to love or sex. Gradually, both become extinct. My relationships are hollowed out. Imperceptibly, I switch to a-sexual co-habitation.

But the vitriolic environment that I create is only one hand of the equation. The other hand is the woman herself.

I am heterosexual, so I am attracted to women. But I am simultaneously repelled, horrified, bewitched and provoked by them. I seek to frustrate and humiliate them. Psychodynamically, I am probably visiting upon them my mother's sin – but I think such an instant explanation does the subject great injustice.

Most narcissists I know – myself included – are misogynists. Their sexual and emotional lives are perturbed and chaotic. They are unable to love in any true sense of the word – nor are they capable of developing any measure of intimacy. Lacking empathy, they are incapable of offering to the partner emotional sustenance.

I have been asked many times if I miss loving, whether I would have liked to love and if I am angry with my parents for crippling me so. There is no way I can answer these questions. I never loved. I do not know what is it that I am missing. Observing it from the outside, love seems to me to be a risible pathology. But I am only guessing.

I am not angry for being unable to love. I equate love with weakness. I hate being weak and I hate and despise weak people (and, by implication, the very old and the very young). I do not tolerate stupidity, disease and dependence – and love seems to encompass all three. These are not sour grapes. I really feel this way.

I am an angry man – but not because I never experienced love and probably never will. No, I am angry because I am not as powerful, awe inspiring and successful as I wish to be and as I deserve to be. Because my daydreams refuse so stubbornly to come true. Because I am my worst enemy. And because, in my unmitigated paranoia, I see adversaries plotting everywhere and feel discriminated against and contemptuously ignored. I am angry because I know that I am sick and that my sickness prevents me from realising even a small fraction of my potential.

My life is a mess as a direct result of my disorder. I am a vagabond, avoiding my creditors, besieged by hostile media in more than one country, hated by one and all. Granted, my disorder also gave me "Malignant Self Love", the rage to write as I do (I am referring to my political essays), a fascinating life and insights a healthy man is unlikely to attain. But I find myself questioning the trade-off ever more often.

But at other times, I imagine myself healthy and I shudder. I cannot conceive of a life in one place with one set of people, doing the same thing, in the same field with one goal within a decades-old game plan. To me, this is death. I am most terrified of boredom and whenever faced with its haunting prospect, I inject drama into my life, or even danger. This is the only way I feel alive.

I guess all the above portrays a lonely wolf. I am a shaky platform, indeed, on which to base a family, or future plans. I know as much. So, I pour wine to both of us, sit back and watch with awe and with amazement the delicate contours of my female partner. I savour every minute. In my experience, it might well be the last.

Return

Narcissist, the Machine

I always think of myself as a machine. I say to myself things like "You have an amazing brain" or "You are not functioning today, your efficiency is low". I measure things, I constantly compare performance. I am acutely aware of time and how it is utilised. There is a meter in my head, it ticks and tocks, a metronome of self-reproach and grandiose assertions. I talk to myself in third person singular. It lends objectivity to what I think, as though it comes from an external source, from someone else. That low is my self-esteem that, to be trusted, I have to disguise myself, to hide myself from myself. It is the pernicious and all-pervasive art of unbeing.

I like to think about myself in terms of automata. There is something so aesthetically compelling in their precision, in their impartiality, in their harmonious embodiment of the abstract. Machines are so powerful and so emotionless, not prone to be hurting weaklings like me. Machines don't bleed. Often I find myself agonising over the destruction of a laptop in a movie, as its owner is blown to smithereens as well. Machines are my folk and kin. They are my family. They allow me the tranquil luxury of unbeing.

And then there is data. My childhood dream of unlimited access to information has come true and I am the happiest for it. I have been blessed by the Internet. Information was power and not only figuratively.

Information was the dream, reality the nightmare. My knowledge was my flying info-carpet. It took me away from the slums of my childhood, from the atavistic social milieu of my adolescence, from the sweat and stench of the army – and into the perfumed existence of international finance and media exposure.

So, even in the darkness of my deepest valleys I was not afraid. I carried with me my metal constitution, my robot countenance, my superhuman knowledge, my inner timekeeper, my theory of morality and my very own divinity – myself.

When N. left me, I discovered the hollowness of it all. It was the first time that I experienced my True Self consciously. It was a void, annulment, a gaping abyss, almost audible, an hellish iron fist gripping, tearing my chest apart. It was horror. A transubstantiation of my blood and flesh into something primordial and screaming.

It was then that I came to realised that my childhood was difficult. At the time, it seemed to me to be as natural as sunrise and as inevitable as pain.

But in hindsight, it was devoid of emotional expression and abusive to the extreme. I was not sexually abused – but I was physically, verbally and psychologically tormented for 16 years without one minute of respite.

Thus, I grew up to be a narcissist, a paranoid and a schizoid. At least that's what I wanted to believe. Narcissists have alloplastic defences – they tend to blame others for their troubles. In this case, psychological theory itself was on my side. The message was clear: people who are abused in their formative years (0-6) tend to adapt by developing personality disorders, amongst them the Narcissistic Personality Disorder. I was absolved, an unmitigated relief.

I want to tell you how much I am afraid of pain. To me, it is a pebble in Indra's Net – lift it and the whole net revives. My pains do not come isolated – they live in families of anguish, in tribes of hurt, whole races of agony. I cannot experience them insulated from their kin. They rush to drown me through the demolished floodgates of my childhood. These floodgates, my inner dams – this is my narcissism, there to contain the ominous onslaught of stale emotions, repressed rage, a child's injuries.

Pathological narcissism is useful – this is why it is so resilient and resistant to change. When it is "invented" by the tormented individual – it enhances his functionality and makes life bearable for him. Because it is so successful, it attains religious dimensions – it become rigid, doctrinaire, automatic and ritualistic. In other words, it becomes a PATTERN of behaviour.

I am a narcissist and I can feel this rigidity as though it were an outer shell. It constrains me. It limits me. It is often prohibitive and inhibitive. I am afraid to do certain things. I am injured or humiliated when forced to engage in certain activities. I react with rage when the mental edifice supporting my disorder is subjected to scrutiny and criticism – no matter how benign.

Narcissism is ridiculous. I am pompous, grandiose, repulsive and contradictory. There is a serious mismatch between who I really am and what I really achieved – and how I feel myself to be. It is not that I THINK that I am far superior to other humans intellectually. Thought implies volition – and willpower is not involved here. My superiority is ingrained in me, it is a part of my every mental cell, an all-pervasive sensation, an instinct and a drive. I feel that I am entitled to special treatment and outstanding consideration because I am such a unique specimen. I know this to be true – the same way you know that you are surrounded by air. It is an integral part of my identity. More integral to me than my body.

This opens a gap – rather, an abyss – between me and other humans. Because I consider myself so special, I have no way of knowing how it is to be THEM.

In other words, I cannot empathise. Can you empathise with an ant? Empathy implies identity or equality, both abhorrent to me. And being so inferior, people are reduced to cartoonish, two-dimensional representations of functions. They become instrumental or useful or functional or entertaining – rather than loving or interacting emotionally. It leads to ruthlessness and exploitativeness. I am not a bad person – actually, I am a good person. I have helped people – many people – all my life. So, I am not evil. What I am is indifferent. I couldn't care less. I help people because it is a way to secure attention, gratitude, adulation and admiration. And because it is the fastest and surest way to get rid of them and their incessant nagging.

I realise these unpleasant truths cognitively – but there is no corresponding emotional reaction (emotional correlate) to this realisation.

There is no resonance. It is like reading a boring users' manual pertaining to a computer you do not even own. It is like watching a movie about yourself. There is no insight, no assimilation of these truths. When I write this now, I feel like writing the script of a mildly interesting docudrama.

It is not I.

Still, to further insulate myself from the improbable possibility of confronting these facts – the gulf between reality and grandiose fantasy (the Grandiosity Gap, in my writings) – I came up with the most elaborate mental structure, replete with mechanisms, levers, switches and flickering alarm lights. My narcissism does two things for me – it always did:

1. Isolate me from the pain of facing reality;
2. Allow me to inhabit the fantasyland of ideal perfection and brilliance.

These once-vital function are bundled in what is known to psychologists as my "False Self".

Return

Looking for a Family

I don't have a family of my own. I don't have children and marriage is a remote prospect. Families, to me, are hotbeds of misery, breeding grounds of pain and scenes of violence and hate. I do not wish to create my own.

Even as adolescent I was looking for another family. Social workers offered to find foster families. I spent my vacations begging Kibbutzim to accept me as an underage member. It pained my parents and my mother expressed her agony the only way she knew how – by abusing me physically and psychologically. I threatened to have her committed. It was not a nice place, our family. But in its thwarted way, it was the only place. It had the warmth of a familiar disease.

My father always said to me that their responsibilities end when I am 18. But they couldn't wait that long and signed me to the army a year earlier, though at my behest. I was 17 and terrified witless. After a while my father told me not to visit them again – so the army became my second, nay, my only home. When I was hospitalised for a fortnight with kidney disease, my parents came to see me only once, bearing stale chocolates. A person never forgets such slights – they go to the very core of one's identity and self-worth.

I dream about them often, my family whom I haven't seen for five years now. My little brothers and one sister, all huddled around me listening cravingly to my stories of fantasy and black humour. We are all so white and luminescent and innocent. In the background is the music of my childhood, the quaintness of the furniture, my life in sepia colour. I remember every detail in stark relief and I know how different it could all have been. I know how happy we could all have been. I dream about my mother and my father. A great vortex of sadness threatens to suck me in. I wake up suffocating.

I spent the first vacation in jail – voluntarily – locked up in a sizzling barrack writing a children's story. I refused to go "home".

Everyone did, though – so, I was the only prisoner in jail. I had it all to myself and I was content in the quite manner of the dead. I was to divorce N. in a few weeks. Suddenly, I felt unshackled, ethereal. I guess that, at the bottom of it all, I do not want to live. They took away from me the will to live. If I allow myself to feel – this is what I overwhelmingly experience – my own non-existence. It is an ominous, nightmarish sensation which I am fighting to avoid even at the cost of forgoing my emotions. I deny myself three times for fear of being crucified. There is in me a deeply repressed seething ocean of melancholy, gloom and self-worthlessness awaiting to engulf me, to lull me into oblivion. My shield is my narcissism. I let the medusas of my soul be petrified by their own reflections in it.

Return

The Magic of My Thinking

When deprived of Narcissistic Supply – Primary AND Secondary – I feel annulled. It is a strange sensation, I am not sure it can be described.

Words, after all, do exist. But it is very much like being hollowed out, mentally disembowelled or watching oneself die. It is a cosmic evaporation, disintegrating into molecules of terrified anguish, helplessly and inexorably.

I lived through this twice and I would do anything not to go through it again. It is by far the most nightmarish experience I ever had in a rather febrile life.

I want to tell you now what happens to narcissists when deprived of Narcissistic Supply of any kind (Secondary or Primary). Perhaps it will make it easier for you to understand why the narcissist pursues Narcissistic Supply so fervently, so relentlessly and so ruthlessly. Without Narcissistic Supply – the narcissist crumbles, he disintegrates like the zombies or the vampires in horror movies. It is terrifying and the narcissist will do anything to avoid it. Think about the narcissist as a drug addict. His withdrawal symptoms are identical: delusions, physiological effects, irritability, emotional liability.

I want to tell you now about the two times in my life that I faced an utter absence of Narcissistic Supply and what happened to me as a result.

The first time was after Nomi abandoned me as I was in jail, deprived of all means of obtaining Narcissistic Supply and subject to the dehumanising existence of a brutal penal colony. I reacted by retreating into a life-threatening dysphoria.

The second time was even more frightening.

I found myself in Russia in the throes of its worst economic crisis ever. I was a fugitive, having escaped the displeasure of a nasty regime I dared criticise and attack openly. Gaining access to Sources of Narcissistic Supply was a tedious and narcissistically injurious process and my girlfriend was far away, in Macedonia. I lived in a decrepit apartment, with no hot water, with furniture in wooden death and tried to get accustomed to the brutish nastiness of everyday life there. I had no Narcissistic Supply of any kind – and this lasted for months. All my frantic efforts to generate supply – failed.

At the beginning it was a mere thought – following an exceedingly stormy night which I spent reading about Jack the Ripper. I imagined a decomposing body of a young woman emerging from the rusty bathroom (its creaking door half-hidden from where I slept). She leaned casually against the doorframe and said: "So, you finally came". Gradually, this gruesome image obsessed me to the point of terror. I was reduced to scribbling crosses on all doors together with special mantras I invented. At last, I could not stay there any longer and I moved to live for a few days with my client, a jolly, young and entrepreneurial Macedonian. His interpretation was that I was simply too lonely.

He couldn't understand why I was so uninterested in the ravishing girls that worked for him. He could not fathom my behaviour – reading and writing 16 hours a day, day in and day out, without a break.

But I knew better. I knew that my decomposing apparition was a manifestation of a psychotic break, the zombie of my disorder, my self-destructiveness embodied and my virulent self-hatred projected. I knew that "she" was as real an enemy as any I have ever come across. Narcissists often experience brief psychotic episodes when they are disassembled – either in therapy or following a life-crisis accompanied by a major narcissistic injury.

Psychotic episodes may be closely allied to another feature of narcissism: magical thinking. Narcissists are like children in this sense. I, for instance, fully believe in two things: that whatever happens – I will prevail and that good things will happen to me. It is not a belief, really.

There is no cognitive component in it. I just KNOW it, the same way I know gravity – in a direct and immediate and secure way.

I believe that, no matter what I do, I will always be forgiven, I will always prevail and triumph, I will always land safely on all my fours. I, therefore, am fearless in a manner perceived by others to be both admirable and insane. I attribute to myself divine and cosmic immunity – I cloak myself in it, it renders me invisible to my enemies and to the powers of evil. It is a childish phantasmagoria – but to me it is very real.

The second thing I know with religious certainty is that good things will happen to me. Good things always have, I was never disproved, on the very contrary – my belief only grows stronger as I grow older. With equal certitude, I know that I will squander my good fortune time and again in a bedevilled effort to defeat myself and to vindicate my mother and her transubstantiations, all other authority figures. She – and other role models that substituted for her in later life – insisted with a vengeance that I was corrupt and vain and empty. My life is a continuous effort to prove them right.

So, no matter what serendipity, what lucky circumstance, what blessing I shall receive – I will always strive with blind fury to deflect them, to deform, to ruin. And being the talented person that I am – I will succeed spectacularly.

I have lived in fairy tales come true all my life. I was adopted by a billionaire, an admiring student of mine became Minister of Finance and summoned me to his side, I was given millions to invest and have been the subject of many other miracles – but I was and am intent on bringing myself to biblical destitution and devastation.

Perhaps in this – in the belief that I have the omnipotence to conspire against a universe that constantly smiles upon me – lies the real magic of my thinking. The day I stop resisting my endowments and my good fortune is the day I die.

Return

The Music of My Emotions

I feel sad only when I listen to music. My sadness is tinged with the decomposing sweetness of my childhood. So, sometimes, I sing or think about music and it makes me unbearably sad. I know that somewhere inside me there are whole valleys of melancholy, oceans of pain but they remain untapped because I want to live. I cannot listen to music – any music – for more than a few minutes. It is too dangerous, I cannot breathe.

But this is the exception. Otherwise, my emotional life is colourless and eventless, as rigidly blind as my disorder, as dead as me. Oh, I feel rage and hurt and inordinate humiliation and fear. These are very dominant, prevalent and recurrent hues in the canvass of my daily existence. But there is nothing except these atavistic gut reactions. There is nothing else – at least not that I am aware of.

Whatever it is that I experience as emotions – I experience in reaction to slights and injuries, real or imagined. My emotions are all reactive, not active. I feel insulted – I sulk. I feel devalued – I rage. I feel ignored – I pout. I feel humiliated – I lash out. I feel threatened – I fear. I feel adored – I bask in glory. I am virulently envious of one and all.

I can appreciate beauty but in a cerebral, cold and "mathematical" way. I have no sex drive I can think of. My emotional landscape is dim and grey, as though observed through thick mist in a particularly dreary day.

I can intelligently discuss other emotions, which I never experienced – like empathy, or love – because I make it a point to read a lot and to correspond with people who claim to experience them. Thus, I gradually formed working hypotheses as to what people feel. It is pointless to try to really understand – but at least I can better predict their behaviour than in the absence of such models.

I am not envious of people who feel. I disdain feelings and emotional people because I think that they are weak and vulnerable and I deride human weaknesses and vulnerabilities. Such derision makes me feel superior and is probably the ossified remains of a defence mechanism gone berserk. But, there it is, this is I and there is nothing I can do about it.

To all of you who talk about change – there is nothing I can do about myself. And there is nothing you can do about yourself. And there is nothing anyone can do for you, either. Psychotherapy and medications are concerned with behaviour modification – not with healing. They are concerned with proper adaptation because maladaptation is socially costly. Society defends itself against misfits by lying to them. The lie is that change and healing are possible. They are not. You are what you are. Period. Go live with it.

So, here I am. An emotional hunchback, a fossil, a human caught in amber, observing my environment with dead eyes of calcium. We shall never meet amicably because I am a predator and you are the prey. Because I do not know what it is like to be you and I do not particularly care to know. Because my disorder is as essential to me as your feelings are to you. My normal state is my very illness. I look like you, I walk the walk and talk the talk and I – and my ilk – deceive you magnificently. Not out of the cold viciousness of our hearts – but because that is the way we are.

I have emotions and they are buried in a pit down below. All of my emotions are acidulously negative, they are vitriol, the "not for internal consumption" type. I cannot feel anything, because if I open the floodgates of this cesspool of my psyche, I will drown.

And I will carry you with me.

And all the love in this world, and all the crusading women who think that they can "fix" me by doling out their saccharine compassion and revolting "understanding" and all the support and the holding environments and the textbooks – cannot change one iota in this maddening, self-imposed verdict meted out by the most insanely, obtusely, sadistically harsh judge:

By me.

Return

I Love to be Hated

If I had to distil my quotidian existence in two pithy sentences, I would say: I love to be hated and I hate to be loved.

Hate is the complement of fear and I like being feared. It imbues me with an intoxicating sensation of omnipotence. I am veritably inebriated by the looks of horror or repulsion on people's faces. They know that I am capable of anything. Godlike, I am ruthless and devoid of scruples, capricious and unfathomable, emotion-less and asexual, omniscient, omnipotent and omni-present, a plague, a devastation, an inescapable verdict. I nurture my ill-repute, stoking it and fanning the flames of gossip. It is an enduring asset.

Hate and fear are sure generators of attention. It is all about Narcissistic Supply, of course – the drug which we, the narcissists consume and which consumes us in return. So, attack sadistically authority figures, institutions, my hosts and I make sure they know about my eruptions.

I purvey only the truth and nothing but the truth – but I tell it bluntly told in an orgy of evocative baroque English.

The blind rage that this induces in the targets of my vitriolic diatribes provokes in me a surge of satisfaction and inner tranquillity not obtainable by any other means. I like to think about their pain, of course – but that is the lesser part of the equation.

It is my horrid future and inescapable punishment that carries the irresistible appeal. Like some strain of alien virus, it infects my better judgement and I succumb.

In general, my weapon is the truth and human propensity to avoid it. In tactless breaching of every etiquette, I chastise and berate and snub and offer vitriolic opprobrium. A self-proclaimed Jeremiah, I hector and harangue from my many self-made pulpits. I understand the prophets. I understand Torquemada.

I bask in the incomparable pleasure of being RIGHT. I derive my grandiose superiority from the contrast between my righteousness and the humanness of others.

But it is not that simple. It never is with narcissists. Fostering public revolt and the inevitable ensuing social sanctions fulfils two other psychodynamic goals.

The first one I alluded to. It is the burning desire – nay, NEED – to be punished.

In the grotesque mind of the narcissist, his punishment is equally his vindication.

By being permanently on trial, the narcissist claims high moral ground and the position of the martyr: misunderstood, discriminated against, unjustly roughed, outcast by his very towering genius or other outstanding qualities. To conform to the cultural stereotype of the "tormented artist" – the narcissist provokes his own suffering. He is thus validated.

His grandiose fantasies acquire a modicum of substance. "If I were not so special – they wouldn't have persecuted me so."

The persecution of the narcissist IS his uniqueness. He must be different, for better or for worse. The streak of paranoia embedded in him, makes the outcome inevitable. He is in constant conflict with lesser beings: his spouse, his shrink, his boss, his colleagues. Forced to stoop to their intellectual level, the narcissist feels like Gulliver: a giant strapped by Lilliputians. His life is a constant struggle against the self-contented mediocrity of his surroundings. This is his fate which he accepts, though never stoically. It is a calling, a mission and a recurrence in his stormy life.

Deeper still, the narcissist has an image of himself as a worthless, bad and dysfunctional extension of others. In constant need of Narcissistic Supply, he feels humiliated. The contrast between his cosmic fantasies and the reality of his dependence, neediness and, often, failure (the "Grandiosity Gap") is an emotionally harrowing experience. It is a constant background noise of devilish, demeaning laughter. The voices say: "You are a fraud", "You are a zero", "You deserve nothing", "If only they knew how worthless you are".

The narcissist attempts to silence these tormenting voices not by fighting them but by agreeing with them. Unconsciously – sometimes consciously – he says to them: "I do agree with you. I am bad and worthless and deserving of the most severe punishment for my rotten character, bad habits, addiction and the constant fraud that is my life. I will go out and seek my doom.

Now that I have complied – will you leave me be? Will you leave me alone?"

Of course, they never do.

Return

Grandiosity Deconstructed

Sometimes I find myself bemused (though rarely amused) by my own grandiosity. Not by my fantasies – they are common to many "normal people".

It is healthy to daydream and fantasise. It is the antechamber of life and its circumstances. It is a process of preparing for eventualities, embellished and decorated. No, I am talking about feeling grandiose.

This feeling has four components.

Omnipotence

I believe that I will live forever. "Believe" in this context is a weak word. I know. It is a cellular certainty, almost biological, it flows with my blood and permeates every niche of my being. I can do anything I choose to do and excel in it. What I do, what I excel at, what I achieve depends only on my volition. There is no other determinant. Hence my rage when confronted with disagreement or opposition – not only because of the audacity of my, evidently inferior, adversary. But because it threatens my world view, it endangers my feeling of omnipotence. I am fatuously daring, adventurous, experimentative and curious precisely due to this hidden assumption of "can-do". I am genuinely surprised and devastated when I fail, when the Universe does not arrange itself, magically, to accommodate my unlimited powers, when it (and people in it) does not comply with my whims and wishes. I often deny such discrepancies, delete them from my memory. As a result, my life is remembered as a patchy quilt of unrelated events.

Omniscience

Until very recently I pretended to know everything – I mean EVERYTHING, in every field of human knowledge and endeavour. I lied and invented to avoid proof of my ignorance. I pretended to know and resorted to numerous subterfuges to support my God-like omniscience (reference books hidden in my clothes, frequent visits to the restroom, cryptic notation or sudden illness, if all else failed). Where my knowledge failed me – I feigned authority, faked superiority, quoted from non-existent sources, embedded threads of truth in a canvass of falsehoods. I transformed myself into an artist of intellectual prestidigitation. As I advanced in age, this invidious quality has receded, or, rather, metamorphosed. I now claim more confined expertise. I am not ashamed to admit my ignorance and need to learn outside the fields of my self-proclaimed expertise. But this "improvement" is merely optical. Within my "territory", I am still as fiercely defensive and possessive as I have ever been. And I am still an avowed autodidact, unwilling to subject my knowledge and insights to peer scrutiny, or, for this matter, to any scrutiny. I keep re-inventing myself, adding new fields of knowledge as I go: finance, economics, psychology, philosophy, physics, politics... This crawling intellectual annexation is a round about way of reverting to my old image as the erudite "Renaissance Man".

Omnipresence

Even I – the master of self-deception – cannot pretend that I am everywhere at once in the PHYSICAL sense. Instead, I feel that I am the centre and the axis of my Universe, that all things and happenstances revolve around me and that disintegration would ensue if I were to disappear or to lose interest in someone or in something. I am convinced, for instance, that I am the main, if not the only, topic of discussion in my absence. I am often surprised and offended to learn that I was not even mentioned. When invited to a meeting with many participants, I assume the position of the sage, the guru, or the teacher/guide whose words survive his physical presence. My books, articles and Web sites are extensions of my presence and, in this restricted sense, I do seem to exist everywhere. In other words, I "stamp" my environment. I "leave my mark" upon it. I "stigmatise" it.

Narcissist the Omnivore
(Perfectionism and Completeness)

There is another "omni" component in grandiosity. The narcissist is an omnivore. It devours and digests experiences and people, sights and smells, bodies and words, books and films, sounds and achievements, his work and his leisure, his pleasure and his possessions. The narcissist is incapable of ENJOYING anything because he is in constant pursuit of the twin attainments of perfection and completeness. Classic narcissists interact with the world as predators would with their prey. They want to do it all, own it all, be everywhere, experience everything. They cannot delay gratification. They do not accept "no" for an answer. And they settle for nothing less than the ideal, the sublime, the perfect, the all-inclusive, the all-encompassing, the engulfing, the all-pervasive, the most beautiful, the cleverest, the richest. The narcissist is shattered by discovering that a collection he possesses is incomplete, that his colleague's wife is more glamorous, that his son is better than he in math, that his neighbour has a new, impressive car, that his roommate got promoted, that the "love of his life" signed a recording contract. It is not plain old jealousy, not even pathological envy (though it is definitely a part of the psychological make-up of the narcissist). It is the discovery that the narcissist is NOT perfect, or ideal, or complete – that does him in.

Return

The Entitlement of Routine

I hate routine. When I find myself doing the same things over and over again, I get depressed. I oversleep, over-eat, over-drink and, in general, engage in addictive, impulsive and compulsive behaviours. This is my way of re-introducing risk and excitement into what I (emotionally) perceive to be a barren life.

The problem is that even the most exciting and varied existence becomes routine after a while. Living in the same country or apartment, meeting the same people, doing essentially the same things (though with changing content) - all "qualify" as stultifying rote. I feel entitled to more. I feel it is my right - due to my intellectual superiority - to lead a thrilling, rewarding, kaleidoscopic life. I feel entitled to force life itself, or, at least, people around me - to yield to my wishes and needs, supreme among them the need for stimulating variety.

This rejection of habit is part of a larger pattern of aggressive entitlement. I feel that the very existence of a sublime intellect (such as myself) warrants concessions and allowances. Standing in line is a waste of time best spent pursuing knowledge, inventing and creating. I should avail myself of the best medical treatment proffered by the most prominent medical authorities - lest the asset that is I be lost to Mankind. I should not be bothered with proofreading my articles (or even re-reading them) - these lowly jobs best be assigned to the less gifted. The devil is in paying precious attention to details.

Entitlement is sometimes justified in a Picasso or an Einstein. But I am neither. My achievements are grotesquely incommensurate with my overwhelming sense of entitlement. I am but a mediocre and forgettable scribbler who, at the age of 39, is a colossal under-achiever, if anything.

Of course, the feeling of supremacy often serves to mask a cancerous complex of inferiority. Moreover, I infect others with my projected grandiosity and their feedback constitutes the edifice upon which I construct my self-esteem. I regulate my sense of self-worth by rigidly insisting that I am above the madding crowd while deriving my Narcissistic Supply from this very thus despised source.

But there is a second angle to this abhorrence of the predictable. As a narcissist, I employ a host of Emotional Involvement Prevention Mechanisms (EIPM). Despising routine and avoiding it is one of these mechanisms. Their function is to prevent me from getting emotionally involved and, subsequently, hurt. Their application results in an "approach-avoidance repetition complex". The narcissist, fearing and loathing intimacy, stability and security – yet craving them – approaches and then avoids significant others or important tasks in a rapid succession of apparently inconsistent and disconnected behaviours.

Here is a partial (and truncated) list of other EIPMs. In this text – "objects" means "others".

From "Malignant Self Love – Narcissism Revisited":

Emotional Involvement Preventive Measures

Personality and Conduct

Lack of enthusiasm, anhedonia, and constant boredom
A wish to "vary", to "be free",
to hop from one subject matter or object to another.
Laziness, constantly present fatigue
Dysphoria to the point of depression
leads to reclusiveness, detachment, low energies.
Repression of the affect and uniform emotional "hues"
Self-hatred disables capacity to love or
to develop emotional involvement.
Externalised transformations of aggression:
Envy, rage, cynicism, vulgar honesty, black humour
(all lead to disintimisation and distancing
and to pathological emotional and sexual communication)
Narcissistic compensatory and defence mechanisms:
Grandiosity and grandiose fantasies
(Feelings of) uniqueness
Lack of empathy, or the existence of functional empathy,
or empathy by proxy.
Demands for adoration and adulation
A feeling that he deserves everything ("entitlement")
Exploitation of objects
Objectification/symbolisation (abstraction)
and fictionalisation of objects.

Manipulative behaviour
(using personal charm, ability to
psychologically penetrate the object, ruthlessness,
and knowledge and information regarding the object
obtained, largely, by interacting with the object)
Intellectualisation through generalisation,
differentiation and categorisation of objects.
Feelings of omnipotence and omniscience
Perfectionism and performance anxiety (repressed)
These mechanisms lead to emotional substitution
(adulation and adoration instead of love),
to the distancing and repulsion of objects, to disintimisation
(not possible to interact with the "real" narcissist)

The results:
Narcissistic vulnerability to narcissistic injury
(more bearable than emotional vulnerability
and can be more easily recovered from)
"Becoming a child" and infantilism
(the narcissist's inner dialogue: "No one will hurt me",
"I am a child and I am loved unconditionally, unreservedly,
non-judgementally, and disinterestedly")
Adults don't expect such unconditional love and acceptance
and they constitute a barrier to mature, adult relationships.
Intensive denial of reality
(perceived by others as innocence, naiveté, or pseudo-stupidity)
Constant lack of confidence
concerning matters not under full control
leads to hostility towards objects and towards emotions.
Compulsive behaviours intended to neutralise
a high level of anxiety and compulsive seeking of
love substitutes (money, prestige, power)...

Instincts and Drives

The Cerebral Narcissist

Sexual abstinence, low frequency of sexual activity
lead to less emotional involvement.
Frustration of emotional objects through sex avoidance
encourages abandonment by the object.
Sexual disintimisation by preferring autoerotic,
anonymous sex with immature or incompatible objects
(who do not represent an emotional threat or pose demands).
Sporadic sex with long intervals

and drastic alterations of sexual behaviour patterns.
Dissociation of pleasure centres:
Pleasure avoidance (unless "for and on behalf" of the object)
Refraining from child rearing or family formation
Using the object as an "alibi"
not to form new sexual and emotional liaisons,
extreme marital and monogamous faithfulness,
to the point of ignoring all other objects
leads to object inertia.
This mechanism defends the narcissist
from the need to make contact with other objects.
Sexual frigidity with significant other
and sexual abstinence with others.

The Somatic Narcissist

The somatic narcissist treats others
as sex objects or sex slaves or masturbatory aides.
High frequency of unemotional sex,
lacking in intimacy and warmth.

Object Relations

Manipulative attitudes, which in conjunction with
feelings of omnipotence and omniscience,
create a mystique of infallibility and immunity.
Partial reality test
Social friction leads to social sanctions (up to imprisonment)
Refraining from intimacy
Absence of emotional investment or presence
Reclusive life, avoiding neighbours, family
(both nuclear and extended), spouse and friends.
The narcissist is often a schizoid
Active misogyny (women-hatred)
with sadistic and anti-social elements.
Narcissistic dependence serves as
substitute for emotional involvement.
Immature emotional dependence and habit
Object interchangeability
(dependence upon ANY object – not upon a specific object)...
Limitation of contacts with objects
to material and "cold" transactions.
The narcissist prefers fear, adulation, admiration
and narcissistic accumulation to love.
To the narcissist, objects have no autonomous existence

except as PNSSs and SNSSs
(Primary and Secondary Sources of Narcissistic Supply).
Knowledge and intelligence serve as control mechanisms and
extractors of adulation and attention (Narcissistic Supply).
The object is used to re-enact early life conflicts:
The narcissist is bad and asks to be punished anew
and thus obtain confirmation that people are angry at him.
The object is kept emotionally distant through deterrence
and is constantly tested by the narcissist
who reveals his negative sides to the object.
The aim of negative, off-putting behaviours
is to check whether the narcissist's uniqueness will
override and offset them in the mind of the object.
The object experiences emotional absence,
repulsion, deterrence and insecurity.
It is thus encouraged not to develop
emotional involvement with the narcissist
(emotional involvement requires a positive emotional feedback).
The erratic and demanding relationship with the narcissist
is experienced as an energy-depleting burden.
It is punctuated by a series of "eruptions" followed by relief.
The narcissist is imposing, intrusive, compulsive and tyrannical.
Reality is interpreted cognitively so that negative aspects,
real and imagined, of the object are highlighted.
This preserves the emotional distance
between the narcissist and his objects,
fosters uncertainty, prevents emotional involvement
and activates narcissistic mechanisms (such as grandiosity) which,
in turn, increase the repulsion and the aversion of the partner.
The narcissist claims to have chosen the object because of
an error/circumstances/pathology/loss of control/
immaturity/partial or false information, etc.

Functioning and Performance

A grandiosity shift:

A preference to be emotionally invested in grandiose
career-related fantasies in which the narcissist does not have to
face practical, rigorous and consistent demands.
The narcissist avoids success in order to avoid
emotional involvement and investment.
He shuns success because it obliges him to follow through
and to identify himself with some goal or group.

He emphasises areas of activity in which he is unlikely to succeed.
The narcissist ignores the future and does not plan.
Thus he is never emotionally committed.
The narcissist invests the necessary minimum
in his job (emotionally).
He is not thorough and under-performs,
his work is shoddy and defective or partial.
He evades responsibility and tends to pass it on to others
while exercising little control.
His decision-making processes are ossified and rigid
(he presents himself as a man of "principles" –
usually referring to his whims and moods).
The narcissist reacts very slowly to a changing environment
(change is painful).
He is a pessimist, knows that he will lose his job/business –
so, he is constantly engaged in seeking alternatives
and constructing plausible alibis.
This yields a feeling of temporariness, which prevents
engagement, involvement, commitment, dedication,
identification and emotional hurt in case of change or failure.

The alternative to having a spouse/companion:
Solitary life (with vigorous emphasis on PNSS)
or frequent changes of partners.
Serial vocations prevent the narcissist from having
a clear career path and obviate the need to persevere.
All the initiatives adopted by the narcissist are egocentric,
sporadic and discrete (they focus on one skill or trait of
the narcissist, are randomly distributed in space and in time,
and do not form a thematic or other continuum
– they are not goal or objective oriented).

*Sometimes, as a substitute,
the narcissist engages in performance shifting:*
He comes up with imaginary, invented goals
with no correlation to reality and its constraints.
To avoid facing performance tests
and to maintain grandiosity and uniqueness
the narcissist refrains from acquiring skills and training
(such as a driver's licence, technical skills, any systematic
– academic or non-academic – knowledge).
The "child" in the narcissist is reaffirmed this way –
because he avoids adult activities and attributes.
The gap between the image projected by the narcissist

(charisma, unusual knowledge, grandiosity, fantasies)
and his actual achievements – create in him
permanent feelings that he is a crook, a hustler,
that his life is unreal life and movie-like
(derealisation and depersonalisation).
This gives rise to ominous feelings of imminent threat
and, concurrently, to compensatory assertions
of immunity and omnipotence.
The narcissist is forced to become a manipulator.

Locations and Environment

A feeling of not belonging and of detachment
Bodily discomfiture (the body feels as depersonalised,
alien and a nuisance, its needs are totally ignored, its signals
re-routed and re-interpreted, its maintenance neglected)
Keeping his distance from relevant communities
(his neighbourhood, coreligionists, his nation and countrymen)
Disavowing his religion, his ethnic background, his friends
The narcissist often adopts the stance of a "scientist-observer".
This is narcissistic detachment – the feeling that
he is a director or an actor in a movie about his own life.
The narcissist avoids "emotional handles":
photographs, music identified with a certain period in his life,
familiar places, people he knew,
mementoes and emotional situations.
The narcissist lives on borrowed time in a borrowed life.
Every place and period are transitory
and lead to the next, unfamiliar environment.
The narcissist feels that the end is near.
He lives in rented apartments, is an illegal alien,
is fully mobile on a short notice,
does not buy real estate or immovables.
He travels light and he likes to travel.
He is peripatetic and itinerant.
The narcissist cultivates feelings of incompatibility
with his surroundings.
He considers himself superior to others
and keeps criticising people, institutions and situations.
The above behaviour patterns constitute a denial of reality.
The narcissist defines a rigid, impenetrable, personal territory
and is physically revolted when it is breached.

Return

Wasted Lives

I think a lot about the desultory waste that is my biography. Ask anyone who shared a life with a narcissist, or knew one and they are likely to sigh: "What a waste". Waste of potential, waste of opportunities, waste of emotions, a wasteland of arid addiction and futile pursuit.

Narcissists are as gifted as they come. The problem is to disentangle their tales of fantastic grandiosity from the reality of their talents and skills.

They always tend either to over-estimate or to devalue their potency. They often emphasise the wrong traits and invest in their mediocre or (dare I say) less than average capacities. Concomitantly, they ignore their real potential, squander their advantage and under-rate their gifts.

The narcissist decides which aspects of his self to nurture and which to neglect. He gravitates towards activities commensurate with his pompous auto-portrait. He suppresses these tendencies and aptitudes in him which don't conform to his inflated view of his uniqueness, brilliance, might, sexual prowess, or standing in society. He cultivates these flairs and predilections which he regards as befitting his overweening self-image and ultimate grandeur.

A slave to this pressing need to preserve a fake and demanding self, I dedicated years to commerce. I projected the spectre of a rich man (I never came close) of great power (I never had) and multitudinous connections throughout the world (mostly shallow and ephemeral). I hated every minute of wheeling and dealing, of cutting throats and second guessing, of the nauseatingly boring repetition that is the essence of this world. But I kept on trudging, unable to forsake the fear and adulation and media attention and frivolous gossip that gave me sustenance and constituted my very self-worth.

It took a catastrophic, Job-like, turn of events to wean me from this self-made dependency. Having emerged from prison, with nothing but the proverbial shirt on my back, I finally was able to be me. I finally decided to partake of both the joys and the successes of writing, my true skill and knack. Thus, I became an author.

But, the narcissist, no matter how self-aware and well-meaning is accursed.

His grandiosity, his fantasies, the compelling, overriding urge to feel unique, invested with some cosmic significance, unprecedentedly bestowed – these thwart the best intentions. These structures of obsession and compulsion, these deposits of insecurity and pain, the stalactites and stalagmites of years of abuse and then abandonment – they all conspire to frustrate the gratification, however circumspect, of the narcissist's true nature.

Consider, yet again, my writing. I am at my most effective when I write "from the heart", about my personal experiences and in a thoughtful-reminiscing mode. But, to my mind, such style serves the purpose of showcasing my sparkling intellect and my remarkable brilliance poorly. I need to impress and inspire awe more than I need to communicate with my readers and affect them. I act the academic which my laziness and sense of entitlement and lack of commitment prevented me from being. I am looking, once more, for a short cut.

I am blind to the fact that my prolix and babblative prose inspires more ridicule than awe. I ignore my incomprehensibility and the irritation I provoke with my moribund vocabulary, convoluted syntax and tortured grammar.

I present my half-baked ideas, based on a shaky and fragmented foundation of knowledge haphazardly gleaned, with the certitude of confidence of an authority – or a trickster.

Tis a waste. I have written heart-rending short fiction and powerful poetry. I have touched the hearts of people. I have made them cry and rage and smile. But I have laid this part of my writing to rest because it does injustice to my grandiose perception of myself. Anyone can write a short story or a poem. Only the few – the unique, the erudite, the brilliant – can comment on the Measurement Problem, analyse Church-Turing machines and use words such as "atrabilious", "sesquipedalian" and "apothegm". I count myself among those few. By doing so, I betray my inner sanctum, my real potential, my gift.

This betrayal and the helpless rage that it provokes in one, if you ask me, is the very essence of narcissism.

Return

The Split Narcissist

That the narcissist possesses a prominent False Self as well as a suppressed and dilapidated True Self is common knowledge. Yet, how intertwined and inseparable are these two? Do they interact? How do they influence each other? And what behaviours can be attributed squarely to one or the other of these protagonists? Moreover, does the False Self assume traits and attributes of the True Self in order to deceive?

Two years ago, I suggested a methodological framework. I compared the narcissist to a person suffering from the Dissociative Identity Disorder (DID) – formerly known as the Multiple Personality Disorder (MPD).

Here is what I wrote:

"A debate is starting to stir: is the False Self an alter? In other words: is the True Self of a narcissist the equivalent of a host personality in a DID (Dissociative Identity Disorder) – and the False Self one of the fragmented personalities, also known as 'alters'?

My personal opinion is that the False Self is a mental construct, not a self in the full sense. It is the locus of the fantasies of grandiosity, the feelings of entitlements, omnipotence, magical thinking, omniscience and magical immunity of the narcissist. It lacks so many elements that it can hardly be called a 'self'.

Moreover, it has no 'cut-off' date. DID alters have a date of inception, being reactions to trauma or abuse. The False Self is a process, not an entity, it is a reactive pattern and a reactive formation. All taken into account, the choice of words was poor. The False Self is not a Self, nor is it False. It is very real, more real to the narcissist than his True Self. A better choice would have been 'abuse reactive self' or something like this.

This is the core of my work. I say that narcissists have vanished and have been replaced by a False Self (bad term, but not my fault, write to Kernberg). There is NO True Self in there. It's gone. The narcissist is a hall of mirrors – but the hall itself is an optical illusion created by the mirrors... This is a little like the paintings of Escher.

MPD (DID) is more common than believed. The emotions are the ones to get segregated. The notion of 'unique separate multiple whole personalities' is primitive and untrue. DID is a continuum. The inner language breaks down into a polyglottal chaos. Emotions cannot communicate with each other for fear of the pain (and its fatal results). So, they are kept apart by various mechanisms (a host or birth personality, a facilitator, a moderator and so on).

And here we come to the crux of the matter: All PDs – except NPD – suffer from a modicum of DID, or incorporate it. Only the narcissists don't. This is because the narcissistic solution is to emotionally disappear so thoroughly that not one personality/emotion is left. Hence, the tremendous, insatiable need of the narcissist for external approval. He exists ONLY as a reflection. Since he is forbidden from loving his True Self – he chooses to have no self at all. It is not dissociation – it is a vanishing act.

This is why I regard pathological narcissism as THE source of all PDs. The total, 'pure' solution is NPD: self-extinguishing, self-abolishing, totally fake. Then come variations on the self-hate and perpetuated self-abuse themes: HPD (NPD with sex or the body as the Source of Narcissistic Supply), BPD (emotional liability, movement between poles of life wish and death wish) and so on.

Why are narcissists not prone to suicide? Simple: they died a long time ago. They are the true zombies of the world. Read vampire and zombie legends and you will see how narcissistic these creatures are."

Many researchers and scholars and therapists tried to grapple with the void at the core of the narcissist. The common view is that the remnants of the True Self are so ossified, shredded, cowed into submission and repressed – that, for all practical purposes, they are functionless and useless. In treating the narcissist, the therapist often tries to invent a healthy self, rather than build upon the distorted wreckage strewn across the narcissist's psyche.

But what of the rare glimpses of True Self that the unfortunates who interact with narcissists keep reporting?

If the pathological narcissistic element is but one of many other disorders – the True Self may well have survived. Gradations and shades of narcissism occupy the narcissistic spectrum. Narcissistic traits (overlay) are often co-diagnosed with other disorders (co-morbidity). Some people have a narcissistic personality – but NOT NPD! These distinctions are important.

A person may well appear to be a narcissist – but is not, in the strict, psychiatric, sense of the word.

In a full-fledged narcissist, the False Self IMITATES the True Self.

To do so artfully, it deploys two mechanisms:

Re-Interpretation

It causes the narcissist to re-interpret certain emotions and reactions in a flattering, True Self-compatible, light. A narcissist may, for instance, interpret FEAR – as compassion. If I hurt someone I fear (e.g., an authority figure) – I may feel bad afterwards and interpret my discomfort as EMPATHY and COMPASSION. To be afraid is humiliating – to be compassionate is commendable and earns me social acceptance and understanding.

Emulation

The narcissist is possessed of an uncanny ability to psychologically penetrate others. Often, this gift is abused and put at the service of the narcissist's control freakery and sadism. The narcissist uses it liberally to annihilate the natural defences of his victims by faking unprecedented, almost inhuman, empathy.

This capacity is coupled with the narcissist's ability to frighteningly imitate emotions and their attendant behaviours. The narcissist possesses "resonance tables". He keeps records of every action and reaction, every utterance and consequence, every datum provided by others regarding their state of mind and emotional make-up. From these, he then constructs a set of formulas which often result in impeccably and eerily accurate renditions of emotional behaviour. This is enormously deceiving.

The narcissist is our first encounter with carbon-based artificial intelligence. Many wish it were the last.

Return

The Anxiety of Boredom

I often find myself worried. I say "find myself" because it is usually unconscious, like a nagging pain, a permanence, like being immersed in a gelatinous liquid, trapped and helpless. Perhaps the phrase I am looking for is the DSM favourite "all-pervasive". Still, it is never diffuse. I am worried about specific people, or possible events, or more or less plausible scenarios. It is just that I seem to constantly conjure up some reason or another to be worried. Positive past experiences have not dissuaded me from this preoccupation. I seem to believe that the world is a cruelly arbitrary, ominously contrarian, contrivingly cunning and indifferently crushing place. I know it will all end badly and for no good reason. I know that life is too good to be true and too bad to endure. I know that civilisation is an ideal and that the deviation from it are what we call "history". I am incurably pessimistic, an ignoramus by choice and incorrigibly blind to evidence to the contrary.

Underneath all this is a Great Anxiety. I fear life and what people do unto each other. I fear my fear and what it does to me. I know I am a participant in a game whose rules I will never know and that my very existence is at stake. I trust no one, I believe in nothing, I know only two certainties: evil exists and life is meaningless. I am convinced that no one cares. I am a pawn without a chessboard with the chess players long departed. In other words: I float.

This existential angst that permeates my every cell is atavistic and irrational. It has no name or likeness. It is like the monsters in every child's bedroom with the lights turned off. But being the rationalising and intellectualising cerebral narcissist that I am - I must instantly label it, explain it, analyse it and predict it. I must attribute this poisonous cloud that weighs on me from the inside to some external cause. I must set it in a pattern, embed it in a context, transform it into a link in the great chain of my being. Hence, diffuse anxiety become my focused worries. Worries are known and measurable quantities. They have a mover which can be tackled and eliminated. They have a beginning and an end.

They are tied to names, to places, faces and to people. Worries are human – anxiety divine. I thus, transform my demons into notation in my diary: check this, do that, apply preventive measures, do not allow, pursue, attack, avoid. The language of human conduct in the face of real and immediate danger is cast as blanket over the underlying abyss that harbours my anxiety.

But such excessive worrying – whose sole intent is to convert irrational anxiety into the mundane and tangible – is the stuff of paranoia. For what is paranoia if not the attribution of inner disintegration to external persecution, the assignment of malevolent agents from the outside to the turmoil inside? The paranoid seeks to alleviate his voiding by irrationally clinging to rationality. Things are so bad, he says, mainly to himself, because I am a victim, because "they" are after me and I am hunted by the juggernaut of state, or by the Freemasons, or by the Jews, or by the neighbourhood librarian. This is the path that leads from the cloud of anxiety, through the lamp posts of worry to the consuming darkness of paranoia.

Paranoia is a defence against anxiety and against aggression. The latter is projected outwards, upon imaginary other, the agents of one's crucifixion.

Anxiety is also a defence against aggressive impulses. Therefore, anxiety and paranoia are sisters, the latter but a focused form of the former. The mentally disordered defend against their own aggressive propensities by either being anxious or by becoming paranoid.

Aggression has numerous faces. One of its favourite disguises is boredom.

Like its relation, depression, it is aggression directed inwards. It threatens to drown the bored in a primordial soup of inaction and energy depletion. It is anhedonic (pleasure depriving) and dysphoric (leads to profound sadness). But it is also threatening, perhaps because it is so reminiscent of death.

I find myself most worried when I am bored. It goes like this: I am aggressive. I channel my aggression and internalise it. I experience my bottled wrath as boredom. I am bored. I feel threatened by it in a vague, mysterious way. Anxiety ensues. I rush to construct an intellectual edifice to accommodate all these primitive emotions and their transubstantiations. I identify reasons, causes, effects and possibilities in the outer world. I build scenarios. I spin narratives. I feel no more anxiety. I know the enemy (or so I think). And now I am worried. Or paranoid.

Return

A Great Admiration

To paraphrase what Henry James' once said of Louisa May Alcott, my experience of genius is small but my admiration for it is, nevertheless, great. When I visited the "Figarohaus" in Vienna – where Mozart lived and worked for two crucial years – I experienced a great fatigue, the sort that comes with acceptance. In the presence of real genius, I slumped into a chair and listened for one listless hour to its fruits: symphonies, the divine Requiem, arias, a cornucopia.

I always wanted to be a genius. Partly as a sure-fire way to secure constant Narcissistic Supply, partly as a safeguard against my own mortality. As it became progressively more evident how far I am from it and how ensconced in mediocrity – I, being a narcissist, resorted to short cuts. Ever since my fifth year I pretended to be thoroughly acquainted with issues I had no clue about. This streak of con-artistry reached a crescendo in my puberty, when I convinced a whole township (and later, my country, by co-opting the media) that I was a new Einstein. While unable to solve even the most basic mathematical equations, I was regarded by many – including world class physicists – as somewhat of an epiphanous miracle. To sustain this false pretence, I plagiarised liberally. Only 15 years later did an Israeli physicist discover the (Australian) source of my major plagiarised "studies" in advanced physics. Following this encounter with the abyss – the mortal fear of being mortifyingly exposed – I stopped plagiarising at the age of 23 and has never done so since.

I then tried to experience genius vicariously, by making friends with acknowledged ones and by supporting up and coming intellectuals. I became this bathetic sponsor of the arts and sciences that forever name drops and attributes to himself undue influence over the creative processes and outcomes of others. I created by proxy. The (sad, I guess) irony is that, all this time, I really did have a talent (for writing). But talent was not enough – being short of genius. It is the divine that I sought, not the average. And so, I kept denying my real self in pursuit of an invented one.

As the years progressed, the charms of associating with genius waned and faded. The gap between what I wanted to become and what I have has made me bitter and cantankerous, a repulsive, alien oddity, avoided by all but the most persistent friends and acolytes. I resent being doomed to the quotidian. I rebel against being given to aspirations which have so little in common with my abilities. It is not that I recognise my limitations – I don't. I still wish to believe that had I only applied myself, had I only persevered, had I only found interest – I would have been nothing less of a Mozart or an Einstein or a Freud. It is a lie I tell myself in times of quiet despair when I realise my age and compare it to the utter lack of my accomplishments.

I keep persuading myself that many a great man reached the apex of their creativity at the age of 40, or 50, or 60. That one never knows what of one's work shall be deemed by history to have been genius. I think of Kafka, of Nietzsche, of Benjamin – the heroes of every undiscovered prodigy. But it sounds hollow. Deep inside I know the one ingredient that I miss and that they all shared: an interest in other humans, a first hand experience of being one and the fervent wish to communicate – rather than merely to impress.

Return

The Narcissist in Love

The narcissist can get better, but rarely does he get well ("heal"). The reason is the narcissist's enormous life-long, irreplaceable and indispensable emotional investment in his disorder. It serves two critical functions, which together maintain the precariously balanced house of cards called the narcissist's personality. His disorder endows the narcissist with a sense of uniqueness, of "being special" – and it provides him with a rational explanation of his behaviour (an "alibi").

Most narcissists reject the notion or diagnosis that they are mentally disturbed. Absent powers of introspection and a total lack of self-awareness are part and parcel of the disorder. Pathological narcissism is founded on alloplastic defences – the firm conviction that the world or others are to blame for one's behaviour. The narcissist firmly believes that people around him should be held responsible for his reactions or have triggered them.

With such a state of mind so firmly entrenched, the narcissist is incapable of admitting that something is wrong with HIM.

But that is not to say that the narcissist does not experience his disorder.

He does. But he re-interprets this experience. He regards his dysfunctional behaviours – social, sexual, emotional, mental – as conclusive and irrefutable proof of his superiority, brilliance, distinction, prowess, might, or success. Rudeness to others is reinterpreted as efficiency.

Abusive behaviours are cast as educational. Sexual absence as proof of preoccupation with higher functions. His rage is always just and a reaction to injustice or being misunderstood by intellectual dwarves.

Thus, paradoxically, the disorder becomes an integral and inseparable part of the narcissist's inflated self-esteem and vacuous grandiose fantasies.

His False Self (the pivot of his pathological narcissism) is a self-reinforcing mechanism. The narcissist thinks that he is unique BECAUSE he has a False Self. His False Self IS the centre of his "specialness". Any therapeutic "attack" on the integrity and functioning of the False Self constitutes a threat to the narcissist's ability to regulate his wildly fluctuating sense of self-worth and an effort to "reduce" him to other people's mundane and mediocre existence.

The few narcissists that are willing to admit that something is terribly wrong with them, displace their alloplastic defences. Instead of blaming the world, other people, or circumstances beyond their control - they now blame their "disease". Their disorder become a catch-all, universal explanation for everything that is wrong in their lives and every derided, indefensible and inexcusable behaviour. Their narcissism becomes a "licence to kill", a liberating force which sets them outside human rules and codes of conduct.

Such freedom is so intoxicating and empowering that it is difficult to give up.

The narcissist is emotionally attached to only one thing: his disorder. The narcissist loves his disorder, desires it passionately, cultivates it tenderly, is proud of its "achievements" (and in my case, makes a living off it). His emotions are misdirected. Where normal people love others and empathise with them, the narcissist loves his False Self and identifies with it to the exclusion of all else - his True Self included.

Return

Why Do I Write Poetry?

They say, with a knowing smile: "If he is really a narcissist - how come he writes such beautiful poetry?"

"Words are the sounds of emotions" - they add - "and he claims to have none". They are smug and comfortable in their well classified world, my doubters.

But I use words as others use algebraic signs: with meticulousness, with caution, with the precision of the artisan. I sculpt in words. I stop. I tilt my head. I listen to the echoes. The tables of emotional resonance. The fine tuned reverberations of pain and love and fear. Air waves and photonic ricochets answered by chemicals secreted in my listeners and my readers.

I know beauty. I have always known it in the biblical sense, it was my passionate mistress. We made love. We procreated the cold children of my texts. I measured its aesthetics admiringly. But this is the mathematics of grammar. It was merely the undulating geometry of syntax.

Devoid of all emotions, I watch your reactions with the sated amusement of a Roman nobleman.

I wrote:

"My world is painted in shadows of fear and sadness. Perhaps they are related - I fear the sadness. To avoid the overweening, sepia melancholy that lurks in the dark corners of my being - I deny my own emotions. I do so thoroughly, with the single-mindedness of a survivor. I persevere through dehumanisation. I automate my processes. Gradually, parts of my flesh turn into metal and I stand there, exposed to sheering winds, as grandiose as my disorder.

I write poetry not because I need to. I write poetry to gain attention, to secure adulation, to fasten on to the reflection in the eyes of others that passes for my Ego. My words are fireworks, formulas of resonance, the periodic table of healing and abuse.

These are dark poems. A wasted landscape of pain ossified, of scarred remnants of emotions. There is no horror in abuse. The terror is in the endurance, in the dreamlike detachment from one's own existence that follows. People around me feel my surrealism. They back away, alienated, discomfited by the limpid placenta of my virtual reality.

Now I am left alone and I write umbilical poems as others would converse.

Before and after prison, I have written reference books and essays. My first book of short fiction was critically acclaimed and commercially successful.

I tried my hand at poetry before, in Hebrew, but failed. Tis strange. They say that poetry is the daughter of emotion. Not in my case.

I never felt except in prison – and yet there, I wrote in prose. The poetry I authored as one does math. It was the syllabic music that attracted me, the power to compose with words. I wasn't looking to express any profound truth or to convey a thing about myself. I wanted to recreate the magic of the broken metric. I still recite aloud a poem until it SOUNDS right. I write upright – the legacy of prison. I stand and type on a laptop perched atop a cardboard box. It is ascetic and, to me, so is poetry. A purity. An abstraction. A string of symbols open to exegesis. It is the most sublime intellectual pursuit in a world that narrowed down and has become only my intellect."

Return

The Sad Dreams of the Narcissist

I dream of my childhood. And in my dreams we are again one big unhappy family. I sob in my dreams, I never do when I am awake. When I am awake, I am dry, I am hollow, mechanically bent upon the maximisation of Narcissistic Supply. When asleep, I am sad. The all-pervasive, engulfing melancholy of somnolence. I wake up sinking, converging on a black hole of screams and pain. I withdraw in horror. I don't want to go there. I cannot go there.

People often mistake depression for emotion. They say: "But you are sad" and they mean: "But you are human", "But you have emotions". And this is wrong.

True, depression is a big component in a narcissist's emotional make-up. But it mostly has to do with the absence of Narcissistic Supply.

It mostly has to do with nostalgia to more plentiful days, full of adoration and attention and applause. It mostly occurs after the narcissist has depleted his Secondary Source of Narcissistic Supply (spouse, mate, girlfriend, colleagues) for a "replay" of his days of glory. Some narcissists even cry – but they cry exclusively for themselves and for their lost paradise. And they do so conspicuously and publicly – to attract attention.

The narcissist is a human pendulum hanging by the thread of the void that is his False Self. He swings between brutal and vicious abrasiveness – and mellifluous, saccharine sentimentality. It is all a simulacrum. A verisimilitude. A facsimile. Enough to fool the casual observer. Enough to extract the drug – other people's glances – the reflection that sustains this house of cards somehow.

But the stronger and more rigid the defences – and nothing is more resilient than narcissism – the bigger and deeper the hurt they aim to compensate for.

One's narcissism stands in direct relation to the seething abyss and the devouring vacuum that one harbours in one's True Self.

I know it's there. I catch glimpses of it when I am tired, when I hear music, when reminded of an old friend, a scene, a sight, a smell. I know it is awake when I am asleep. I know that it subsists of pain – diffuse and inescapable. I know my sadness. I have lived with it and I have encountered it full force.

Perhaps I choose narcissism, as I have been "accused". And if I do, it is a rational choice of self-preservation and survival. The paradox is that being a self-loathing narcissist may be the only act of self-love I have ever committed.

Return

The Lonely Narcissist

NPD (Narcissistic Personality Disorder) is often diagnosed with other mental health disorders (such as the Borderline, Histrionic, or Antisocial Personality Disorder). This is called "co-morbidity". It is also often accompanied by substance abuse and other reckless and impulsive behaviours and this is called "dual diagnosis".

But there is one curious match, one logic-defying co-appearance of mental health disorders: narcissism and the Schizoid Personality Disorder.

The basic dynamic of this particular brand of co-morbidity goes like this:

1. The narcissist feels superior, unique, entitled and better than his fellow men. He thus tends to despise them, to hold them in contempt and to regard them as lowly and subservient beings.
2. The narcissist feels that his time is invaluable, his mission of cosmic importance, his contributions priceless. He, therefore, demands total obedience and catering to his ever-changing needs. Any demands on his time and resources is deemed to be both humiliating and wasteful.
3. But the narcissist is DEPENDENT on input from other people for the performance of certain ego functions (such as the regulation of his sense of self-worth). Without Narcissistic Supply (adulation, adoration, attention), the narcissist shrivels and withers and is dysphoric (depressed).
4. The narcissist resents this dependence (described in point 3). He is furious at himself for his neediness and – in a typical narcissistic manoeuvre (called "alloplastic defence") – he blames OTHERS for his anger. He displaces his rage and its roots.
5. Many narcissists are paranoids. This means that they are afraid of people and of what people might do to them. Think about it: wouldn't you be scared and paranoid if your very life depended continually on the goodwill of others? The

narcissist's very life depends on others providing him with Narcissistic Supply. He becomes suicidal if they stop doing so.
6. To counter this overwhelming feeling of helplessness (dependence on Narcissistic Supply), the narcissist becomes a control freak. He sadistically manipulates others to his needs. He derives pleasure from the utter subjugation of his human environment.
7. Finally, the narcissist is a latent masochist. He seeks punishment, castigation and ex-communication. This self-destruction is the only way to validate powerful voices he internalised as a child ("You are a bad, rotten, hopeless child").

As you can easily see, the narcissistic landscape is fraught with contradictions. The narcissist depends on people – but hates and despises them. He wants to control them unconditionally – but is also looking to punish himself savagely. He is terrified of persecution ("persecutory delusions") – but seeks the company of his own "persecutors" compulsively.

The narcissist is the victim of incompatible inner dynamics, ruled by numerous vicious circles, pushed and pulled simultaneously by irresistible forces.

A minority of narcissist (I am one) choose the SCHIZOID SOLUTION. They choose, in effect, to disengage, both emotionally and socially.

Return

The Green Eyed Narcissist

Today I wrote to someone:
"The biggest source of personal strength is loneliness. The fountain of vigour and clarity and tranquillity and creativity erupts from extreme deprivation. It is when we cannot rely on others, nor depend on them (not even for our sexual fulfilment), when we neither expect, nor wish, nor dream - that we are invincible. It is when we lose everything purposefully - that we gain it back. Naked, in the moonlight, we extend a hand to the stars and are one with them, primordially and unconditionally.

When we discover ourselves - we naturally shed the world. We have no need for it, this empty shell of failed communication. We are perfectly and entirely neutral - not sad, nor elated, not scared and not proud. A state of nothingness contrasted to the former and depraved state of being. We crave no more. Are at peace.

I congratulate you on your independence."

I am constantly envious of people. This is my way of interacting with the world. I begrudge others their success, or brilliance, or happiness, or good fortune. I am driven to excesses of paranoia and guilt and fear that subside only after I "act out" or punish myself. It is a vicious cycle in which I am entrapped.

From "Cronos and His Children - Envy and Reparation" by Mary Ashwin - Chapter II, "Everyday Envy":

"Envy is forever looking upwards. It does not look sideways.

In 'Facial Justice' Hartley [1960] describes a life after a catastrophic war. A Dictator has decreed that envy is so destructive that it has to be eliminated. The citizens are coerced to be as alike each other as possible.

The worst crime is not envy itself but to excite envy.

'Equality and Envy - the two E's were ... the positive and negative poles on which the New State rotated' [p.12]. In order to exterminate envy everything that was enviable has been destroyed. Of course that in itself is the very essence of envy.

Neither envy nor equality are spoken of as words but referred to as Good and Bad E's. All tall buildings had been destroyed in the war except the tower of Ely Cathedral and none are allowed to be built – a horizontal view of life is required. No comparisons are to be made, women are encouraged to undertake an operation so they all looked alike, to be pretty would excite envy. The result is that the populace loses its humanity and becomes a non-thinking mass. The independently minded heroine, Jael, visits the Ely and looks up at the tower and leads a dance round it. She pays the price of having her more than averagely pretty face (an Alpha face) changed to a Beta face by cosmetic surgery and so made indistinguishable from the others."

The New Oxford Dictionary of English defines envy as:

"A feeling of discontented or resentful longing aroused by someone else's possessions, qualities, or luck."

And an earlier version (The Shorter Oxford English Dictionary) adds:

"Mortification and ill-will occasioned by the contemplation of another's superior advantages."

Pathological envy – the second deadly sin – is a compounded emotion. It is brought on by the realisation of some lack, deficiency, or inadequacy in oneself. It is the result of unfavourably comparing oneself to others: to their success, their reputation, their possessions, their luck, their qualities. It is misery and humiliation and impotent rage and a tortuous, slippery path to nowhere. The effort to break the padded walls of this self-visited purgatory often leads to attacks on the perceived source of frustration.

There is a spectrum of reactions to this pernicious and cognitively distorting emotion:

Subsuming the Object of Envy Through Imitation

Some narcissists seek to imitate or even emulate their (ever changing) role models. It is as if by imitating the object of his envy, the narcissist BECOMES that object. So, narcissists are likely to adopt their boss' typical gestures, the vocabulary of a successful politician, the views of an esteemed tycoon, even the countenance and actions of the (fictitious) hero of a movie or a novel.

In his pursuit of peace of mind, in his frantic effort to alleviate the burden of consuming jealousy, the narcissist often deteriorates to conspicuous and ostentatious consumption, impulsive and reckless behaviours and substance abuse.

Elsewhere I wrote:

"In extreme cases, to get rich quick through schemes of crime and corruption, to out-wit the system, to prevail is thought by these people to be the epitome of cleverness (providing one does not get caught), the sport of living, a winked-at vice, a spice."

Destroying the Frustrating Object

Other narcissists "choose" to destroy the object that gives them so much grief by provoking in them feelings of inadequacy and frustration. They display obsessive, blind animosity and engage in a compulsive acts of rivalry often at the cost of self-destruction and self-isolation.

In my essay "The Dance of Jael", I wrote:

"This hydra has many heads. From scratching the paint of new cars and flattening their tyres, to spreading vicious gossip, to media-hyped arrests of successful and rich businessmen, to wars against advantaged neighbours.

The stifling, condensed vapours of envy cannot be dispersed.

They invade their victims, their rageful eyes, their calculating souls, they guide their hands in evil doings and dip their tongues in vitriol...

(The envious narcissist's existence is) a constant hiss, a tangible malice, the piercing of a thousand eyes. The imminence and immanence of violence.

The poisoned joy of depriving the other of that which you don't or cannot have."

Self-Deprecation

From my essay, "The Dance of Jael":

"There are those narcissists who idealise the successful and the rich and the lucky. They attribute to them super-human, almost divine, qualities...

In an effort to justify the agonising disparities between themselves and others, they humble themselves as they elevate the others.

They reduce and diminish their own gifts, they disparage their own achievements, they degrade their own possessions and look with disdain and contempt upon their nearest and dearest, who are unable to discern their fundamental shortcomings. They feel worthy only of abasement and punishment. Besieged by guilt and remorse, voided of self-esteem, perpetually self-hating and self-deprecating – this is by far the more dangerous species of narcissist.

For he who derives contentment from his own humiliation cannot but derive happiness from the downfall of others. Indeed, most of them end up driving the objects of their own devotion and adulation to destruction and decrepitude..."

Cognitive Dissonance

"...But the most common reaction is the good old cognitive dissonance. It is to believe that the grapes are sour rather than to admit that they are craved.

These people devalue the source of their frustration and envy. They find faults, unattractive features, high costs to pay, immorality in everything they really most desire and aspire to and in everyone who has attained that which they so often can't. They walk amongst us, critical and self-righteous, inflated with a justice of their making and secure in the wisdom of being what they are rather than what they could have been and really wish to be. They make a virtue of jejune abstention, of wishful constipation, of judgmental neutrality, this oxymoron, the favourite of the disabled."

Avoidance - The Schizoid Solution

And then, of course, there is my favourite solution: avoidance. To witness the success and joy of others is too painful, too high a price to pay. So, I stay home, alone and incommunicado. I inhabit the artificial bubble that is my world where I am king and country, I am the law and yardstick, I am the one and only. There, in the penumbral recesses of my study, my flickering laptop for company, the only noises are electronic and I am the resident of my own burgeoning delusions. I am happy and soothed. I am what I can dream and dream my very being. I am no longer real, simply a narrative, an invention of my fervent mind, a colourful myth - sustaining and engulfing. I am content.

Return

The Discontinuous Narcissist

"But you hate kiwi!" – protests my girl – "How can anyone detest kiwi and then eat it so eagerly?" She is baffled. She is hurt. To some extent, she is even frightened to find herself with this kiwi-guzzling stranger.

How can I tell her that, in the absence of a self, there are no likes or dislikes, preferences, predictable behaviour or characteristics? It is not possible to know the narcissist. There is no one there.

The narcissist was conditioned – from an early age of abuse and trauma – to expect the unexpected. His was a world in motion where (sometimes sadistically) capricious caretakers and peers often engaged in arbitrary behaviour. He was trained to deny his True Self and nurture a False one.

Having invented himself, the narcissist sees no problem in re-inventing that which he designed in the first place. The narcissist is his own creator.

Hence his grandiosity.

Moreover, the narcissist is a man for all seasons, forever adaptable, constantly imitating and emulating, a human sponge, a perfect mirror, a non-entity that is, at the same time, all entities combined.

The narcissist is best described by Heidegger's phrase: "Being and Nothingness". Into this reflective vacuum, this sucking black hole, the narcissist attracts the Sources of his Narcissistic Supply.

To an observer, the narcissist appears to be fractured or discontinuous.

Pathological narcissism has been compared to the Dissociative Identity Disorder (formerly the Multiple Personality Disorder). By definition, the narcissist has at least two selves. His personality is very primitive and disorganised. Living with a narcissist is a nauseating experience not only because of what he is – but because of what he is NOT. He is not a fully formed human – but a dizzyingly kaleidoscopic gallery of mercurial images, which melt into each other seamlessly. It is incredibly disorienting.

It is also exceedingly problematic. Promises made by the narcissist are easily disowned by him. His plans are ephemeral. His emotional ties – a simulacrum. Most narcissists have one island of stability in their life (spouse, family, their career, a hobby, their religion, country, or idol) – pounded by the turbulent currents of a dishevelled existence.

Thus, to invest in a narcissist is a purposeless, futile and meaningless activity. To the narcissist, every day is a new beginning, a hunt, a new cycle of idealisation or devaluation, a newly invented self.

There is no accumulation of credits or goodwill because the narcissist has no past and no future. He occupies an eternal and timeless present. He is a fossil caught in the frozen lava of a volcanic childhood.

The narcissist does not keep agreements, does not adhere to laws, regards consistency and predictability as demeaning traits. The narcissist hates kiwi one day – and devours it passionately the next.

Return

Dr. Jackal and Mr. Hide

Narcissists are either cerebral or somatic. In other words, they either generate their Narcissistic Supply by applying their bodies or by applying their minds.

The somatic narcissist flaunts his sexual conquests, parades his possessions, exhibits his muscles, brags about his physical aesthetics or sexual prowess or exploits, is often a health freak and a hypochondriac. The cerebral narcissist is a know-it-all, haughty and intelligent "computer". He uses his awesome intellect, or knowledge (real or pretended) to secure adoration, adulation and admiration. To him, his body and its maintenance are a burden and a distraction.

Both types are auto-erotic (psychosexually in love with themselves, with their bodies and with their brain). Both types prefer masturbation to adult, mature, interactive, multi-dimensional and emotion-laden sex.

The cerebral narcissist is often celibate (even when he has a girlfriend or a spouse). He prefers pornography and sexual auto-stimulation to the real thing. The cerebral narcissist is sometimes a latent (hidden, not yet outed) homosexual.

The somatic narcissist uses other people's bodies to masturbate. Sex with him – pyrotechnics and acrobatics aside – is likely to be an impersonal and emotionally alienating and draining experience. The partner is often treated as an object, an extension of the somatic narcissist, a toy, a warm and pulsating vibrator.

It is a mistake to assume type-constancy. In other words, all narcissists are BOTH cerebral and somatic. In each narcissist, one of the types is dominant. So, the narcissist is either OVERWHELMINGLY cerebral – or DOMINANTLY somatic. But the other type, the recessive (manifested less frequently) type, is there. It is lurking, waiting to erupt.

The narcissist swings between his dominant type and his recessive type. The latter is expressed mainly as a result of a major narcissistic injury or life crisis.

I can give you hundreds of examples from my correspondence but, instead, let's talk about me (of course).

I am a cerebral narcissist. I brandish my brainpower, exhibit my intellectual achievements, bask in the attention given to my mind and its products. I hate my body and neglect it. It is a nuisance, a burden, a derided appendix, an inconvenience, a punishment. Needless to add that I rarely have sex (often years apart). I masturbate regularly, very mechanically, as one would change water in an aquarium. I stay away from women because I perceive them to be ruthless predators who are out to consume me and mine.

I have had quite a few major life crises. I got divorced, lost millions a few times, did time in one of the worst prisons in the world, fled countries as a political refugee, was threatened, harassed and stalked by powerful people and groups. I have been devalued, betrayed, denigrated and insulted.

Invariably, following every life crisis, the somatic narcissist in me took over. I became a lascivious lecher. When this happened, I had a few relationships – replete with abundant and addictive sex – going simultaneously. I participated in and initiated group sex and mass orgies. I exercised, lost weight and honed my body into an irresistible proposition.

This outburst of unrestrained, primordial lust waned in a few months and I settled back into my cerebral ways. No sex, no women, no body.

These total reversals of character stun my mates. My girlfriends and spouse found it impossible to digest this eerie transformation from the gregarious, darkly handsome, well-built and sexually insatiable person that swept them off their feet – to the bodiless, bookwormish hermit with not an inkling of interest in either sex or other carnal pleasures.

I miss my somatic half. I wish I could find a balance, but I know it is a doomed quest. This sexual beast of mine will forever be trapped in the intellectual cage that is I, Sam Vaknin, the Brain.

Return

Portrait of the Narcissist as a Young Man

Abuse has many forms. Expropriating someone's childhood in favour of adult pursuits is one of the subtlest varieties of soul murder.

I never was a child. I was a "wunderkind", the answer to my mother's prayers and intellectual frustration. A human computing machine, a walking-talking encyclopaedia, a curiosity, a circus freak. I was observed by developmental psychologists, interviewed by the media, endured the envy of my peers and their pushy mothers. I constantly clashed with figures of authority because I felt entitled to special treatment, immune to prosecution and superior. It was a narcissist's dream. Abundant Narcissistic Supply – rivers of awe, the aura of glamour, incessant attention, open adulation, country-wide fame.

I refused to grow up. In my mind, my tender age was an integral part of the precocious miracle that I became. One looks much less phenomenal and one's exploits and achievements are much less awe-inspiring at the age of 40, I thought. Better stay young forever and thus secure my Narcissistic Supply.

So, I wouldn't grow up. I never took out a driver's licence.

I do not have children. I rarely have sex. I never settle down in one place. I reject intimacy. In short: I refrain from adulthood and adult chores. I have no adult skills. I assume no adult responsibilities. I expect indulgence from others. I am petulant and haughtily spoiled. I am capricious, infantile and emotionally labile and immature. In short: I am a 40 years old brat.

When I talk to my girlfriend, I do so in a baby's voice, making baby faces and baby gestures. It is a pathetic and repulsive sight, very much like a beached whale trying to imitate a seaborne trout. I want to be her child, you see, I want to regain my lost childhood. I want to be admired as I was when I was one year old and recited poems in three languages to stunned visiting high school teachers. I want to be four again, when I first read a daily paper to the silent astonishment of the neighbours.

I am not preoccupied with my age, nor am I obsessed with my dwindling, fat flapping body. I am no hypochondriac. But There is a streak of sadness in me, like an undercurrent and a defiance of Time itself. Like Dorian Gray, I want to remain as I was when I became the centre of attention, the focus of adoration, the heart of a twister of media attention. I know I can't. And I know that I have failed not only at arresting Chronos – but on a more mundane, degrading level. I failed as an adult.

Interview with Arllen

Q: As a narcissist, did you go to school? If so, what kind? What did you think of the facilities? The other students? The teachers? And what was your overall experience of the school years?

A: I attended both primary and high school in my hometown in Israel – a community of immigrants hardened by economic duress and constant insecurity. The facilities – sponsored by wealthy American Jews out to immortalise themselves – were more than adequate. I especially loved the library, an oasis of serene knowledge in a sea of boorishness and irrationality. I was a bespectacled, flabby, smelly and inert student but considered myself, haughtily and unjustly, intellectually superior to both my fellow pupils and our youngish and inexperienced teachers. Overall, I felt, school was a drudgery I had to endure before my meteoric rise to unbridled fame commences.

Q: Was any of the subject matter they taught of any interest to you, if so, what and why? What was your most favourite and least favourite subject and why?

A: My most favourite subject was history because I was allowed to teach it and thus to indulge in theatrics and power plays. I detested math because my inaptitude in it deflated my grandiosity and my claim to be a Renaissance Man.

Q: How were you treated by the other students? By the teachers?

A: Largely with pity and disdain, I guess. Though a few – both students and teachers – succumbed to my dubious charms and admired my accomplishments, whether real and imaginary. These acolytes were at the mercy of my capricious and overweening conduct. They formed my fan club, a source of adulation, affirmation and obsequious applause.

Earlier on I was allowed to skip one year and go directly from fourth to sixth grade. For a short while, I became the toast of the town. I then leveraged this fortuitous celebrity by brazenly lying about the extent of my academic achievements. I learned a few crucial lessons: you are what you say you are, people crave to be manipulated, victims prefer fantasies to reality and it is obscenely easy to gain fame.

Q: Did you have a pet during your school years, if so, what happened to it?

A: I never had a pet, though I came close by sharing a turtle with my siblings and a snail with my ex-wife.

Q: Did you happen to make any friends from the student body? If so, do you still keep in contact with them?

A: My life is rigidly compartmentalised. "Friends" belong to time periods, forever locked in mental boxes. The minute I move from one period to the next, relocate, or find a new interest - I lose my "friendships" and "relationships" as that much ballast. I never look back and I actively refuse contact with figures from my former lives.

I did have "buddies" in both primary and high school - mainly collaborators in nasty deeds conceived largely by me and, at the time, deemed hilarious by all of us. But these were shallow and ephemeral liaisons. My prankish creativity did not buy me he other students' love or affiliation. They regarded me as a freak whose very freakishness allowed him to innovate.

Additionally, I attached myself to a series of mentally disordered or challenged students and deliberately played meticulously executed mind games on them intended to gain unmitigated control over their mental functions. One of the victims ended up in an asylum. This propensity did not survive primary school, I am glad to say.

Q: Did you have favourite teachers, if so why were they your favourites?

A: I had two favourite teachers - one in primary school and one in high school. The first was chosen due to a confluence of circumstances. She taught me English in my aforementioned brief days of glory and was, therefore, associated in my mind with the "good old times". I had a crush on her - the urbanite, sexually liberated, glamorous, well-read woman that she was. She was the first person I dared disclose my overwhelming emotional distress to.

The other favourite instructor, in high school, was her antithesis. Fat, a-feminine, brooding, moody - but she worshipped the ground I walked on. I needed this kind of unconditional acceptance. I was going through a rough patch. My grades deteriorated. My budding sexuality was thwarted by my perverted self-image. She gave me hope and restored in me a modicum of self-confidence by surrendering her classes. I taught as she sat at the back of the class, glowing.

Q: Were you involved in any extracurricular activities such as clubs, sports, or theatre?

A: I lectured a lot and made numerous appearances in school plays. I was the town crier and the master of ceremonies of the local municipality. I published poetry and, by the age of 16, had my own column in a regional rag. I worked in the local library and also tutored immigrants, mainly from Russia and Soviet Georgia. I was a very active lad. I even invented an extremely detailed and micromanaged daily schedule to better myself through a self-imposed syllabus of reading and theatre-going.

Q: Did you attend parties or dances during the school years?

A: Not even once.

Q: Did you learn how to play any musical instruments, sing or dance? Is art something you enjoy? If so, why?

A: The only form of art I really enjoy – to the point of addiction – is cinema. I do pretend, of course, to be interested in higher-brow pursuits: painting, sculpture and music. But at heart I am not, it is merely perfunctory. I played the flute when I was young because my mother wanted to. I stopped the minute she lost interest.

Q: What activities did you do for fun?

A: Reading and – far more rarely – watching movies.

Q: Did you seek out or were approached by suitors?

A: In hindsight I now understand that some girls found me attractive – though why, it eludes me. But I was unable – and, at times, resentfully unwilling – to decipher their increasingly desperate signals. I, myself, never courted. I haven't had sex until the age of 25and have first fully masturbated – with ejaculation – only when I was 19. I was – and am still – very retarded sexually, on the verge of being a-sexual.

Q: What role did your parents play in your life during the school years?

A: I perceived my mother as both an evil entity, out to harm me, hating and contemptuous – and the driving force in my life. For a stretch of time, everything I did was geared to impress her and disprove her lowly opinion of me. When it was clear that I do not stand a fighting chance against her searing disappointment and disdain, I gave up completely. I did not proceed to university and have been peripatetic ever since with little to show for my efforts.

My father was tyrannical but also more lovable because he was mostly absent, toiling hard to extract us from the slums. When present, he was so manifestly sad and frustrated, so down-trodden and ineffectually rebellious that my insurrection against his arbitrariness was inevitably interspersed with moments of great pity.

Q: Did you have any siblings? If so, what role did they play in your life then?

A: I am the first born and my siblings are far younger than me. I, thus, emulated my father's despotism in my relationships with them. In later years, as I became economically independent, I endeavoured to secure their affection with numerous gifts. In all, I was a fun brother, always full of stories and wild poems – but, more typically, remote, uninterested and ensconced in an imaginary escapist Universe of my own making. My prolonged and recurrent emotional – and, later, physical – absences have deeply injured my siblings who, throughout their childhoods, were my most ardent, persistent and blind admirers.

Q: Did you notice any racism or prejudice amongst the students?

A: I belong to a minority – the Moroccan Jews – much derided in Israel for its alleged backwardness, ignorance, proneness to superstition, paranoia and hot temper. Inevitably, I was judged more by the stereotype than by any biographical fact. This greatly affected my anyhow volatile sense of self-worth, self-esteem and self-confidence. For a short time I was even active in divisive ethnic politics in Israel.

Q: How did you tend to dress while attending school?

A: We wore obligatory school uniforms so personal choice was never an issue. Off-school, though, I fitted my unwieldy body into whatever clothes my parents bought me. To this very day, I dress shabbily and inappropriately – when at home, virtually in tattered rags.

Return

Pseudologica Fantastica

In "Streetcar Named Desire", Blanche, the sister in law of Marlon Brando, is accused by him of inventing a false biography, replete with exciting events and desperate wealthy suitors. She responds that it is preferable to lead an imaginary but enchanted life – then a real but dreary one.

This, approximately, is my attitude, as well. My biography needs no embellishments. It is chock full of adventures, surprising turns of events, governments and billionaires, prisons and luxury hotels, criminals and ministers, fame and infamy, wealth and bankruptcy. I have lived a hundred lives. All I need to do is tell it straight. And yet I can't.

Moreover, I exaggerate everything. If a newspapers publishes my articles, I describe it as "the most widely circulated", or "the most influential". If I meet someone, I make him out to be "the most powerful", "most enigmatic", "most something". If I make a promise, I always promise the impossible or undoable.

To put it less gently, I lie. Compulsively and needlessly.

All the time.

About everything. And I often contradict myself.

Why do I need to do this?

To make myself interesting or attractive. In other words, to secure Narcissistic Supply (attention, admiration, adulation, gossip). I refuse to believe that I can be of interest to anyone as I am. My mother was interested in me only when I achieved something. Since then I flaunt my achievements – or invent ones. I feel certain that people are more interested in my fantasies than in me.

This way I also avoid the routine, the mundane, the predictable, the boring.

In my mind, I can be anywhere, do anything and I am good at convincing people to participate in my scripts. It is movie-making. I should have been a director.

Pseudologica Fantastica is the compulsive need to lie consistently and about everything, however inconsequential – even if it yields no benefits to the liar. I am not that bad. But when I want to impress – I lie.

I love to see people excited, filled with wonder, bedazzled, dreamy, starry eyed, or hopeful. I guess I am a little like the myth spinners, legend tellers and troubadours of yore. I know that at the end of my rainbow there is nothing but a broken pot. But I so want to make people happy! I so want to feel the power of a giver, a God, a benefactor, a privileged witness.

So, I lie. Do you believe me?

Return

I Cannot Forgive

I am cursed with mental X-ray vision. I see through people's emotional shields, their petty lies, their pitiable defences, their grandiose fantasies. I know when they deviate from the truth and by how much. I intuitively grasp their self-interested goals and accurately predict the strategy and tactics they will adopt in order to achieve them.

I cannot stand self-important, self-inflated, pompous, bigoted, self-righteous, and hypocritical people. I rage at the inefficient, the lazy, the hapless and the weak.

Perhaps this is because I recognise myself in them. I try to break the painful reflection of my own flaws in theirs.

I home in on the chinks in their laboriously constructed armours. I spot their Achilles heel and attach to it. I prick the gasbags that most people are. I deflate them. I force them to confront their finiteness and helplessness and mediocrity. I negate their sense of uniqueness. I reduce them to proportion and provide them with a perspective. I do so cruelly and abrasively and sadistically and lethally efficiently. I have no compassion. And I prey on their vulnerabilities, however microscopic, however well-concealed.

I expose their double-talk and deride their double standards. I refuse to play their games of prestige and status and hierarchy. I draw them out of their shelters. I destabilise them. I deconstruct their narratives, their myths, their superstitions, their hidden assumptions, their polluted language. I call a spade a spade.

I force them to react and, by reacting, to confront their true, dilapidated selves, their dead end careers, their mundane lives, the death of their hopes and wishes and their shattered dreams. And all that time I observe them with the passionate hatred of the outcast and the dispossessed.

The truths about them, the ones they are trying so desperately to conceal, especially from themselves. The facts denied, so ugly and uncomfortable. Those things that never get mentioned in proper company, the politically incorrect, the personally hurtful, the dark, ignored, and hidden secrets, the tumbling skeletons, the taboos, the fears, the atavistic urges, the pretensions, the social lies, the distorted narratives of life – piercing, bloodied and ruthless – these are my revenge, the settling of scores, the levelling of the battlefield.

I lance them – the high and mighty and successful and the happy people, those who possess what I deserve and never had, the object of my green eyed monsters. I inconvenience them, I make them think, reflect on their own misery and wallow in its rancid outcomes. I coerce them to confront their zombie state, their own sadism, their unforgivable deeds and unforgettable omissions. I dredge the sewer that is their mind, forcing to the surface long repressed emotions, oft suppressed pains, their nightmares and their fears.

And I pretend to do so selflessly, "for their own good". I preach and hector and pour forth vitriolic diatribes and expose and impose and writhe and foam in the proverbial mouth – all for the greater good. I am so righteous, so true, so geared to help, so meritorious. My motives are unassailable. I am always so chillingly reasoned, so algorithmically precise. I am a the frozen wrath. I play their alien game by their very own rules. But I am so foreign to them, that I am unbeatable. Only they do not realise it yet.

Return

The Ghost in the Machine

I have no roots. I was born in Israel but left it many times and now have been away for five years. I haven't seen my parents since 1996. I have met my sister (and my niece and nephew) for the first time last week. I haven't been in touch with any of my "friends". I haven't exchanged one additional word with my ex after we split up. I – an award winning author – am slowly forgetting my Hebrew. I do not celebrate any nation's holidays or festivals. I stay away from groups and communities. I wander, an itinerant lone wolf. I was born in the Middle East, I write about the Balkan and my readers are mostly American.

This reads like a typical profile of the modern expatriate professional the world over – but it is not. It is not a temporary suspension of self-identity, of group-identity, of location, of mother tongue and of one's social circle. In my case, I have nowhere to go back to. I either burn the bridges or keep walking. I never look back. I detach and vanish.

I am not sure why I behave this way. I like to travel and I like to travel light. On the way, in between places, in the twilight zone of neither here not there and not now – I feel like I am unburdened. I do not need to – indeed, I cannot – secure Narcissistic Supply. My obscurity and anonymity are excused ("I am a stranger here", "I just arrived"). I can relax and take refuge from my inner tyranny and from the anxious depletion of energy that is my existence as a narcissist.

I love freedom. With no possessions, devoid of all attachments, to fly away, to be carried, to explore, not to be me. It is the ultimate depersonalisation. Only then do I feel real. Sometimes I wish I were so rich that I could afford to travel incessantly, without ever stopping. I guess it sounds like escaping and avoiding oneself. I guess it is.

I do not like myself. In my dreams, I find myself an inmate in a concentration camp, or in a tough prison, or a dissident in a murderously dictatorial country. These are all symbols of my inner captivity, my debilitating addiction, the death amidst me. Even in my nightmares, though, I keep fighting and sometimes I win. But my gains are temporary and I am so tired...

In my mind, I am not human. I am a machine at the service of a madman that snatched my body and invaded my being when I was very young. Imagine the terror I live with, the horror of having an alien within your own self. A shell, a nothingness, I keep producing articles at an ever accelerating pace. I write maniacally, unable to cease, unable to eat, or sleep, or bathe, or enjoy. I am possessed by me. Where does one find refuge if one's very abode, one's very soul is compromised and dominated by one's mortal enemy – oneself?

Return

That Thing Between a Man and a Woman...

... I lack.

That moistly energy, the hungry eyes, the imperceptible tilt of bodies lusting, that magnetism. I do not have it. I do not know the frequency of the silent broadcasts of sexuality. My face is handsome in a man-child way. My features broad but quite agreeable. Sometimes I am rich and powerful or famous. Women are curious.

Until a few years back I was able to disguise my illness. I mimicked the behaviours, the intricate messages, the subtle bodily perfumes, the long and longing looks. But now I can't. I am exhausted. These rites of procreation drain me of the energy I need so abundantly in my pursuit of my supply. Freud called it sublimation. I am a prolific author. My seeds are verbal. My passion is abstract. I rarely fuck.

In women I induce confusion. They are attracted, then repelled by something they cannot explain, nor name. "He is so unpleasant" - they say, hesitantly - "He is so... violent... and so... disagreeable". They mean to say I am not a healthy person altogether. The animals we are, they sense my illness. I read somewhere that female birds avoid the sickly males in mating season. I am one sickly bird and they avoid me with the hurt perplexity of the frustrated. In this modern world of "what you see is what you get", the narcissist is an exception. A packaged deception, a diversion, a virtual reality with awry programming.

Not long ago, I was still able to control myself, to hide my vile thoughts, to play the social game, to mimetically engage in human intercourse. I can no longer. I am the denuded narcissist - bereft of old defences. This transparency is the ultimate - and psychopathic - act of sheer contempt. People are not even worth maintaining my defences anymore. This frightens women. They sense the danger. Psychic annihilation is often irresistible, the brinkmanship of self-destruction luring. That evil is aesthetic we all know. But it is also so alien, like waking from a nightmare into its continuation in reality.

But I am not an evil man, I am simply indifferent and wish not to be bothered. This schizoid streak conflicts with my narcissism and with my virility. The narcissist devours people, consumes their output, and casts the empty, writhing shells aside. The schizoid avoids them at all costs. As a man, I am very much attracted to the opposite sex. I am imaginative in my fantasies and prone to sexual abandon. But to a schizoid, women are nuisance and annoyance. Obtaining voluntary sex requires too much effort and waste of scarce resources.

Most narcissists go through schizoid phases in their inexorable orbits of gloom and mania. Sometimes the schizoid prevails. A narcissist that is also a schizoid is an unnatural hybrid, a chimera, a shattered personality. The push and pull, the approach and the avoidance, the compulsive search for the drugs that only humans can provide and the no less compulsive urge to avoid them altogether... it is a sorry sight. The narcissist shrivels and withers as the battle is prolonged. He becomes almost psychotic at the tug of war inside him. Alienated even from his False Self by his schizoid disorder, such a narcissist is turned into a gaping black hole, out to suck the vitality of those around him.

So, you see, that thing between a woman and a man – I lack it.

Return

The Malignant Optimism of the Abused

I often come across sad examples of the powers of self-delusion that the narcissist provokes in his victims. It is what I call "malignant optimism". People refuse to believe that some questions are unsolvable, some diseases incurable, some disasters inevitable. They see a sign of hope in every fluctuation. They read meaning and patterns into every random occurrence, utterance, or slip. They are deceived by their own pressing need to believe in the ultimate victory of good over evil, health over sickness, order over disorder. Life appears otherwise so meaningless, so unjust and so arbitrary... So, they impose upon it a design, progress, aims, and paths. This is magical thinking.

"If only he tried hard enough", "If he only really wanted to heal", "If only we found the right therapy", "If only his defences were down", "There MUST be something good and worthy under the hideous facade", "NO ONE can be that evil and destructive", "He must have meant it differently", "God, or a higher being, or the spirit, or the soul is the solution and the answer to our prayers".

The Pollyanna defences of the abused against the emerging and horrible understanding that humans are specks of dust in a totally indifferent universe, the playthings of evil and sadistic forces, of which the narcissist is one – as well as against the unbearable realisation that their pain means nothing to anyone but themselves. Nothing whatsoever. It has all been in vain.

The narcissist holds such thinking in barely undisguised contempt. To him, it is a sign of weakness, the scent of prey, a gaping vulnerability. He uses and abuses this human need for order, good, and meaning – as he uses and abuses all other human needs. Gullibility, selective blindness, malignant optimism – these are the weapons of the beast. And the abused are hard at work to provide it with its arsenal.

Return

No One Counts to Ten

I make it a point to triumphantly ignore and belittle figures of authority. Knowing that their options of retaliation are rather limited by my official position, or by law – I abuse them flagrantly. When a security guard or a policeman halts me, I pretend I haven't heard him and proceed with callous disregard. When threatened, I go unpredictably wild. In doing so I (very often) provoke repulsion and pity and (much less often) fear and amazement. Often I find myself in danger, always punished, forever the losing party.

So, why do it?

First, because it feels great. To experience immunity, shielded behind an invisible wall, untouchable, and, therefore, by implication, omnipotent.

Second, because I actively and knowingly seek to be punished, perceived as the "bad man", the corrupt, no good, vile, heartless, villain.

Third, I project my own shortcomings, deficiencies, pain, and rage onto these mother and father substitutes. I then react to these behaviours and negative emotions I perceive in others with righteous and furious indignation.

My inability to work in a team, to be instructed, to accept orders, to admit to ignorance, to listen to reason, and to succumb to social conventions, or to superior knowledge and credentials – transformed me into a reclusive and clownish disappointment. People are always misled by my intelligence into predicting a bright future for me and my work. I end up shattering their hopes. Mine is a heartless march to heartbreak.

So, what now?

I am a little over forty and a lot overweight. My teeth are rotting and my breath is bad. I am entirely celibate. I am a ruptured nervous wreck. I communicate almost exclusively through rage attacks and vitriolic diatribes. I cannot go back to my own disintegrating country – and am trapped in another. I desperately seek Narcissistic Supply. I delude myself regarding my achievements and status, fully aware of my self-delusion. It is surrealistic, this infinite regression of mirrors, true and false. Mine is the on going nightmare of reality itself.

And beneath it all, there is an ominous spring of sadness. The flotsam that is my being in the murky puddle of my pain. I do not feel it anymore, I just recognise its existence, like a presence in the dark.

I am devoid of energy. I am denuded of defences. I stumble. I get up. I stumble again. Floored, no one bothers to count to ten. I know I will revive. I know I will survive. I just don't know what for.

Return

The Ubiquitous Narcissist

The narcissist feels omnipresent, all-pervasive, the prime mover and shaker, the cause of all things. Hence his constant projection of his own traits, fears, behaviour patterns, beliefs, and plans onto others. The narcissist is firmly convinced that he is the generator of other people's emotions, that they depend on him for their well-being, that without him their lives will crumble into grey mediocrity. He regards himself as the most important part in the life of his nearest and dearest. To avoid painful contradictions with reality, the narcissist aims to micromanage and control his human environment.

But this only one aspect of the pathology.

The second aspect is malignant cynicism. A healthy modicum of doubt and caution is... well... healthy. But the narcissist is addicted to excess doses of both. To the narcissist, all people are narcissists – others are simply hypocritical when they pretend to be "normal". They are weak and fear society's reactions, so they adhere to its edicts and behavioural-moral codes. The narcissist magically feels strong, immune to punishment, and invincible and thus able to express his true nature fearlessly and openly.

Consider generosity and altruism, the daughters of empathy – that which the narcissist is absolutely devoid of.

I cannot digest or fathom true generosity. I immediately suspect ulterior motives (though not necessarily sinister ones). I ask myself: Why the helping hand? How come the trust placed in me? What do they really want from me? How (unbeknownst to me) do I benefit them? What is the disguised self-interest which drives their perplexing behaviour? Don't these people know better? Don't they realise that people are all, without exception, self-centred, interest-driven, unnecessarily malevolent, ignorant, and abusive? In other words, I am surprised that my true nature does not show instantly. I feel like an incandescent lamp. I feel that people can see through my transparent defences and that what they see must surely horrify and repel them.

When this does not happen, I am shocked.

I am shocked because altruistic, loving, caring, and generous behaviours expose as false the hidden assumptions underlying my mental edifice. Not everyone is a narcissist. People do care for each other for no immediate reward. And, most damaging of all, I am loveable.

Return

The Disappearance of the Witnesses

I live through others. I inhabit their memories of me. Bits and pieces of Sam are strewn across continents, among hundreds of casual acquaintances, friends, lovers, teachers, admirers, and despisers. I exist by reflection. This is the essence of Secondary Narcissistic Supply - the secure knowledge that I am replicated in the minds of many. I want to be remembered because without being remembered I am not. I need to be discussed because I have no being except as a topic of discussion. So, passive memory is not enough. I need to be actively reminded of my achievements, of my moments of glory, of past adulation. The constancy of these streams of memories smoothes the inevitable fluctuations in Primary Narcissistic Supply. In lean moments, when I am all but forgotten, or when I feel humiliated by the gap between my reality and my grandiosity - these memories of past grandeur, related to me by outside "observers" lift my spirits. It is the main function of people in my life: to tell me how great I am because of how great I was.

I was a precocious child. Always the wunderkind with oversized spectacles, the freak. I befriended only men many years my senior. At the age of 20, the youngest of my best friends - among which I counted a mafia don, a political scientist, businessmen, authors, and journalists - was 40. Their age, experience and social standing made them ideal Sources of Narcissistic Supply. They fed me, hosted me in their homes, bought me reference books, introduced me to each other, interviewed me, and took me on expensive trips to foreign lands. I was their darling, the subject of much awe and adulation.

Now, twenty years and some later, these are old people and they are dying. Their kids are in their late twenties. They are out of the loop. And when they die, their memories of me die with them. They take to their grave my Secondary Narcissistic Supply. I slightly fade with every passing one of them. They, the dying and the dead, are the only ones who know. They are the witnesses of who I was back then and why. They are my only chance at ever getting to know myself at all. When the last of them is interred - I will be no more. I will have lost my stab at proper self-introduction. It feels so sad never to know Sam. It feels so lonely, like a child's grave in autumn.

Return

Physique Dysmorphique

For most of my childhood and adolescence I believed that I had an enormous, elephantine skull. I didn't. Actually, I am told that my head is unusually small in comparison to my body. This is especially true after I put on another 20 kilos in weight.

So, why was I wrong about the size of my head for such a long and critical period of my life?

I am a cerebral narcissist. I derive my Narcissistic Supply from people's reactions to my intellectual achievements – real or fictitious. No wonder that I exaggerated the dimensions of the site and exclusive source of my life sustaining gratification. Children draw adults as giants. Budding cerebral narcissists misconstrue the size of their skulls.

Possessing a distorted physical self-image is called a Body Dysmorphic Disorder. All narcissists have it to some degree. Somatic narcissists are especially prone to misjudge their bodies – either positively or negatively. They believe themselves to be physically irresistible, exuding sex and energy, statuesquely shaped, and, in general, stunning hunks. This grandiose self-image rarely corresponds with reality, though.

Aware of this, the somatic narcissist dedicates inordinate amounts of time and effort to body building, exercising, mastering sexual advances and foreplay and the intricacies of the coital act itself. To enhance his belief system, the somatic narcissist co-opts others by forcing them to compliment his build, shape, constitution, health, sexual prowess, physical regime and attractiveness. The somatic narcissist is a compulsive consumer of "body complements or extensions" – objects that he thinks increase his attraction, irresistibility, appeal, and the value of his propositions. Fancy cars, flashy clothing, sumptuous residences, first class flights, luxury hotels, platinum credit cards, lavish parties, name-dropping, celebrity "friends", hi-tech gadgetry – all serve to enhance the narcissist's self-image and to bolster his grandiose fantasies.

Thus, this positive Dysmorphic Disorder serves to elicit Narcissistic Supply and buttress a distorted, unreal, self-image. But it is also a control mechanism. It allows the narcissist's False Self to manipulate both the narcissist and his human environment. It is as though by morphing his body – the narcissist moulds and designs his world, his nearest and dearest, his self in flux, his projected image and the reactions to it. By lying about his body, his health, his sex appeal, his longevity, his possessions (his bodily extensions), his sexual prowess, his attractiveness, his irresistibility, his friends and lovers, adventures and affairs – the narcissist transforms the REAL world. To him, the REAL world – is how people PERCEIVE him to be. By changing their perceptions, by indoctrinating and "brainwashing" them – the narcissist secures a Pathological Narcissistic Space in which his Self False can thrive, fully nourished.

This phenomenon is not limited to the somatic narcissist. The cerebral narcissist also deforms the true image of his body in his mind. He may exaggerate the dimensions of his head, the height of his forehead, or the length of his (sensitive) fingers. He may attribute to himself ailments and syndromes typical of high powered intellectuals – consumption (tuberculosis), tendonitis, headaches. The cerebral narcissist almost always lies about his IQ, his mental capacities, his skills. He tends to completely ignore and belittle the rest of his body. To him, it is a burdensome and unnecessary appendage. He may complain of the need to "maintain" the flesh and of the derided dependence of his magnificent brain on his abject and decaying body. "I would have willingly placed my brain in a laboratory jar, to be artificially nourished there, and given up my body" – they may say. They rarely exercise and regard with disdain the activities, proclivities, and predilections of the somatic narcissist. Physical pursuits – sex included – are perceived by them to be bestial, demeaning, common, wasteful, and meaningless. This is also a result of Body Dysmorphic Disorder. The cerebral narcissist underestimates the needs of his own body, misreads its signals, and ignores its processes. The body, to him, becomes abstract, a background noise, or nuisance.

Cerebral narcissists sometimes go through somatic phases and somatic narcissists – if capable – adopt cerebral behaviour patterns. Their attitudes change accordingly. The temporarily somatic narcissist suddenly begins to exercise, groom himself, seduce, and have creative and imaginative sex. The somatic made cerebral tries to read more, becomes contemplative and a-social, and consumes culture. But these are passing phases and the narcissist always reverts to true – or should I say, false – form.

Return

Being There

I am often shocked when presented with incontrovertible evidence to an event in my past, something I said, or did, a person I knew, a sentence I have written. I do not remember having done, said, or written what is attributed to me. I do not recall having met the person, having felt anything, having been there. It is not that it looks alien to me, as though it happened to someone else. I simply have no recollection whatsoever, I draw a blank. Hence my enormous and recurrent and terrifyingly helpless state of surprise. These cognitive distortions, these lapses of memory are as close as I ever get to losing control.

My terror is mixed with voyeuristic fascination. Through the writings, through the reconstructed utterances, through a careful study of what that other, previous, "Sam" has done, or said, or written – I come to learn myself. I meet myself on numerous occasions, reflections in the shattered mirrors of my dysfunctional, selective memory. These frequent occurrences of dissociative amnesia – when I repress the painful, the irrelevant, the useless – are the fabric of the punctuated being that is I.

But what are the rules determining this ruthless and automatic censorship? What governs the selection process? What events, people, writings, thoughts, emotions, hopes are cast into my oblivion – and why do others etch themselves indelibly? Is the repository of my discarded reality – my True Self, that dilapidated, immature, scared and atrophied little child inside me? Am I afraid to get in touch with memory itself, spun from the yarn of pains and disappointments? In short: is this an emotional involvement prevention mechanism?

It's not. On introspection, I simply erase and atomise that which is no longer of use in the pursuit of Narcissistic Supply. I read books, magazines, Web pages, research papers, official memoranda, and daily papers. I then retain in accessible long-term memory only the facts, the views, the news, the theories, the words that can help me elicit Narcissistic Supply. Like the proverbial squirrel, I amass intellectual assets that yield the maximum astonishment, adulation, and attention in my listeners. All the rest I discard contemptuously, though, by now, after decades of self-training, unconsciously. I, therefore, rarely remember anything I read just minutes after having read it. I cannot recall movie plots, story lines of novels, a reasoned argument in an article, the history of any nation, or things I myself have authored. No matter how many times I re-read my own essays, I find them absolutely new, none of the sentences recognisable. I then proceed to forget them instantly.

Similarly, I alter my biography at will, to suit the potential Sources of Narcissistic Supply who happen to be listening. I say things not because I believe in them, nor because I know them to be true (in truth, I know very little and ignorant of much). I say things because I am desperately trying to impress, provoke responses, bask in the glow of affirmation, extract applause. Naturally, I very soon forget what I said. Not the result of a coherent structure of deeply assimilated and integrated knowledge, or of a set of convictions – my utterances, judgements, opinions, beliefs, wishes, plans, analyses, comments, and narratives are ephemeral improvisations. Here today, gone tomorrow, unbeknownst to me.

Before I meet someone, I learn everything I can about him. I then proceed to acquire superficial knowledge that is certain to create the impression of genius bordering on omniscience. If I am to meet a politician from Turkey, whose hobby is farming, and is the author of books about ancient pottery – I will while away days and nights studying Turkish history, ancient pottery, and farming. Not an hour after the meeting – having inspired awesome admiration in my new acquaintance - all the facts I so meticulously memorised evaporate, never to return. The original views I expressed so confidently vanish from my mind. I am preoccupied with my next prey and with his predilections and interests.

My life is not a thread, it is a patchwork of chance encounters, haphazard exams, and the drug of Narcissistic Supply consumed. I feel like a series of still frames, somehow improperly animated. I know the audience is there. I crave their adulation. I try to reach out, to break the mould of the album of photographs that I became – to no avail. I am trapped in there forever. And if none of you chooses to inspect my image at a given moment, I fade, in sepia colours. Until I am no longer.

Return

Other People's Pain

Most narcissists enjoy an irrational and brief burst of relief after having suffered emotionally ("narcissistic injury") or after having sustained a loss. It is a sense of freedom, which comes with being unshackled. Having lost everything, the narcissist often feels that he has found himself, that he has been re-born, that he has been charged with natal energy, able to take on new challenges and to explore new territories. This elation is so addictive, that the narcissist often seeks pain, humiliation, punishment, scorn, and contempt – as long as they are public and involve the attention of peers and superiors. Being punished accords with the tormenting inner voices of the narcissist which keep telling him that he is bad, corrupt, and worthy of penalty.

This is the masochistic streak in the narcissist. But the narcissist is also a sadist – albeit an unusual one.

The narcissist inflicts pain and abuse on others. He devalues Sources of Supply, callously and off-handedly abandons them, and discards people, places, partnerships, and friendships unhesitatingly. Some narcissists – though by no means the majority – actually ENJOY abusing, taunting, tormenting, and freakishly controlling others ("gaslighting"). But most of them do these things absentmindedly, automatically, and, often, even without good reason.

What is unusual about the narcissist's sadistic behaviours – premeditated acts of tormenting others while enjoying their anguished reactions – is that they are goal orientated. "Pure" sadists have no goal in mind except the pursuit of pleasure – pain as an art form (remember the Marquis de Sade?). The narcissist, on the other hand, haunts and hunts his victims for a reason – he wants them to reflect his inner state. It is all part of a mechanism called Projective Identification.

When the narcissist is angry, unhappy, disappointed, injured, or hurt – he feels unable to express his emotions sincerely and openly since to do so would be to admit his frailty, his neediness, and his weaknesses. He deplores his own humanity – his emotions, his vulnerability, his susceptibility, his gullibility, his inadequacies, and his failures. So, he makes use of other people to express his pain and his frustration, his pent up anger and his aggression. He achieves this by mentally torturing other people to the point of madness, by driving them to violence, by reducing them to scar tissue in search of outlet, closure, and, sometimes, revenge. He forces people to lose their own character traits – and adopt his own instead. In reaction to his constant and well-targeted abuse, they become abusive, vengeful, ruthless, lacking empathy, obsessed, and aggressive. They mirror him faithfully and thus relieve him of the need to express himself directly.

Having constructed this writhing hall of human mirrors, the narcissist withdraws. The goal achieved, he lets go. As opposed to the sadist, he is no in it, indefinitely, for the pleasure of it. He abuses and traumatises, humiliates and abandons, discards and ignores, insults and provokes – only for the purpose of purging his inner demons. By possessing others, he purifies himself, cathartically, and exorcises his demented self.

This accomplished, he acts almost with remorse. An episode of extreme abuse is followed by an act of great care and by mellifluous apologies. The Narcissistic Pendulum swings between the extremes of torturing others and empathically soothing the resulting pain. This incongruous behaviour, these "sudden" shifts between sadism and altruism, abuse and "love", ignoring and caring, abandoning and clinging, viciousness and remorse, the harsh and the tender – are, perhaps, the most difficult to comprehend and to accept. These swings produce in people around the narcissist emotional insecurity, an eroded sense of self-worth, fear, stress, and anxiety ("walking on eggshells"). Gradually, emotional paralysis ensues and they come to occupy the same emotional wasteland inhabited by the narcissist, his prisoners and hostages in more ways than one – and even when he is long out of their life.

Return

The Weapon of Language

In the narcissist's surrealistic world, even language is pathologised. It mutates into a weapon of self-defence, a verbal fortification, a medium without a message, replacing words with duplicitous and ambiguous vocables.

Narcissists (and, often, by contagion, their unfortunate victims) don't talk, or communicate. They fend off. They hide and evade and avoid and disguise. In their planet of capricious and arbitrary unpredictability, of shifting semiotic and semantic dunes – they perfect the ability to say nothing in lengthy, Castro-like speeches.

The ensuing convoluted sentences are arabesques of meaninglessness, acrobatics of evasion, lack of commitment elevated to an ideology. The narcissist prefers to wait and see what waiting brings. It is the postponement of the inevitable that leads to the inevitability of postponement as a strategy of survival.

It is often impossible to really understand a narcissist. The evasive syntax fast deteriorates into ever more labyrinthine structures. The grammar tortured to produce the verbal Doppler shifts essential to disguise the source of the information, its distance from reality, the speed of its degeneration into rigid "official" versions.

Buried under the lush flora and fauna of idioms without an end, the language erupts, like some exotic rash, an autoimmune reaction to its infection and contamination. Like vile weeds it spread throughout, strangling with absent minded persistence the ability to understand, to feel, to agree, to disagree and to debate, to present arguments, to compare notes, to learn and to teach.

Narcissists, therefore, never talk to others – rather, they talk at others, or lecture them. They exchange subtexts, camouflage-wrapped by elaborate, florid, texts. They read between the lines, spawning a multitude of private languages, prejudices, superstitions, conspiracy theories, rumours, phobias and hysterias. Theirs is a solipsistic world – where communication is permitted only with oneself and the aim of language is to throw others off the scent or to obtain Narcissistic Supply.

This has profound implications. Communication through unequivocal, unambiguous, information-rich symbol systems is such an integral and crucial part of our world - that its absence is not postulated even in the remotest galaxies which grace the skies of science fiction. In this sense, narcissists are nothing short of aliens. It is not that they employ a different language, a code to be deciphered by a new Freud. It is also not the outcome of upbringing or socio-cultural background.

It is the fact that language is put by narcissists to a different use - not to communicate but to obscure, not to share but to abstain, not to learn but to defend and resist, not to teach but to preserve ever less tenable monopolies, to disagree without incurring wrath, to criticise without commitment, to agree without appearing to do so. Thus, an "agreement" with a narcissist is a vague expression of intent at a given moment - rather than the clear listing of long-term, iron-cast and mutual commitments.

The rules that govern the narcissist's universe are loopholed incomprehensibles, open to an exegesis so wide and so self-contradictory that it renders them meaningless. The narcissist often hangs himself by his own verbose Gordic knots, having stumbled through a minefield of logical fallacies and endured self-inflicted inconsistencies. Unfinished sentences hover in the air, like vapour above a semantic swamp.

In the case of the inverted narcissist, who was suppressed and abused by overbearing caregivers, there is the strong urge not to offend. Intimacy and inter-dependence are great. Parental or peer pressures are irresistible and result in conformity and self-deprecation. Aggressive tendencies, strongly repressed in the social pressure cooker, teem under the veneer of forced civility and violent politeness. Constructive ambiguity, a non-committal "everyone is good and right", an atavistic variant of moral relativism and tolerance bred of fear and of contempt - are all at the service of this eternal vigilance against aggressive drives, at the disposal of a never ending peacekeeping mission.

With the classic narcissist, language is used cruelly and ruthlessly to ensnare one's enemies, to saw confusion and panic, to move others to emulate the narcissist (Projective Identification), to leave the listeners in doubt, in hesitation, in paralysis, to gain control, or to punish. Language is enslaved and forced to lie. The language is appropriated and expropriated. It is considered to be a weapon, an asset, a piece of lethal property, a traitorous mistress to be gang raped into submission.

With cerebral narcissists, language is a lover. The infatuation with its very sound leads to a pyrotechnic type of speech which sacrifices its meaning to its music. Its speakers pay more attention to the composition than to the content. They are swept by it, intoxicated by its perfection, inebriated by the spiralling complexity of its forms. Here, language is an inflammatory process. It attacks the very tissues of the narcissist's relationships with artistic fierceness. It invades the healthy cells of reason and logic, of cool headed argumentation and level headed debate.

Language is a leading indicator of the psychological and institutional health of social units, such as the family, or the workplace. Social capital can often be measured in cognitive (hence, verbal-lingual) terms. To monitor the level of comprehensibility and lucidity of texts is to study the degree of sanity of family members, co-workers, friends, spouses, mates, and colleagues. There can exist no hale society without unambiguous speech, without clear communications, without the traffic of idioms and content that is an inseparable part of every social contract. Our language determines how we perceive our world. It IS our mind and our consciousness. The narcissist, in this respect, is a great social menace.

Based on my Balkan and Central and Eastern Europe essays:
http://ceeandbalkan.tripod.com
http://samvak.tripod.com/guide.html

Return

Studying My Death

I study death as one would an especially curious insect, part metal, part decomposing flesh. I am detached and cold as I contemplate my own demise. The death of others is but a statistic. I would have made a great American governor, or general, or statesman – sentencing people to a bureaucratic, emotionless, end. Death is a constant presence in my life, as I disintegrate from within and from without. It is no stranger, but a comforting horizon. I would not seek it actively – but I am often terrified by the abhorrent thought of immortality. I would have gladly lived forever as an abstract entity. But, as I am, ensconced in my decaying corpse, I would rather die on schedule.

Hence my aversion to suicide. I love life – its surprises, intellectual challenges, technological innovations, scientific discoveries, unsolved mysteries, diverse cultures and societies. In short, I like the cerebral dimensions of my existence. I reject only the corporeal ones. I am enslaved to my mind and enthralled by it. It is my body that I hold in increasing contempt.

While I fear not death – I do fear dying. The very thought of pain makes me dizzy. I am a confirmed hypochondriac. I go into a frenzy at the sight of my own blood. I react with asthma to stress. I don't mind BEING dead – I mind the torture of getting there. I loathe and dread prolonged, body dissolving, maladies such as cancer or diabetes.

Yet none of this motivates me to maintain my health. I am obese. I do not exercise. I am internally inundated by cholesterol. My teeth crumble. My eyesight fails. I can barely hear when spoken to. I do nothing to ameliorate these circumstances beyond superstitiously popping assorted vitamin pills and drinking wine. I know I am rushing towards a crippling stroke, a devastating heart attack, or a diabetic meltdown.

But I keep still, hypnotised by the on-coming headlights of physical doom. I rationalise this irrational behaviour. My time, I argue with myself, is too precious to be wasted on jogging and muscle stretching. Anyhow it would do no good. The odds are overwhelmingly adverse. It is all determined by heredity.

I used to find my body sexually arousing – its pearly whiteness, its effeminate contours, the pleasure it yielded once stimulated. I no longer do. All self-eroticism was buried under the gellous, translucent, fat that is my constitution now. I hate my sweat – this salty adhesive that clings to me relentlessly. At least my scents are virile. Thus, I am not very attached to the vessel that contains me. I wouldn't mind to see it go. But I resent the farewell price – those protracted, bilious, and bloody agonies we call "passing away". Afflicted by death – I wish it only to be inflicted as painlessly and swiftly as possible. I wish to die as I have lived – detached, oblivious, absent minded, apathetic, and on my terms.

[Return](#)

Beware the Children

I see in children feigned innocence, relentless and ruthless manipulation, the cunning of the weak. They are ageless. Their narcissism is disarming in its directness, in its cruel and absolute lack of empathy. They demand with insistence, punish absent-mindedly, idealise and devalue capriciously. They have no loyalty. They do not love, they cling. Their dependence is a mighty weapon and their neediness – a drug. They have no time, neither before, nor after. To them, existence is a play, they are the actors, and we all – are but the props. They raise and drop the curtain of their mock emotions at will. The bells of their laughter often tintinnabulate. They are the fresh abode of good and evil pure and pure they are.

Children, to me, are both mirrors and competitors. They reflect authentically my constant need for adulation and attention. Their grandiose fantasies of omnipotence and omniscience are crass caricatures of my internal world. The way they abuse others and mistreat them hits close to home. Their innocuous charm, their endless curiosity, their fount of energy, their sulking, nagging, boasting, bragging, lying, and manipulating are mutations of my own behaviour. I recognise my thwarted self in them. When they make their entrance, all attention is diverted. Their fantasies endear them to their listeners. Their vainglorious swagger often causes smiles. Their trite stupidities are invariably treated as pearls of wisdom. Their nagging is yielded to, their threats provoke to action, their needs accommodated urgently. I stand aside, an abandoned centre of attention, the dormant eye of an intellectual storm, all but ignored and neglected. I watch the child with envy, with rage, with wrath. I hate its effortless ability to defeat me.

Children are loved by mothers, as I was not. They are bundled emotions, and happiness and hope. I am jealous of them, I am infuriated by my deprivation, I am fearful of the sadness and hopelessness that they provoke in me. Like music, they reify a threat to the precariously balanced emotional black hole that is myself. They are my past, my dilapidated and petrified True Self, my wasted potentials, my self-loathing and my defences. They are my pathology projected. I revel in my Orwellian narcissistic newspeak. Love is weakness, happiness is a psychosis, hope is malignant optimism. Children defy all this. They are proof positive of how different it could all have been.

But what I consciously experience is disbelief. I cannot understand how anyone can love these thuggish brats, their dripping noses, gelatinous fat bodies, whitish sweat, and bad breath. How can anyone stand their cruelty and vanity, their sadistic insistence and blackmail, their prevarication and deceit? In truth, no one except their parents can.

Children are always derided by everyone except their parents. There is something sick and sickening in a mother's affections. There is a maddening blindness involved, an addiction, a psychotic episode, it's sick, this bond, it's nauseous. I hate children. I hate them for being me.

Return

It is My World

"The new narcissist is haunted not by guilt but by anxiety. He seeks not to inflict his own certainties on others but to find a meaning in life. Liberated from the superstitions of the past, he doubts even the reality of his own existence. Superficially relaxed and tolerant, he finds little use for dogmas of racial and ethnic purity but at the same time forfeits the security of group loyalties and regards everyone as a rival for the favours conferred by a paternalistic state. His sexual attitudes are permissive rather than puritanical, even though his emancipation from ancient taboos brings him no sexual peace. Fiercely competitive in his demand for approval and acclaim, he distrusts competition because he associates it unconsciously with an unbridled urge to destroy. Hence he repudiates the competitive ideologies that flourished at an earlier stage of capitalist development and distrusts even their limited expression in sports and games. He extols cooperation and teamwork while harbouring deeply antisocial impulses. He praises respect for rules and regulations in the secret belief that they do not apply to himself. Acquisitive in the sense that his cravings have no limits, he does not accumulate goods and provisions against the future, in the manner of the acquisitive individualist of nineteenth-century political economy, but demands immediate gratification and lives in a state of restless, perpetually unsatisfied desire."
   [Christopher Lasch – The Culture of Narcissism: American Life in an age of Diminishing Expectations, 1979]

"A characteristic of our times is the predominance, even in groups traditionally selective, of the mass and the vulgar. Thus, in intellectual life, which of its essence requires and presupposes qualification, one can note the progressive triumph of the pseudo-intellectual, unqualified, unqualifiable..."
   [Jose Ortega y Gasset – The Revolt of the Masses, 1932]

Look around you. Self absorption. Greed. Frivolity. Social anxiety. Lack of empathy. Exploitation. Abuse. These are not marginal phenomena. These are the defining traits of the West and its denizens. The West's is a narcissistic civilisation. It upholds narcissistic values and penalises the alternative value-systems. From an early age, children are taught to avoid self-criticism, to deceive themselves regarding their capacities and achievements, to feel entitled, to exploit others. Litigiousness is the flip side of this inane sense of entitlement. The disintegration of the very fabric of society is its outcome. It is a culture of self-delusion. People adopt grandiose fantasies, often incommensurate with their real, dreary, lives. Consumerism is built on this common and communal lie of "I can do anything I want and possess everything I desire if I only apply myself to it".

There is one incriminating piece of evidence - the incidence of NPD among men and women. There is no proof that NPD is a genetic disorder or has genetic roots. There is overwhelming evidence that it is the sad outcome of faulty upbringing. Still, if NPD is not related to cultural and social contexts, then it should occur equally among men and women. It doesn't. It occurs three times more among men than it does among women.

This seems to be because the Narcissistic Personality Disorder (as opposed, for instance, to the Borderline or the Histrionic Personality Disorders, which afflict women more than men) seems to conform to masculine social mores and to the prevailing ethos of capitalism.

Ambition, achievements, hierarchy, ruthlessness, drive - are both social values and narcissistic male traits. Social thinkers like Lasch speculated that modern American culture - a narcissistic, self-centred one - increases the rate of incidence of the Narcissistic Personality Disorder.

To this Kernberg answered, rightly:

"The most I would be willing to say is that society can make serious psychological abnormalities, which already exist in some percentage of the population, seem to be at least superficially appropriate."

From my ["Gender and the Narcissist"](#):

"In the manifestation of their narcissism, female and male narcissists, inevitably, do tend to differ. They emphasise different things. They transform different elements of their personality and of their life into the cornerstones of their disorder. They both conform to cultural stereotypes, gender roles, and social expectations.

Women, for instance, concentrate on their body (as they do in eating disorders: Anorexia Nervosa and Bulimia Nervosa). They flaunt and exploit their physical charms, their sexuality, their socially and culturally determined 'femininity'. In its extreme form this is known as HPD or the Histrionic Personality Disorder.

Many female narcissists secure their Narcissistic Supply through their more traditional gender roles: the home, children, suitable careers, their husbands ('the wife of...'), their feminine traits, their role in society, etc. It is no wonder than narcissists – both men and women – are chauvinistically conservative. They depend to such an extent on the opinions of people around them – that, with time, they are transformed into ultra-sensitive seismographs of public opinion, barometers of prevailing winds and guardians of conformity. Narcissists cannot afford to seriously alienate those who reflect to them their False Self. The very proper and on-going functioning of their Ego depends on the goodwill and the collaboration of their human environment.

Even the self-destructive and self-defeating behaviours of narcissists conform to traditional masculine and feminine roles.

Besieged and consumed by pernicious guilt feelings – many a narcissist seek to be punished. The self-destructive narcissist plays the role of the 'bad guy' (or 'bad girl'). But even then it is within the traditional socially allocated roles. To ensure social opprobrium (read: attention, i.e., Narcissistic Supply), the narcissist cartoonishly exaggerates these roles. A woman is likely to label herself a 'whore' and a male narcissist to style himself a 'vicious, unrepentant criminal'. Yet, these again are traditional social roles. Men are likely to emphasise intellect, power, aggression, money, or social status. Women are likely to emphasise body, looks, charm, sexuality, feminine 'traits', homemaking, children and childrearing – even as they seek their masochistic punishment.

There are mental disorders, which afflict a specific sex more often.

This has to do with hormonal or other physiological dispositions, with social and cultural conditioning through the socialisation process, and with role assignment through the gender differentiation process. None of these seem to be strongly correlated to the formation of malignant narcissism."

I belong. I am a narcissist. And you? You are deviants. You have mal-adapted to my brave new world. The world of the narcissist.

Return

Conspicuous Existence

The narcissist is a shell. Uncertain of his own reality, he engages in "conspicuous existence".

"Conspicuous existence" is a form of "conspicuous consumption", in which the consumed commodity is Narcissistic Supply. The narcissist elaborately stage manages his very being. His every movement, his tone of voice, his inflection, his poise, his text and subtext and context are carefully orchestrated to yield the maximum effect and to garner the most attention.

Narcissists appear to be unpleasantly deliberate. They are somehow "wrong", like automata gone awry. They are too human, or too inhuman, or too modest, or too haughty, or too loving, or too cold, or too empathic, or too stony, or too industrious, or too casual, or too enthusiastic, or too indifferent, or too courteous, or too abrasive.

They are excess embodied. They act their part and their acting shows. Their show invariably unravels at the seams under the slightest stress. Their enthusiasm is always manic, their emotional expression unnatural, their body language defies their statements, their statements belie their intentions, their intentions are focused on the one and only drug – securing Narcissistic Supply from other people.

The narcissist authors his life and scripts it. To him, time is the medium upon which he, the narcissist, records the narrative of his recherché biography. He is, therefore, always calculated, as though listening to an inner voice, to a "director", or a "choreographer" of his unfolding history. His speech is tumid. His motion stunted. His emotional palette, a mockery of true countenances.

But the narcissist's constant invention of his self is not limited to outward appearances.

The narcissist does nothing and says nothing – or even thinks nothing – without first having computed the quantity of Narcissistic Supply his actions, utterances, or thoughts may yield. The visible narcissist is the tip of a gigantic, submerged, iceberg of seething reckoning. The narcissist is incessantly engaged in energy draining gauging of other people and their possible reactions to him. He estimates, he counts, he weighs and measures, he determines, evaluates, and enumerates, compares, despairs, and re-awakens. His fatigued brain is bathed with the drowning noise of stratagems and fears, rage and envy, anxiety and relief, addiction and rebellion, meditation and pre-meditation. The narcissist is a machine which never rests, not even in his dreams, and it has one purpose only – the securing and maximisation of Narcissistic Supply.

Small wonder the narcissist is tired. His exhaustion is all-pervasive and all-consuming. His mental energy depleted, the narcissist can hardly empathise with others, love, or experience emotions. "Conspicuous existence" malignantly replaces "real existence". The myriad, ambivalent, forms of life are supplanted by the single obsession-compulsion of being seen, being observed, being reflected, being by proxy, through the gaze of others. The narcissist ceases to exist when not in company. His being fades when not discerned. Yet, he is unable to return the favour. He is a captive, oblivious to everything but his preoccupation. Emptied from within, devoured by his urge, the narcissist blindly stumbles from one relationship to another, from one warm body to the next, forever in search of that elusive creature – himself.

Return

The Self-Deprecating Narcissist

I have a riotous, subtle, ironic, and sharpened sense of humour. I can be self-deprecating and self-effacing. I do not recoil from making my dilapidated Ego the target of my own barbs. Yet, this is true only when I have Narcissistic Supply aplenty. Narcissistic Supply – attention, adulation, admiration, applause, fame, celebrity, notoriety – neuter the sting of my self-directed jokes. In my more humorous moments I can present myself as the opposite of what is widely known to be true. I can unfold a tale of fatuous decisions followed by clumsy misbehaviour – yet, no one would take me to be fatuous or clumsy. It is as though my reputation protects me from the brunt of my own jocular modesty. I can afford to be magnanimously forgiving of my own shortcomings because they are so outweighed by my gifts and by my widely known achievements or traits.

Still, the gist of what I once wrote stands:

"A narcissist rarely engages in self-directed, self-deprecating humour. If he does, he expects to be contradicted, rebuked and rebuffed by his listeners ('Come on, you are actually quite handsome!'), or to be commended or admired for his courage or for his wit and intellectual acerbity ('I envy your ability to laugh at yourself!'). As everything else in a narcissist's life, his sense of humour is deployed in the interminable pursuit of Narcissistic Supply."

I am completely different when I lack Narcissistic Supply or when in search of sources of such supply. Humour is always an integral part of my charm offensive. But, when Narcissistic Supply is deficient, it is never self-directed. Moreover, when deprived of supply, I react with hurt and rage when I am the butt of jokes and humorous utterances. I counter-attack ferociously and make a complete arse of myself.

Why these extremes?

"The absence of Narcissistic Supply (or the impending threat of such an absence) is, indeed, a serious matter. It is the narcissistic

equivalent of mental death. If prolonged and unmitigated, such absence can lead to the real thing: physical death, a result of suicide, or of a psychosomatic deterioration of the narcissist's health. Yet, to obtain Narcissistic Supply, one must be taken seriously and to be taken seriously one must be the first to take oneself seriously. Hence the gravity with which the narcissist contemplates his life. This lack of levity and of perspective and proportion characterise the narcissist and set him apart.

The narcissist firmly believes that he is unique and that he is thus endowed because he has a mission to fulfil, a destiny, a meaning to his life. The narcissist's life is a part of history, of a cosmic plot and it constantly tends to thicken. Such a life deserves only the most serious attention. Moreover, every particle of such an existence, every action or inaction, every utterance, creation, or composition, indeed every thought, are bathed in this cosmic meaningfulness. They all lead down the paths of glory, of achievement, of perfection, of ideals, of brilliance. They are all part of a design, a pattern, a plot, which inexorably and unstoppably lead the narcissist on to the fulfilment of his task. The narcissist may subscribe to a religion, to a belief, or to an ideology in his effort to understand the source of this strong feeling of uniqueness. He may attribute his sense of direction to God, to history, to society, to culture, to a calling, to his profession, to a value system. But he always does so with a straight face, with a firm conviction and with deadly seriousness.

And because, to the narcissist, the part is a holographic reflection of the whole - he tends to generalise, to resort to stereotypes, to induct (to learn about the whole from the detail), to exaggerate, finally to pathologically lie to himself and to others. This tendency of his, this self-importance, this belief in a grand design, in an all embracing and all-pervasive pattern - make him an easy prey to all manner of logical fallacies and con artistry. Despite his avowed and proudly expressed rationality the narcissist is besieged by superstition and prejudice. Above all, he is a captive of the false belief that his uniqueness destines him to carry a mission of cosmic significance.

All these make the narcissist a volatile person. Not merely mercurial - but fluctuating, histrionic, unreliable, and disproportional. That which has cosmic implications calls for cosmic reactions. The person with an inflated sense of self-import, will react in an inflated manner to threats, greatly inflated by his imagination and by the application to them of his *personal myth. On a cosmic scale, the daily vagaries of life, the mundane, the routine are not important, even damagingly distracting. This is the source of his feelings of exceptional entitlement. Surely, engaged as he is in securing the well being of humanity by the exercise of his unique faculties – the narcissist deserves special treatment! This is the source of his violent swings between opposite behaviour patterns and between devaluation and idealisation of others. To the narcissist, every minor development is nothing less than a new stage in his life, every adversity, a conspiracy to upset his progress, every setback an apocalyptic calamity, every irritation the cause for outlandish outbursts of rage. He is a man of the extremes and only of the extremes. He may learn to efficiently suppress or hide his feelings or reactions – but never for long. In the most inappropriate and inopportune moment, you can count on the narcissist to explode, like a wrongly wound time bomb. And in between eruptions, the narcissistic volcano daydreams, indulges in delusions, plans his victories over an increasingly hostile and alienated environment. Gradually, the narcissist becomes more paranoid – or more aloof, detached and dissociative.*

In such a setting, you must admit, there is not much room for a sense of humour."

Return

A Holiday Grudge

Holiday blues are a common occurrence even among the mentally sound. In me they provoke a particularly virulent strain of pathological envy. I am jealous at others for having a family, or for being able to celebrate lavishly, or for being in the right, festive mood. My cognitive dissonances crumble. I keep telling myself: "Look at those inferior imitations of humans, slaves of their animated corpses, wasting their time, pretending to be happy". Yet, deep inside, I know that I am the defective one. I realise that my inability to rejoice is a protracted and unusual punishment meted out to me by my very self. I am sad and enraged. I want to spoil it for those who can. I want them to share my misery, to reduce them to my level of emotional abstinence and absence.

I hate humans because I am unable to be one.

A long time ago, I wrote:

"I hate holidays and birthdays, including my birthday. It is because I hate it when other people are happy if I am not the cause of it. I have to be the prime mover and shaker of EVERYONE's mood. And no one will tell me HOW I should feel. I am my own master. I feel that their happiness is false, fake, forced. I feel that they are hypocrites, dissimulating joy where there is none. I feel envious, humiliated by my envy, and enraged by my humiliation. I feel that they are the recipients of a gift I will never have: the ability to enjoy life and to feel joy.

And then I do my best to destroy their mood: I bring bad news, provoke a fight, make a disparaging remark, project a dire future, sow uncertainty in the relationship, and when the other person is sour and sad, I feel relieved.

It's back to normal. My mood improves dramatically and I try to cheer her up. Now if she does cheer up - it is REAL. It is my doing. I controlled it.

And I controlled HER."

Holidays remind me of my childhood, of the supportive and loving family I never had, of what could have been, and never was, and, as I grow older, I know, will never be. I feel deprived and, coupled with my rampant paranoia, I feel cheated and persecuted. I rail against the indifferent injustice of a faceless, cold world. Holidays are a conspiracy of the emotional haves against the emotional haves not.

Birthdays are an injury, an imposition, a reminder of vulnerability, a fake event artificially construed. I destroy in order to equalise the misery. I rage in order to induce rage. Holidays create in me an abandon of negative, nihilistic emotions, the only ones I consciously possess.

On holidays and on my birthday, I make it a point to carry on routinely.

I accept no gifts, I do not celebrate, I work till the wee hours of the night. It is a demonstrative refusal to participate, a rejection of social norms, an "in your face" statement of withdrawal. It makes me feel unique. It makes me feel even more deprived and punished. It feeds the furnace of hatred, the bestial anger, the all engulfing scorn I harbour. I want to be drawn out of my sulk and pouting – yet, I decline any such offer, evade any such attempt, hurt those who try to make me smile and to forget. In times like that, in holidays and birthdays, I am reminded of this fundamental truth: my voluptuous, virulent, spiteful, hissing and spitting grudge is all I have. Those who threaten to take it away from me – with their love, affection, compassion, or care – are my mortal enemies indeed.

Return

Ideas of Reference

The narcissist is the centre of the world. He is not merely the centre of HIS world – as far as he can tell, he is the centre of THE world. This Archimedean delusion is one of the narcissist's most predominant and all-pervasive cognitive distortions. The narcissist feels certain that he is the source of all events around him, the origin of all the emotions of his nearest or dearest, the fount of all knowledge, both the first and the final cause, the beginning as well as the end.

This is understandable.

The narcissist derives his sense of being, his experience of his own existence, and his self-worth from the outside. He mines others for Narcissistic Supply – adulation, attention, reflection, fear. Their reactions stalk his furnace. Absent Narcissistic Supply – the narcissist disintegrates and self-annihilates. When unnoticed, he feels empty and worthless. The narcissist MUST delude himself into believing that he is persistently the focus and object of the attentions, intentions, plans, feelings, and stratagems of other people. The narcissist faces a stark choice – either be (or become) the permanent centre of the world, or cease to be altogether.

This constant obsession with one's locus, with one's centrality, with one's position as a hub – leads to referential ideation ("ideas of reference"). This is the conviction that one is at the receiving end of other people's behaviours, speech, and even thoughts. The person suffering from delusional ideas of reference is at an imaginary centre of constant attention.

When people talk – the narcissist is convinced that he is the topic of discussion. When they quarrel – he is most probably the cause. When they smirk – he is the victim of their ridicule. If they are unhappy – he made them so. If they are happy – they are egotists for ignoring him. He is convinced that his behaviour is continuously monitored, criticised, compared, dissected, approved of, or imitated by others. He deems himself so indispensable and important, such a critical component of other people's lives, that his every act, his every word, his every omission – is bound to upset, hurt, uplift, or satisfy his audience.

And, to the narcissist, everyone is but an audience. It all emanates from him – and it all reverts to him. The narcissist's is a circular and closed universe. His ideas of reference are a natural extension of his primitive defence mechanisms (omnipotence, omniscience, omnipresence).

Being omnipresent explains why everyone, everywhere is concerned with him. Being omnipotent and omniscient excludes other, lesser, beings from enjoying the admiration, adulation, and attention of people.

Yet, the attrition afforded by years of tormenting ideas of reference inevitably yields paranoiac thinking.

To preserve his egocentric cosmology, the narcissist is compelled to attribute fitting motives and psychological dynamics to others. Such motives and dynamics have little to do with reality. They are PROJECTED by the narcissist UNTO others so as to maintain his personal mythology.

In other words, the narcissist attributes to others HIS OWN motives and psychodynamics. And since narcissists are mostly besieged by transformations of aggression (rage, hatred, envy, fear) – these they often attribute to others as well. Thus, the narcissist tends to interpret other people's behaviour as motivated by anger, fear, hatred, or envy and as directed at him or revolving around him. The narcissist (often erroneously) believes that people discuss him, gossip about him, hate him, defame him, mock him, berate him, underestimate him, envy him, or fear him. He is (often rightly) convinced that he is, to others, the source of hurt, humiliation, impropriety, and indignation. The narcissist "knows" that he is a wonderful, powerful, talented, and entertaining person – but this only explains why people are jealous and why they seek to undermine and destroy him.

Thus, since the narcissist is unable to secure the long-term POSITIVE love, admiration, or even attention of his Sources of Supply – he resorts to a mirror strategy. In other words, the narcissist becomes paranoid. Better to be the object of (often imaginary and always self-inflicted) derision, scorn, and bile – than to be ignored. Being envied is preferable to being treated with indifference. If he cannot be loved – the narcissist would rather be feared or hated than forgotten.

Return

The Delusional Way Out

The study of narcissism is a century old and the two scholarly debates central to its conception are still undecided. Is there such a thing as HEALTHY adult narcissism (Kohut) – or are all the manifestations of narcissism in adulthood pathological (Freud, Kernberg)? Moreover, is pathological narcissism the outcome of verbal, sexual, physical, or psychological abuse (the overwhelming view) – or, on the contrary, the sad result of spoiling the child and idolising it (Millon, the late Freud)?

The second debate is easier to resolve if one agrees to adopt a more comprehensive definition of "abuse". Overweening, smothering, spoiling, overvaluing, and idolising the child – are all forms of parental abuse.

This is because, as Horney pointed out, the child is dehumanised and instrumentalised. His parents love him not for what he really is – but for what they wish and imagine him to be: the fulfilment of their dreams and frustrated wishes. The child becomes the vessel of his parents' discontented lives, a tool, the magic brush with which they can transform their failures into successes, their humiliation into victory, their frustrations into happiness. The child is taught to ignore reality and to occupy the parental fantastic space. Such an unfortunate child feels omnipotent and omniscient, perfect and brilliant, worthy of adoration and entitled to special treatment. The faculties that are honed by constantly brushing against bruising reality – empathy, compassion, a realistic assessment of one's abilities and limitations, realistic expectations of oneself and of others, personal boundaries, team work, social skills, perseverance and goal-orientation, not to mention the ability to postpone gratification and to work hard to achieve it – are all lacking or missing altogether. The child turned adult sees no reason to invest in his skills and education, convinced that his inherent genius should suffice. He feels entitled for merely being, rather than for actually doing (rather as the nobility in days gone by felt entitled not by virtue of its merit but as the inevitable, foreordained outcome of its birth right). In other words, he is not meritocratic – but aristocratic. In short: a narcissist is born.

But such a mental structure is brittle, susceptible to criticism and disagreement, vulnerable to the incessant encounter with a harsh and intolerant world. Deep inside, narcissists of both kinds (those wrought by "classic" abuse and those yielded by being idolised) – feel inadequate, phoney, fake, inferior, and deserving of punishment. This is Millon's mistake. He makes a distinction between several types of narcissists. He wrongly assumes that the "classic" narcissist is the outcome of overvaluation, idolisation, and spoiling and, thus, is possessed of supreme, unchallenged, self-confidence, and is devoid of all self-doubt. According to Millon, it is the "compensatory" narcissist that falls prey to nagging self-doubts, feelings of inferiority, and a masochistic desire for self-punishment. Yet, the distinction is both wrong and unnecessary. There is only ONE type of narcissist – though there are TWO developmental paths to it. And ALL narcissists are besieged by deeply ingrained (though at times not conscious) feelings of inadequacy, fears of failure, masochistic desires to be penalised, a fluctuating sense of self-worth (regulated by Narcissistic Supply), and an overwhelming sensation of fakeness.

The Grandiosity Gap (between a fantastically grandiose – and unlimited – self-image and actual – limited – accomplishments and achievements) is grating. Its recurrence threatens the precariously balanced house of cards that is the narcissistic personality. The narcissist finds, to his chagrin, that people out there are much less admiring, accommodating and accepting than his parents. As he grows old, the narcissist often becomes the target of constant derision and mockery, a sorry sight indeed. His claims for superiority appear less plausible and substantial the more and the longer he makes them.

Pathological narcissism – originally a defence mechanism intended to shield the narcissist from an injurious world – becomes the main source of hurt, a generator of injuries, counterproductive and dangerous. Overwhelmed by negative or absent Narcissistic Supply, the narcissist is forced to let go of it.

The narcissist then resorts to self-delusion. Unable to completely ignore contrarian opinion and data – he transmutes them. Unable to face the dismal failure that he is, the narcissist partially withdraws from reality. To soothe and salve the pain of disillusionment, he administers to his aching soul a mixture of lies, distortions, half-truths and outlandish interpretations of events around him. These solutions can be classified thus:

The Delusional Narrative Solution

The narcissist constructs a narrative in which he figures as the hero – brilliant, perfect, irresistibly handsome, destined for great things, entitled, powerful, wealthy, the centre of attention, etc. The bigger the strain on this delusional charade – the greater the gap between fantasy and reality – the more the delusion coalesces and solidifies.

Finally, if it is sufficiently protracted, it replaces reality and the narcissist's reality test deteriorates. He withdraws his bridges and may become schizotypal, catatonic, or schizoid.

The Antisocial Solution

The narcissist renounces reality. To his mind, those who pusillanimously fail to recognise his unbound talents, innate superiority, overarching brilliance, benevolent nature, entitlement, cosmically important mission, perfection, etc. – do not deserve consideration. The narcissist's natural affinity with the criminal – his lack of empathy and compassion, his deficient social skills, his disregard for social laws and morals – now erupt and blossom. He becomes a full fledged antisocial (sociopath or psychopath). He ignores the wishes and needs of others, he breaks the law, he violates all rights – natural and legal, he holds people in contempt and disdain, he derides society and its codes, he punishes the ignorant ingrates – that, to his mind, drove him to this state – by acting criminally and by jeopardising their safety, lives, or property.

The Paranoid Schizoid Solution

The narcissist develops persecutory delusions. He perceives slights and insults where none were intended. He becomes subject to ideas of reference (people are gossiping about him, mocking him, prying into his affairs, cracking his e-mail, etc.). He is convinced that he is the centre of malign and mal-intentioned attention. People are conspiring to humiliate him, punish him, abscond with his property, delude him, impoverish him, confine him physically or intellectually, censor him, impose on his time, force him to action (or to inaction), frighten him, coerce him, surround and besiege him, change his mind, part with his values, victimise or even murder him, and so on.

Some narcissists withdraw completely from a world populated with such minacious and ominous objects (really projections of internal objects and processes). They avoid all social contact, except the most necessary. They refrain from meeting people, falling in love, having sex, talking to others, or even corresponding with them. In short: they become schizoids – not out of social shyness, but out of what they feel to be their choice. "This evil, hopeless world does not deserve me" – goes the inner refrain – "and I shall waste none of my time and resources on it."

The Paranoid Aggressive (Explosive) Solution

Other narcissists who develop persecutory delusions, resort to an aggressive stance, a more violent resolution of their internal conflict. They become verbally, psychologically, situationally (and, very rarely, physically) abusive. They insult, castigate, chastise, berate, demean, and deride their nearest and dearest (often well wishers and loved ones). They explode in unprovoked displays of indignation, righteousness, condemnation, and blame. Theirs is an exegetic Bedlam. They interpret everything – even the most innocuous, inadvertent, and innocent comment – as designed to provoke and humiliate them. They sow fear, revulsion, hate, and malignant envy. They flail against the windmills of reality – a pathetic, forlorn, sight. But often they cause real and lasting damage – fortunately, mainly to themselves.

The Masochistic Avoidant Solution

The narcissist is angered by the lack of Narcissistic Supply. He directs some of this fury inwards, punishing himself for his "failure". This masochistic behaviour has the added "benefit" of forcing the narcissist's closest to assume the roles of dismayed spectators or of persecutors and thus, either way, to pay him the attention that he craves.

Self-administered punishment often manifests as self-handicapping masochism – a narcissistic cop-out. By undermining his work, his relationships, and his efforts, the increasingly fragile narcissist avoids additional criticism and censure (negative supply). Self-inflicted failure is the narcissist's doing and thus proves that he is the master of his own fate.

Masochistic narcissists keep finding themselves in self-defeating circumstances which render success impossible – and *"an objective assessment of their performance improbable"* [Millon, 2000]. They act carelessly, withdraw in mid-effort, are constantly fatigued, bored, or disaffected and thus passive-aggressively sabotage their lives. Their suffering is defiant and by "deciding to abort" they reassert their omnipotence.

The narcissist's pronounced and public misery and self-pity are compensatory and *"reinforce (his) self-esteem against overwhelming convictions of worthlessness"* [Millon, 2000]. His tribulations and anguish render him, in his eyes, unique, saintly, virtuous, righteous, resilient, and significant. They are, in other words, self-generated Narcissistic Supply.

Thus, paradoxically, the worst his anguish and unhappiness, the more relieved and elated such a narcissist feels!

[Additional reading: Millon, Theodore and Davis, Roger – Personality Disorders in Modern Life, 2nd Edition – New York, John Wiley and Sons, 2000]

Return

The Selfish Gene

The Genetic Underpinnings of Narcissism

Is pathological narcissism the outcome of inherited traits – or the sad result of abusive and traumatising upbringing? Or, maybe it is the confluence of both? It is a common occurrence, after all, that, in the same family, with the same set of parents and an identical emotional environment – some siblings grow to be malignant narcissists, while others are perfectly "normal". Surely, this indicates a predisposition of some people to developing narcissism, a part of one's genetic heritage.

This vigorous debate may be the offshoot of obfuscating semantics.

When we are born, we are not much more than the sum of our genes and their manifestations. Our brain – a physical object – is the residence of mental health and its disorders. Mental illness cannot be explained without resorting to the body and, especially, to the brain. And our brain cannot be contemplated without considering our genes. Thus, any explanation of our mental life that leaves out our hereditary makeup and our neurophysiology is lacking. Such lacking theories are nothing but literary narratives. Psychoanalysis, for instance, is often accused of being divorced from corporeal reality.

Our genetic baggage makes us resemble a personal computer. We are an all-purpose, universal, machine. Subject to the right programming (conditioning, socialisation, education, upbringing) – we can turn out to be anything and everything. A computer can imitate any other kind of discrete machine, given the right software. It can play music, screen movies, calculate, print, paint. Compare this to a television set – it is constructed and expected to do one, and only one, thing. It has a single purpose and a unitary function. We, humans, are more like computers than like television sets.

True, single genes rarely account for any behaviour or trait. An array of coordinated genes is required to explain even the minutest human phenomenon. "Discoveries" of a "gambling gene" here and an "aggression gene" there are derided by the more serious and less publicity-prone scholars. Yet, it would seem that even complex behaviours such as risk taking, reckless driving, and compulsive shopping have genetic underpinnings.

What about the Narcissistic Personality Disorder?

It would seem reasonable to assume – though, at this stage, there is not a shred of proof – that the narcissist is born with a propensity to develop narcissistic defences. These are triggered by abuse or trauma during the formative years in infancy or during early adolescence [see http://samvak.tripod.com/faq64.html]. By "abuse" I am referring to a spectrum of behaviours which objectifies the child and treats it as an extension of the caregiver (parent) or an instrument. Doting and smothering are as much abuse as beating and starving. And abuse can be dished out by peers as well as by adult role models.

Still, I would have to attribute the development of NPD mostly to nurture. The Narcissistic Personality Disorder is an extremely complex battery of phenomena: behaviour patterns, cognitions, emotions, conditioning, and so on. NPD is a PERSONALITY disordered and even the most ardent proponents of the school of genetics do not attribute the development of the whole personality to genes.

From "The Interrupted Self":

"'Organic' and 'mental' disorders (a dubious distinction at best) have many characteristics in common (confabulation, antisocial behaviour, emotional absence or flatness, indifference, psychotic episodes and so on)."

From "On Dis-ease":

"Moreover, the distinction between the psychic and the physical is hotly disputed, philosophically. The psychophysical problem is as intractable today as it ever was (if not more so). It is beyond doubt that the physical affects the mental and the other way around. This is what disciplines like psychiatry are all about. The ability to control 'autonomous' bodily functions (such as heartbeat) and mental reactions to pathogens of the brain are proof of the artificialness of this distinction.

It is a result of the reductionist view of nature as divisible and summable. The sum of the parts, alas, is not always the whole and there is no such thing as an infinite set of the rules of nature, only an asymptotic approximation of it. The distinction between *the patient and the outside world is superfluous and wrong. The patient AND his environment are ONE and the same. Disease is a perturbation in the operation and management of the complex ecosystem known as patient-world. Humans absorb their environment and feed it in equal measures. This on-going interaction IS the patient. We cannot exist without the intake of water, air, visual stimuli and food. Our environment is defined by our actions and output, physical and mental.*

Thus, one must question the classical differentiation between 'internal' and 'external'. Some illnesses are considered 'endogenic' (generated from the inside). Natural, 'internal', causes – a heart defect, a biochemical imbalance, a genetic mutation, a metabolic process gone awry – cause disease. Aging and deformities also belong in this category.

In contrast, problems of nurturance and environment – early childhood abuse, for instance, or malnutrition – are 'external' and so are the 'classical' pathogens (germs and viruses) and accidents.

But this, again, is a counter-productive approach. Exogenic and Endogenic pathogenesis is inseparable. Mental states increase or decrease the susceptibility to externally induced disease. Talk therapy or abuse (external events) alter the biochemical balance of the brain.

The inside constantly interacts with the outside and is so intertwined with it that all distinctions between them are artificial and misleading. The best example is, of course, medication: it is an external agent, it influences internal processes and it has a very strong mental correlate (its efficacy is influenced by mental factors as in the placebo effect).

The very nature of dysfunction and sickness is highly culture-dependent.

Societal parameters dictate right and wrong in health (especially mental health). It is all a matter of statistics. Certain diseases are accepted in certain parts of the world as a fact of life or even a sign of distinction (e.g., the paranoid schizophrenic as chosen by the gods). If there is no dis-ease there is no disease. That the physical or mental state of a person CAN be different – does not imply that it MUST be different or even that it is desirable that it should be different. In an over-populated world, sterility might be the desirable thing – or even the occasional epidemic. There is no such thing as ABSOLUTE dysfunction. The body and the mind ALWAYS function. They adapt themselves to their environment and if the latter changes – they change.

Personality disorders are the best possible responses to abuse. Cancer may be the best possible response to carcinogens. Aging and death are definitely the best possible response to over-population. Perhaps the point of view of the single patient is incommensurate with the point of view of his species – but this should not serve to obscure the issues and derail rational debate.

As a result, it is logical to introduce the notion of 'positive aberration'. Certain hyper- or hypo- functioning can yield positive results and prove to be adaptive. The difference between positive and negative aberrations can never be 'objective'. Nature is morally-neutral and embodies no 'values' or 'preferences'. It simply exists. WE, humans, introduce our value systems, prejudices and priorities into our activities, science included. It is better to be healthy, we say, because we feel better when we are healthy. Circularity aside – this is the only criterion that we can reasonably employ. If the patient feels good – it is not a disease, even if we all think it is. If the patient feels bad, ego-dystonic, unable to function – it is a disease, even when we all think it isn't. Needless to say that I am referring to that mythical creature, the fully informed patient. If someone is sick and knows no better (has never been healthy) – then his decision should be respected only after he is given the chance to experience health.

All the attempts to introduce 'objective' yardsticks of health are plagued and philosophically contaminated by the insertion of values, preferences and priorities into the formula – or by subjecting the formula to them altogether. One such attempt is to define health as 'an increase in order or efficiency of processes' as contrasted with illness which is 'a decrease in order (increase of entropy) and in the efficiency of processes'. While being factually disputable, this dyad also suffers from a series of implicit value-judgements. For instance, why should we prefer life over death? Order to entropy? Efficiency to inefficiency?"

Return

The Silver Pieces of the Narcissist

When I have money, I can exercise my sadistic urges freely and with little fear of repercussions. Money shields me from life itself, from the outcomes of my actions, it insulates me warmly and safely, like a benevolent blanket, like a mother's good night kiss. Yes, money is undoubtedly a love substitute. And it allows me to be my ugly, corrupt, and dilapidated self. Money buys me absolution and my own friendship, forgiveness, and acceptance. With money in the bank, I feel at ease with myself, free, arrogantly soaring supreme above the contemptible masses.

I can always find people poorer than I, a cause for great disdain and bumptiousness on my part.

I rarely use money to buy, corrupt, and intimidate. I wear 15 year old tattered clothes, I have no car, no house, no property. It is so even when I am wealthy. Money has nothing to do with my physical needs or with my social interactions. I never deploy it to acquire status, or to impress others. I hide it, hoard it, accumulate it and, like the proverbial miser, count it daily and in the dark. It is my licence to sin, my narcissistic permit, a promise and its fulfilment all at once. It unleashes the beast in me and, with abandon, encourages it – nay, seduces it – to be itself.

I am not tight-fisted. I spend money on restaurants and trips abroad and books and health products. I buy gifts (though reluctantly). I speculate and have lost hundreds of thousands of dollars in wanton gambling in the stock exchanges. I am insatiable, always want more, always lose the little that I have. But I do all this not for the love of money, for I do not use it to gratify my self or to cater to my needs. No, I do not crave money, nor care for it. I need the power that it bestows on me to dare, to flare, to conquer, to oppose, to resist, to taunt, and to torment.

In all my relationships, I am either the vanquished or the vanquisher, either the haughty master, or his abject slave, either the dominant, or the recessive. I interact along the up-down axis, rather than along the left-right one. My world is rigidly hierarchical and abusively stratified. When submissive, I am contemptibly so. When domineering, I am contemptuously so. My life is a pendulum swinging between oppressed and oppressor.

To subjugate another, one must be capricious, unscrupulous, ruthless, obsessive, hateful, vindictive, and penetrating. One must spot the cracks of vulnerability, the crumbling foundations of susceptibility, the pains, the trigger mechanisms, the Pavlovian reactions of hate, and fear, and hope, and anger. Money liberates my mind. It endows it with the tranquillity, detachment, and incisiveness of a natural scientist. With my mind free of the quotidian, I can concentrate on attaining the desired position – on top, dreaded, derided, avoided – yet obeyed and deferred to. I then proceed with cool disinterest to unscramble the human jigsaw puzzles, to manipulate their parts, to enjoy their writhing as I expose their petty misbehaviours, harp on their failures, compare them to their betters, and mock their incompetence, hypocrisy, and cupidity. Oh, I disguise it in socially acceptable cloak – only to draw the dagger. I cast myself in the role of a brave, incorruptible iconoclast, a fighter for social justice, for a better future, for more efficiency, for good causes. But it is all about my sadistic urges, really. It is all about death, not life.

Still, antagonising and alienating my potential benefactors is a pleasure that I cannot afford on an empty purse. When impoverished, I am altruism embodied – the best of friends, the most caring of tutors, a benevolent guide, a lover of humanity, and a fierce fighter against narcissism, sadism, and abuse in all their myriad forms. I adhere, I obey, I succumb, I agree wholeheartedly, I praise, condone, idolise, and applaud. I am the perfect audience, an admirer and an adulator, a worm and an amoeba – spineless, adaptable in form, slithery flexibility itself. To behave so is unbearable for a narcissist, hence my addiction to money (really, to freedom) in all its forms. It is my evolutionary ladder from slime to the sublime – to mastery.

[Return](#)

For the Love of God

God is everything the narcissist ever wants to be: omnipotent, omniscient, omnipresent, admired, much discussed, and awe inspiring. God is the narcissist's wet dream, his ultimate grandiose fantasy. But God comes handy in other ways as well.

The narcissist alternately idealises and devalues figures of authority.

In the idealisation phase, he strives to emulate them, he admires them, imitate them (often ludicrously), and defends them. They cannot go wrong, or be wrong. The narcissist regards them as bigger than life, infallible, perfect, whole, and brilliant. But as the narcissist's unrealistic and inflated expectations are inevitably frustrated, he begins to devalue his former idols.

Now they are "human" (to the narcissist, a derogatory term). They are small, fragile, error-prone, pusillanimous, mean, dumb, and mediocre. The narcissist goes through the same cycle in his relationship with God, the quintessential authority figure.

But often, even when disillusionment and iconoclastic despair have set in – the narcissist continues to pretend to love God and follow Him. The narcissist maintains this deception because his continued proximity to God confers on him authority. Priests, leaders of the congregation, preachers, evangelists, cultists, politicians, intellectuals – all derive authority from their allegedly privileged relationship with God.

Religious authority allows the narcissist to indulge his sadistic urges and to exercise his misogynism freely and openly. Such a narcissist is likely to taunt and torment his followers, hector and chastise them, humiliate and berate them, abuse them spiritually, or even sexually. The narcissist whose source of authority is religious is looking for obedient and unquestioning slaves upon whom to exercise his capricious and wicked mastery. The narcissist transforms even the most innocuous and pure religious sentiments into a cultish ritual and a virulent hierarchy. He prays on the gullible. His flock become his hostages.

Religious authority also secures the narcissist's Narcissistic Supply. His coreligionists, members of his congregation, his parish, his constituency, his audience – are transformed into loyal and stable Sources of Narcissistic Supply. They obey his commands, heed his admonitions, follow his creed, admire his personality, applaud his personal traits, satisfy his needs (sometimes even his carnal desires), revere and idolise him.

Moreover, being a part of a "bigger thing" is very gratifying narcissistically. Being a particle of God, being immersed in His grandeur, experiencing His power and blessings first hand, communing with him – are all Sources of unending Narcissistic Supply. The narcissist becomes God by observing His commandments, following His instructions, loving Him, obeying Him, succumbing to Him, merging with Him, communicating with Him – or even by defying him (the bigger the narcissist's enemy – the more grandiosely important the narcissist feels).

Like everything else in the narcissist's life, he mutates God into a kind of inverted narcissist. God becomes his dominant Source of Supply. He forms a personal relationship with this overwhelming and overpowering entity – in order to overwhelm and overpower others. He becomes God vicariously, by the proxy of his relationship with Him. He idealises God, then devalues Him, then abuses Him. This is the classic narcissistic pattern and even God himself cannot escape it.

Return

The Opaque Mirror

I cannot confront my life – that dreary, aimless, unpromising stream of days and nights and days. I am past my prime – a pitiable figure, a has been who never was, a loser and a failure (and not only by my inflated standards). These facts are hard enough to face when one is not burdened with a grandiose False Self and a sadistic inner voice (Superego). I have both.

So, when asked what do I do for a living, I say that I am a columnist and analyst (I am neither – I am a Senior Business Correspondent for United Press International – UPI. In other words, a glorified hack).

I say that I am a successful author (I am far from one). I say that I was the Economic Advisor to the government. True, I was – but at long last I was fired, having pushed my client to the point of nervous breakdown with my endless tantrums and labile fickleness.

But these lies – both outright and borderline – are known to me as such. I can tell the difference between reality and fantasy. I choose fantasy knowingly and consciously – but it doesn't render me oblivious to my true condition.

There is a different sort of self-deception which runs much deeper. It is more pernicious and all-pervasive. It is better at disguising itself as true and veritable. In the absence of outside help and reflection, I can never tell when (and how) I am self-deluded.

On the whole, I am that rarity, the reification of that oxymoron, the self-aware narcissist. I know that my teeth are rotten, my breath is bad, my flesh is flabby. I recognise my preposterous pomposity, my tortured syntax, my often disordered thinking, my compulsions, my obsessions, my regressions, my intellectual mediocrity, my perverted and melancholy sexuality. I know that my cognition is distorted and my emotions thwarted.

What appears to me to be genuine achievements – are often grandiose fantasies. What I take to be admiration – is mockery. I am not loved – I am exploited. And when I am loved – I exploit. I feel entitled – for no good reason. I feel superior – with no commensurate traits or achievements. I know all this. I have written about it extensively. I have expounded about it a thousand times.

And, yet, I keep getting surprised when confronted with reality. My feelings are hurt, my narcissism injured, my self-esteem shaken, my rage provoked.

One becomes aware of one's place in various hierarchies – some implicit, some explicit – through social interactions. One learns that one is not alone in this world, one gets rid of the solipsistic and infantile "I am the (centre of the) world" point of view. The more one meets people – the more one becomes aware of one's relative skills and accomplishment.

In other words, one develops empathy [see: http://samvak.tripod.com/empathy.html].

But the narcissist's social range and repertoire are often limited. The narcissist alienates people. Many narcissists are schizoids [see: http://samvak.tripod.com/faq67.html]. They interactions with others are stunted, partial, distorted, and misleading.

They learn the wrong lessons from the dearth of their social encounters. They are unable to realistically evaluate themselves, their skills, their achievements, their rights and privileges, and their expectations. They retreat to fantasy, denial, and self-delusion. They become rigid and their personality becomes disordered.

The other day, I said to one of my fiancée's girlfriends, full of my usual hubris: "Do you think I am a spy?" (i.e., mysterious, romantic, dark, clever). She looked at me disdainfully and responded: "Frankly, you remind me more of a shopkeeper than a spy."

I am a graphomaniac. I write prolifically about every subject, near and far. I post my work on Web sites and discussion lists, I submit it to the media, I publish it in books, I like to believe that I will be remembered by it. But people mostly find my essays lacking – the verbosity, the triteness, the convolutions of argumentation which often lead to a syllogistic dead-end.

It is when I write about the mundane that I excel. My political and economic columns are reasonable, though by no means spectacular and often in need of thorough editing. My few analytic pieces are good. Some of my poems are excellent. Many of my journal entries are praiseworthy. My work about narcissism is helpful, though badly written. The rest – the bulk of my writing – is trash.

Yet, I respond with outrage and shock when people tell me that. I attribute their well meant words to envy. I reject it fiercely. I counter-attack. I draw my bridges and ensconce myself in a shell of indignation. I know better. I am farsighted, a giant among intellectual dwarves, the tortured genius. The alternative is too painful to contemplate.

I like to think of myself as menacing. I like to think that I impress others with my clout and might. The other day someone said to me: "You know, you want to believe that you are frightening, you want to deter, to instil fear. But when you rage – you are merely being hysterical. It has the opposite effect. It is counter-productive."

I nurture my self-image as a machine: efficient, relentless, industrious, emotionless, reliable, and precise. I am always taken aback when people tell me that I am exceptionally emotional, that I am ruled by my feelings, that I am hyper-sensitive, that I have clear borderline traits.

Once, in response to a contemptuous remark I made about someone (call him "Joe"), his friend retorted: "Joe is cleverer than you because he makes more money than you. If you are so clever and efficient – how come you so poor?"

"I am not as corrupt as he" – I responded – "I wouldn't act as criminally and in collusion with the local venal politicians". I felt self-righteous and triumphant. I really BELIEVED in what I said. I felt indignant and infuriated by Joe's nefarious acts (of which I had no knowledge, nor any proof).

Joe's friend looked at me, not comprehending.

"But, in the last two years, you have served as advisor to these very venal politicians. Joe never worked with them as directly as you did" – she said softly – "And you did spend a year in jail for white collar crimes. Joe never did. What gives you the right to cast the first stone at him?"

There was sad amazement in her voice. And pity. A great pity.

Return

Narcissistic Routines

The behaviour of the narcissist is regulated by a series of routines developed by rote learning and by repetitive patterns of experience. The narcissist finds change extremely distasteful and unsettling. He is a creature of habit. The function of these routines is to reduce his anxiety by transforming a hostile and arbitrary world into a hospitable and manageable one.

Granted, many narcissists are unstable – they often change jobs, apartments, spouses, and vocations. But even these changes are predictable. The narcissistic personality is disorganised – but also rigid. The narcissist finds solace in certainty, in recurrence, in the familiar and the anticipated. It balances his inner precariousness and volatility.

Narcissists often strike their interlocutors as "machine-like", "artificial", "fake", "forced", "insincere", or "spurious". This is because even the narcissist's ostensibly spontaneous behaviours are either planned or automatic. The narcissist is continuously preoccupied with his Narcissistic Supply – how to secure its sources and the next dose. This preoccupation restricts the narcissist's attention span. As a result, he often appears to be aloof, absent-minded, and uninterested in other people, in events around him, and in abstract ideas – unless, of course, they have a direct bearing on his Narcissistic Supply.

The narcissist develops some of his routines to compensate for his inability to attend to his environment. Automatic reactions require much less investment of mental resources (think driving).

Narcissists may fake personal warmth and an outgoing personality – this is the routine of the "narcissistic mask". But as one gets to know the narcissist better, his mask falls, his "narcissistic makeup" wears off, his muscles relax and he reverts to the Narcissistic Tonus. The Narcissistic Tonus is a bodacious air of superiority mixed with disdain.

While routines (such as the various masks) are extraneous and require an (often conscious) investment of energy – the Tonus is the default position: effortless and frequent.

Many narcissists are obsessive-compulsive as well. They conduct daily "rituals", they are overly punctilious, they do things in a certain order, and adhere to numerous "laws", "principles", and "rules". They have rigid and oft-repeated opinions, uncompromising rules of conduct, unalterable views and judgements. These compulsions and obsessions are ossified routines.

Other routines involve paranoid, repetitive, thoughts. Yet others induce shyness and social phobia. The whole range of narcissistic behaviours can be traced to these routines and the various phases of their evolutionary cycles.

It is when these routines break down and are violated – when they become no longer defensible, or when the narcissist can no longer exercise them – that a narcissistic injury occurs. The narcissist expects the outside world to conform to his inner universe. When a conflict between these two realms erupts, thus unsettling the ill-poised mental balance so painstakingly achieved by the narcissist (mainly by exercising his routines) – the narcissist unravels. The narcissist's very defence mechanisms are routines, and so he is left defenceless in a hostile, cold world – the true reflection of his inner landscape.

Return

Pathological Narcissism
A Dysfunction or a Blessing?

Comments on recent research by Roy Baumeister.

Is pathological narcissism a blessing or a malediction?

The answer is: it depends. Healthy narcissism is a mature, balanced love of oneself coupled with a stable sense of self-worth and self-esteem. Healthy narcissism implies knowledge of one's boundaries and a proportionate and realistic appraisal of one's achievements and traits.

Pathological narcissism is wrongly described as too much healthy narcissism (or too much self-esteem). These are two absolutely unrelated phenomena which, regrettably, came to bear the same title. Confusing pathological narcissism with self-esteem betrays a fundamental ignorance of both.

Pathological narcissism involves an impaired, dysfunctional, immature (True) Self coupled with a compensatory fiction (the False Self). The sick narcissist's sense of self-worth and self-esteem derive entirely from audience feedback. The narcissist has no self-esteem or self-worth of his own (no such ego functions). In the absence of observers, the narcissist shrivels to non-existence and feels dead. Hence the narcissist's preying habits in his constant pursuit of Narcissistic Supply. Pathological narcissism is an addictive behaviour.

Still, dysfunctions are reactions to abnormal environments and situations (e.g., abuse, trauma, smothering, etc.).

Paradoxically, his dysfunction allows the narcissist to function. It compensates for lacks and deficiencies by exaggerating tendencies and traits. It is like the tactile sense of a blind person. In short: pathological narcissism is a result of over-sensitivity, the repression of overwhelming memories and experiences, and the suppression of inordinately strong negative feelings (e.g., hurt, envy, anger, or humiliation).

That the narcissist functions at all – is because of his pathology and thanks to it. The alternative is complete decompensation and integration.

In time, the narcissist learns how to leverage his pathology, how to use it to his advantage, how to deploy it in order to maximise benefits and utilities – in other words, how to transform his curse into a blessing.

Narcissists are obsessed by delusions of fantastic grandeur and superiority. As a result they are very competitive. They are strongly compelled – where others are merely motivated. They are driven, relentless, tireless, and ruthless. They often make it to the top. But even when they do not – they strive and fight and learn and climb and create and think and devise and design and conspire. Faced with a challenge – they are likely to do better than non-narcissists.

Yet, we often find that narcissists abandon their efforts in midstream, give up, vanish, lose interest, devalue former pursuits, or slump. Why is that?

A challenge, or even a guaranteed eventual triumph – are meaningless in the absence of onlookers. The narcissist needs an audience to applaud, affirm, recoil, approve, admire, adore, fear, or even detest him. He craves the attention and depends on the Narcissistic Supply only others can provide. The narcissist derives sustenance only from the outside – his emotional innards are hollow and moribund.

The narcissist's enhanced performance is predicated on the existence of a challenge (real or imaginary) and of an audience. Baumeister usefully re-affirmed this linkage, known to theoreticians since Freud.

Return

The Losses of the Narcissist

Narcissists are accustomed to loss. Their obnoxious personality and intolerable behaviours makes them lose friends and spouses, mates and colleagues, jobs and family. Their peripatetic nature, their constant mobility and instability causes them to lose everything else: their place of residence, their property, their businesses, their country, and their language.

There is always a locus of loss in the narcissist's life. He may be faithful to his wife and a model family man – but then he is likely to change jobs frequently and renege on his financial and social obligations. Or, he may be a brilliant achiever – scientist, doctor, CEO, actor, pastor, politician, journalist – with a steady, long-term and successful career – but a lousy homemaker, thrice divorced, unfaithful, unstable, always on the lookout for better Narcissistic Supply.

The narcissist is aware of his propensity to lose everything that could have been of value, meaning, and significance in his life. If he is inclined to magical thinking and alloplastic defences, he blames life, or fate, or country, or his boss, or his nearest and dearest for his uninterrupted string of losses. Otherwise, he attributes it to people's inability to cope with his outstanding talents, towering intellect, or rare abilities. His losses, he convinces himself, are the outcomes of pettiness, pusillanimity, envy, malice, and ignorance. It would have turned out the same way even had he behaved differently, he consoles himself.

In time, the narcissist develops defence mechanisms against the inevitable pain and hurt he incurs with every loss and defeat. He ensconces himself in an ever thicker skin, an impenetrable shell, a make belief environment in which his sense of in-bred superiority and entitlement is preserved. He appears indifferent to the most harrowing and agonising experiences, not human in his unperturbed composure, emotionally detached and cold, inaccessible, and invulnerable. Deep inside, he, indeed, feels nothing.

Four years ago, I had to surrender my collections to my creditors (who then proceeded to loot them egregiously). Over ten years, I have painstakingly recorded thousands of movies, purchased thousands of books, vinyl records, CD's and CD-ROM's. The only copies of many of my manuscripts – hundreds of finished articles, five completed textbooks, poems – were lost as were all my press clippings. It was a great labour of love. But, when I gave all that away, I felt relief. I dream about my lost universe of culture and creativity from time to time. But that is it.

Losing my wife – with whom I spent nine years of my life – was devastating. I felt denuded and annulled. But once the divorce was over, I forgot about her completely. I deleted her memory so thoroughly that I very rarely think and never dream about her. I am never sad. I never stop to think "what if", to derive lessons, to obtain closure. I am not pretending, nor am I putting effort into this selective amnesia. It happened serendipitously, like a valve shut tight. I feel proud of this ability of mine to un-be.

The narcissist cruises through his life as a tourist would through an exotic island. He observes events and people, his own experiences and loved ones – as a spectator would a movie that at times is mildly exciting and at others mildly boring. He is never fully there, entirely present, irreversibly committed. He is constantly with one hand on his emotional escape hatch, ready to bail out, to absent himself, to re-invent his life in another place, with other people. The narcissist is a coward, terrified of his True Self and protective of the deceit that is his new existence. He feels no pain. He feels no love. He feels no life.

Return

Transformations of Aggression

Prone to magical thinking, the narcissist is deeply convinced of the transcendental meaning of his life. He fervently believes in his own uniqueness and "mission". He constantly searches for clues regarding the hidden – though inevitable – meaning of his personal life. The narcissist is forever a "public persona", even when alone, in the confines of his bedroom. His every move, his every act, his every decision and every scribbling is of momentous consequence. The narcissist often documents his life with vigil, for the benefit of future biographers. His every utterance and shred of correspondence are carefully orchestrated as befitting a historical figure of import.

This grandiose background leads to an exaggerated sense of entitlement. The narcissist feels that he is worthy of special and immediate treatment by the most qualified. His time is too precious to be wasted by bureaucratic trifles, misunderstandings, underlings, and social conventions. His mission is urgent. Other people are expected both to share the narcissist's self-assessment – and to behave accordingly: to accommodate his needs, instantly comply with his wishes, and succumb to his whims.

But the world does not always accommodate, comply, and succumb. It often resists the wishes of the narcissist, mocks his comportment, or, worst of all, ignores him. The narcissist reacts to this with a cycle of frustration and aggression.

Still, it is not always possible to express naked aggression. It may be dangerous, or counterproductive, or plain silly. Even the narcissist cannot attack his boss, or a policeman, or the neighbourhood bully with impunity. So, the narcissist's aggression wears many forms. The narcissist suddenly becomes brutally "honest", or bitingly "humorous", or smotheringly "helpful", or sexually "experimental", or socially "reclusive", or behaviourally "different", or find yet another way to express his scathing and repressed hostility.

The narcissist's favourite sadistic cocktail is brutal honesty coupled with "helpful advice" and "concern" for the welfare of the person attacked. The narcissist blurts out – often unprovoked – hurtful observations. These statements are invariably couched in a socially impeccable context.

For instance, "Do you know you have a bad breath? You will be much more popular if you treated it", "You are really too fat, you should take care of yourself, you are not young, you know, who knows what this is doing to your heart", "These clothes do not complement you. Let me give you the name of my tailor…", "You are behaving very strangely lately, I think that talk therapy combined with medication may do wonders", and so on.

The misanthropic and schizoid narcissist at once becomes sociable and friendly when he spots an opportunity to hurt or to avenge. He then resorts to humour – black, thwarted, poignant, biting, sharpened and agonising. Thinly disguises barbs follow thinly disguised threats cloaked in "jokes" or "humorous anecdotes".

Another favourite trick is to harp on the insecurities, fears, weaknesses, and deficiencies of the target of aggression. If married to a jealous spouse, the narcissist emphasises his newfound promiscuity and need to experiment sexually. If his business partner has been traumatised by a previous insolvency, the narcissist berates him for being too cautious or insufficiently entrepreneurial while forcing the partnership to assume outlandish and speculative business risks. If co-habiting with a gregarious mate, the narcissist acts the recluse, the hermit, the social misfit, or the misunderstood visionary – thus forcing the partner to give up her social life.

The narcissist is seething with enmity and venom. He is a receptacle of unbridled hatred, animosity, and hostility. When he can, the narcissist often turns to physical violence. But the non-physical manifestations of his pent-up bile are even more terrifying, more all-pervasive, and more lasting. Beware of narcissists bearing gifts. They are bound to explode in your faces, or poison you. The narcissist hates you wholeheartedly and thoroughly simply because you are. Remembering this has a survival value.

Return

Chronos and Narcissus

Chronos cannibalised his own sons. He devoured them and cast away their remains. This is often what I feel like doing to my more successful protégés. Young people – and not so young – tend to look up to me, stick to me, emulate me, admire me – in short: they are perfect Sources of Narcissistic Supply. I reciprocate. I give them letters of introduction and recommendations suffused with unmitigated enthusiasm. I acquaint them with my business and academic contacts. I help them with their homework. I listen to their dilemmas and give direction to their life. I play the older brother, the friend, the confidant, and the sagacious teacher.

And it often works. They all succeed. They become ministers or bankers or authors or scholars. I then feel left behind, stuck in the proverbial mud that is my life, drowning in a grimy wave of envy and self-pity. I think to myself: I am better than they are – more intelligent and more experienced, more knowledgeable and more creative. Yet, they are there progressing inexorably – and I am here, regressing and decaying.

I consider the numerous chances I was given and how I blew them. The sponsors I eroded with my infantile indecisiveness and amateurish attitude. The businesses I drove to bankruptcy with my narcissistic temper tantrums and superiority contests. The clients and investors I lost to my procrastination, abuse, or treason. The friends who turned to enemies. The enemies who abandoned me in sheer revulsion. The fortunes I squandered, the disgrace of drunken speeches, my barren life – no love, no intimacy, no sex, no family, no children, no country, and no language. I disappointed my benefactors and lovers and well-wishers with glee. I cherished and reveled in my self-annihilation.

A central pillar in my thinking unravels as I age. My intellect is not enough. Not only is it not half as rare or as refined as I imagined it to be – it is simply insufficient. It cannot secure my happiness, or safety, or longevity, or health. It cannot buy me love or friendship. I eke out a living – but that is it. I don't have what it takes. And what it takes is a combination of intelligence with many other things: with empathy, with team work, perseverance, honesty, integrity, stamina, a modicum of optimism, true assessment of reality, sense of proportion, the ability to love, selflessness in measure. Intelligence without these is cold and sterile. It gives birth to nothing but recursive exercises.

To be fully human, it takes much more than memory and analytic skills. In the absence of emotions and empathy, there is only artificial intelligence – a lame and pitiable simulation of the real thing. Artificial intelligence can beat chess masters and memorise entire encyclopaedias. It can blaze a trail of written articles. It can add, subtract, and multiply.

But it can never enjoy another person. It can never intertwine, or care, or warm its heart, or hope. It can produce some poems but never poetry. It is even deprived of the ability to feel lonely. And though it may fully grasp its own deficiencies – try as it may, it can never change. For it is artificial and synthetic – a fiction, a two-dimensional creation, a part and not a whole. It is a narcissist.

Return

The Labours of the Narcissist

I can't hold a job or even run my own business for very long. People – co-workers, clients, suppliers – complain that I create a "bad atmosphere", that I am a "difficult person", that they have to walk on brittle eggshells lest I explode, humiliate them, expose their errors and their weaknesses, or simply walk away.

At the workplace, I connive and collude and spread malicious gossip and complain and grumble and insult profusely and make everyone utterly miserable. I project my fears and foibles unto others. I impose my paranoid set of mind. I am full with ideas of reference – convinced that people are talking about me, conspiring against me, berating me behind my back, out to get me.

I have caused the disintegration of teams and dreams and firms too many to enumerate. Like a ghost, like a poison, I permeated everything, destabilising, provoking, sowing fear and doubt and mutual suspicion, leading inexorably to recriminations and internecine fighting.

Yet, I have done none of this intentionally or with deliberation. These are the unwanted and inadvertent outcomes of my disorder. My grandiose fantasies make me undertake tasks far beyond my capabilities – and then flunk them spectacularly. My sense of entitlement – never commensurate with my achievements – breeds in me a deep-seated conviction of deprivation and discrimination and a wrathful attitude towards those who will not kowtow and instantaneously cater to my inflated needs. My paranoia paints the world in the penumbral hues of suspicion and intrigue.

There is no way to appease me or to stop me. I am the terminator – ever in flux, ever evasive, omnipresent, and all-pervasive. I am the shadow on the wall, the whisper behind the water cooler, the muffled smirking in the corner. I am the traitorous employee, the snitch, the industrial spy, the venomous co-worker, the malicious on-looker. I desert the sinking ship first.

Despite my grandiose self-image, I constantly feel like a cheat. I know that the self people perceive is my FALSE Self. I know that I am false and vain and prone to modulation by the vicissitudes of my Narcissistic Supply. I realise how frivolous, how ephemeral, how unreal I am. In an effort to cover up for these shortcomings I lie and I exaggerate. I dent my credibility and risk my reputation daily in my struggle to sustain a figment of my own pathology. I crush and violently demean any doubter of my skills, any questioner of my qualifications, any threat – perceived or real – to my facade.

I wrote this about the narcissist in the workplace:

"The narcissist always seeks new thrills and stimuli.

The narcissist is notorious for his low threshold of and lack of resistance to boredom. His behaviour is impulsive and his biography tumultuous precisely because of his need to introduce uncertainty and risk to what he regards as 'stagnation' or 'slow death' (i.e., routine). Most interactions in the workplace are part of the rut – and thus constitute a reminder of this routine – deflating the narcissist's grandiose fantasies.

Narcissists do many unnecessary, wrong and even dangerous things in pursuit of the stabilisation of their inflated self-image.

Narcissists forever shift the blame, pass the buck, and engage in cognitive dissonance. They 'pathologise' the other, foster feelings of guilt and shame in her, demean, debase and humiliate in order to preserve their sense of grandiosity and their compulsive control.

Narcissists are pathological liars. They think nothing of it because their very Self is FALSE, an invention.

Here are a few useful guidelines:

- Never disagree with the narcissist or contradict him;
- Never offer him any intimacy;
- Look awed by whatever attribute matters to him (for instance: by his professional achievements or by his good looks, or by his success with women and so on);
- Never remind him of life out there and if you do, connect it somehow to his sense of grandiosity. If the narcissist bought new office equipment – a mundane, drab, and dreary job – so unworthy of the narcissist's time – aggrandise the purchase thus: 'This is the BEST equipment I have ever seen in ANY workplace', 'We got this fax EXCLUSIVELY – it is the FIRST ever sold here', etc.;
- Do not make any comment, which might directly or indirectly impinge on the narcissist's self-image, omnipotence, judgment, omniscience, skills, capabilities, professional record, or even omnipresence;

- *Bad sentences start with: I think you overlooked ... made a mistake here ... you don't know ... do you know ... you were not here yesterday so ... you cannot ... you should ...;*
- *'Should' and 'ought to' are perceived as rude impositions. Narcissists react very badly to instructions, however helpful and given with the best intentions. They interpret them as restrictions on their freedom;*
- *Sentences starting with 'I' are equally disastrous. Never mention the fact that you are a separate, autonomous entity. Narcissists regard others as extensions of their selves."*

Return

The Objects of the Narcissist

The Accumulator

This kind of narcissist jealously guards his possessions – his collections, his furniture, his cars, his children, his women, his money, his credit cards... Objects comfort the narcissist. They remind him of his status. They are linked to gratifying events and, thus, constitute Secondary Sources of Narcissistic Supply. They attest to the narcissist's wealth, his connections, his achievements, his friendships, his conquests, and his glorious past. No wonder he is so attached to them. Objects connected with failures or embarrassments have no place in his abode. They get cast out.

Moreover, owning the right objects often guarantees the uninterrupted flow of Narcissistic Supply. A flashy car or an ostentatious house help the somatic narcissist attract sexual partners. Owning a high powered computer and a broadband connection, or a sizable and expensive library, facilitate the intellectual pursuits of the cerebral narcissist. Sporting a glamorous wife and politically correct kids is indispensable in the careers of the narcissistic politician, or diplomat.

The narcissist parades his objects, flaunts them, consumes them conspicuously, praises them vocally, draws attention to them compulsively, brags about them incessantly. When they fail to elicit Narcissistic Supply – admiration, adulation, marvel – the narcissist feels wounded, humiliated, deprived, discriminated against, the victim of a conspiracy, unloved.

Objects often make the accumulator-narcissist. They are an inseparable part of his pathology. This type of narcissist is possessive. He obsesses about his belongings and collects them compulsively. He "brands" them as his own. He infuses them with his spirit and his personality. He attributes to them his traits. He projects to them his thwarted emotions, his fears, his hopes. They are an integral part of him, inseparable, providing emotional succour.

Such a narcissist will say: "My car is daring and unstoppable", or "How clever is my computer!", or "My dog is cunning", or "My wife craves attention". He often compares people to the inanimate. Himself he sees as a computer or sex machine. His wife he regards as some kind of luxury good. The narcissist loves objects and relates to them – things he fails to do with humans. This is why he objectifies people – it makes it easier for him to interact with them. Objects are predictable, reliable, always there, obedient, easy to control and manipulate, universally desired.

A long time ago I was asked if objects, or pets could serve as Sources of Narcissistic Supply. I described in my response a second type of narcissist – the DISCARDER.

I responded thus (the full text is available here: http://samvak.tripod.com/faq46.html).

The Discarder

Any thing can serve as a Source of Narcissistic Supply, providing that it has the potential to attract people' attention and be the subject of their admiration. This is why narcissists are enamoured of status symbols, i.e., objects, which comprehensively encapsulate and concisely convey a host of data regarding their owners. These data generate a reaction in people: they make them look, admire, envy, dream, compare, or aspire. In short: they elicit Narcissistic Supply.

But, generally, discarder narcissists do not like souvenirs and the memories they bring. They are afraid to get emotionally attached to them and then get hurt if the objects are lost or stolen or expropriated or taken by creditors. Narcissists are sad people. Almost anything can depress them: a tune, a photograph, a work of art, a book, a mental image, or a voice. Narcissists are people who divorced their emotions because their emotions are mostly negative and painful, coloured by their basic trauma, by the early abuses that they suffered.

Objects, situations, voices, sights, colours – can provoke and evoke unwanted memories. The narcissist tries to avoid them. The discarder narcissist callously discards or gives away hard-won objects, memorabilia, gifts, and property. This behaviour sustains his sense of control and lack of vulnerability. It also proves to him that he is unique, not like "other people" who are attached to their material belongings. He is above this.

Accumulators and Narcissistic Handles

Still, not all narcissists are like this. Accumulator narcissists take to objects and memorabilia, to voices and tunes, to sights and to works of art – as reminders of their past glory and of their potential future grandeur. Many narcissists collect proofs and trophies of their sexual prowess, dramatic talent, past wealth, or intellectual achievements. They file them away almost compulsively. These are the "Narcissistic Handles".

The Narcissistic Handle operates through the mechanism of narcissistic branding. An example: objects, which belonged to former lovers, are "stamped" by them and become their full-fledged representations. They are fetishised. By interacting with these objects, the narcissist recreates the Narcissistic-Supply-rich situation, within which the objects were introduced into his life in the first place. This is magical thinking. Some clairvoyants claim to be able to extract all the information regarding the present, past and future states of the owner of an object they hold. It is as though the object, the memory, or the sound carry the narcissist back to where and when Narcissistic Supply was abundant.

This powerful combination of branding and evidencing is what gives rise to the "Narcissistic Contagion". This is the ability of the narcissist to objectify people and to anthropomorphesise objects in order to derive the maximum Narcissistic Supply from them. The narcissist is a pathogen. He transforms his human and non-human environments alike.

On the one hand, he invests as much affection and emotions in an inanimate object as healthier people do in human beings. On the other hand, he transforms people around him into functions, or objects.

In their effort to satisfy the needs of the narcissist – his nearest or dearest very often neglect their own. They feel that something is sick and wrong in their lives. But they are so entrapped, so much part of the narcissist's personal mythology that they cannot cut loose. Manipulated through guilt, leveraged through fear – they are but a shadow of their former selves. They have contracted the disease of narcissism. They have been infected and poisoned. They have been branded.

Return

To Age with Grace

"The permanent temptation of life is to confuse dreams with reality. Then permanent defeat of life comes when dreams are surrendered to reality."
James Michener, Author

The narcissist ages without mercy and without grace. His withered body and his overwrought mind betray him all at once. He stares with incredulity and rage at cruel mirrors. He refuses to accept his growing fallibility. He rebels against his decrepitude and mediocrity. Accustomed to being awe-inspiring and the recipient of adulation – the narcissist cannot countenance his social isolation and the pathetic figure that he cuts.

As a child prodigy, a sex symbol, a stud, a public intellectual, an actor, an idol – the narcissist was at the centre of attention, the eye of his personal twister, a black hole which sucked people's energy and resources dry and spat out with indifference their mutilated carcasses. No longer. With old age comes disillusionment. Old charms wear thin.

Having been exposed for what he is – a deceitful, treacherous, malignant egotist – the narcissist's old tricks now fail him. People are on their guard, their gullibility reduced. The narcissist – being the rigid, precariously balanced structure that he is – can't change. He reverts to old forms, re-adopts hoary habits, succumbs to erstwhile temptations. He is made a mockery by his accentuated denial of reality, by his obdurate refusal to grow up, an eternal, malformed child in the sagging body of a decaying man.

It is the fable of the grasshopper and the ant revisited.

The narcissist – the grasshopper – having relied on supercilious stratagems throughout his life – is singularly ill-adapted to life's rigors and tribulations. He feels entitled – but fails to elicit Narcissistic Supply. Wrinkled time makes child prodigies lose their magic, lovers exhaust their potency, philanderers waste their allure, and geniuses miss their touch. The longer the narcissist lives – the more average he becomes. The wider the gulf between his pretensions and his accomplishments – the more he is the object of derision and contempt.

Yet, few narcissists save for rainy days. Few bother to study a trade, or get a degree, pursue a career, maintain a business, keep their jobs, or raise functioning families, nurture their friendships, or broaden their horizons. Narcissists are perennially ill-prepared. Those who succeed in their vocation, end up bitterly alone having squandered the love of spouse, off-spring, and mates. The more gregarious and family-orientated – often flunk at work, leap from one job to another, relocate erratically, forever itinerant and peripatetic.

The contrast between his youth and prime and his dilapidated present constitutes a permanent narcissistic injury. The narcissist retreats deeper into himself to find solace. He withdraws into the penumbral universe of his grandiose fantasies. There – almost psychotic – he salves his wounds and comforts himself with trophies of his past.

A rare minority of narcissists accept their fate with fatalism or good humour. These precious few are healed mysteriously by the deepest offence to their megalomania – old age. They lose their narcissism and confront the outer world with the poise and composure that they lacked when they were captives of their own, distorted, narrative.

Such changed narcissists develop new, more realistic, expectations and hopes – commensurate with their talents, skills, accomplishments and education. Ironically, it is invariably too late. They are avoided and ignored, rendered transparent by their checkered past. They are passed over for promotion, never invited to professional or social gatherings, cold-shouldered by the media. They are snubbed and disregarded. They are never the recipients of perks, benefits, or awards. They are blamed when not blameworthy and rarely praised when deserving. They are being constantly and consistently punished for who they were. It is poetic justice in more than one way. They are being treated narcissistically by their erstwhile victims. They finally are tasting their own medicine, the bitter harvest of their wrath and arrogance.

Return

Discussing Narcissism

Correspondence with M. William Phelps
Author of "PERFECT POISON" (August, 2003)
Copyright M. William Phelps, Kensington Publishing Corp. 2002

Pathological narcissism pervades every facet of the personality, every behaviour, every cognition, and every emotion. This makes it difficult to treat. Add to this the narcissist's unthinking and deeply-ingrained resistance to authority figures, such as therapists – and healing, or even mere behaviour modification, are rendered unattainable.

Pathological narcissism is often co-morbid with mood disorders, compulsive rituals, substance abuse, paraphilias, or reckless behaviour patterns. Many narcissists are also anti-social. Lacking empathy and convinced of their own magnificence, they feel that they are above social conventions and the Law.

Some of these concomitant problems are amenable to a combination of medication and talk therapy. Not so the core defence mechanisms of the narcissist.

The narcissist is both victimiser and victim. The essence of the narcissistic disorder is a breakdown of internal communication. The narcissist invents and nurtures a False Self intended to elicit attention – positive or negative – from others and thus to fill his innermost void. He is so engrossed in securing Narcissistic Supply from his sources by putting on an energy-sapping show – that he fails to materialise his potential, to have mature, adult relationships, to feel, and, in general, to enjoy life.

To the narcissist, other people are never more than potential Sources of Supply with a useful "shelf life". The narcissist invariably ends up cruelly devaluing and discarding them, like dysfunctional objects. Little wonder that the narcissist – haughty, abrasive, exploitive, manipulative, untruthful – is universally held in contempt, derided, hated, persecuted, and cast out. But we should never forget that he pays a dear price for something which, essentially, is beyond his full control – i.e., for his illness.

Correspondence with Abigail Esman

Upbringing and Narcissism

There are no authoritative studies to back a genetic predisposition to pathological narcissism – nor the oft-heard claim that it is the outcome of abuse. But anecdotal evidence, case studies, and the investigation of population in outpatient clinics and so on – reveals a correlation between abuse in early childhood and infancy and the emergence of pathological narcissism as a defence mechanism.

There are many forms of abuse. The most well-known and frequently discussed include incest, molestation, beatings, constant berating, terrorising, abandonment, arbitrary punishment, capricious and unstable parental behaviour and environment, authoritarian, emotionless, rigid and hierarchical home regime and so on.

But more pernicious are the subtle and socially-acceptable forms of abuse – such as doting, smothering, treating the child as an extension of the parent, forcing the child to realise the parents' unfulfilled dreams and unrealised wishes, putting the child on constant display, maintaining unrealistic expectations of him and so on. These modes of abuse permeate the tenuous self-boundaries formed by the child and teach him that he is loved because of what he accomplishes rather than due to who he is.

Treating Narcissism

Every aspect of the personality is pervaded by pathological narcissism. It colours the narcissist's behaviour, cognition, and emotional landscape. This ubiquity renders it virtually untreatable. Additionally, the narcissist develops deep-set resistance to authority figures, such as therapists. His attitude to treatment is conflictual, competitive, and hostile. When he fails to co-opt the therapist into upholding his grandiose self-image, the narcissist devalues and discards both the treatment and the mental health practitioner administering it.

Mood disorders, compulsive rituals, substance abuse, paraphilias, reckless, or anti-social behaviour patterns often accompany pathological narcissism (they are co-morbid). While some of these coexistent problems can be ameliorated through a combination of medication and talk therapy – not so the core defence mechanisms of the narcissist.

Return

Grandiosity Hangover and Narcissistic Baiting

The grandiose fantasies of the narcissist inevitably and invariably clash with his drab, routine, and mundane reality. We call this constant dissonance the Grandiosity Gap. Sometimes the gap is so yawning that even the narcissist – however dimly – recognises its existence. Still, this insight into his real situation fails to alter his behaviour. The narcissist knows that his grandiose fantasies are incommensurate with his accomplishments, knowledge, status, actual wealth (or lack thereof), physical constitution, or sex appeal – yet, he keeps behaving as though this were untrue.

The situation is further exacerbated by periods of relative success in the narcissist's past. Has-been and also-ran narcissists suffer from a Grandiosity Hangover. They may have once been rich, famous, powerful, brilliant, or sexually irresistible – but they no longer are. Still, they continue to behave as though little has changed.

The balding, potbellied, narcissist still courts women aggressively. The impoverished tycoon sinks deeper into debts, trying to maintain an unsustainable and lavish lifestyle. The one-novel author or one-discovery scholar still demands professional deference and expects attention by media and superiors. The once-potent politician maintains regal airs and holds court in great pomp. The wizened actress demands special treatment and throws temper tantrums when rebuffed. The ageing beauty wears her daughter's clothes and regresses emotionally as she progresses chronologically.

Human collectives – firms, nations, clubs – develop Grandiosity Hangovers as easily and as frequently as do individuals. It is not uncommon to come across a group of people who still live in a bygone buy glorious past. This mass pathology is self-reinforcing. Members feed on each other's delusions, pretensions, and lies. Ostrich-like, they bury their collective head in the sand of time, harking back to happier moments of omnipotence, omniscience, and omnipresence.

The Grandiosity Hangover and the Grandiosity Gap are the two major vulnerabilities of the narcissist. By exploiting them, the narcissist can be effortlessly manipulated. This is especially true when the narcissist is confronted with authority, finds himself in an inferior position, or when his Narcissistic Supply is deficient or uncertain.

From "The Narcissist in Court":

"Here are a few of the things the narcissist finds devastating:

Any statement or fact, which seems to contradict his inflated perception of his grandiose self. Any criticism, disagreement, exposure of fake achievements, belittling of 'talents and skills' which the narcissist fantasises that he possesses, any hint that he is subordinated, subjugated, controlled, owned or dependent upon a third party. Any description of the narcissist as average and common, indistinguishable from many others. Any hint that the narcissist is weak, needy, dependent, deficient, slow, not intelligent, naive, gullible, susceptible, not in the know, manipulated, a victim.

The narcissist is likely to react with rage to all these and, in an effort to re-establish his fantastic grandiosity, he is likely to expose facts and stratagems he had no conscious intention of exposing.

The narcissist reacts with narcissistic rage, hatred, aggression, or violence to an infringement of what he perceives to be his entitlement.

Narcissists believe that they are so unique and that their lives are so cosmically significant that others should defer to their needs and cater to their every whim without ado. The narcissist feels entitled to special treatment by unique individuals, over and above the regular person.

Any insinuation, hint, intimation, or direct declaration that the narcissist is not special at all, that he is average, common, not even sufficiently idiosyncratic to warrant a fleeting interest will inflame the narcissist.

Add to this a negation of the narcissist's sense of entitlement – and the combustion is inevitable. Tell the narcissist that he does not deserve the best treatment, that his needs are not everyone's priority, that he is boring, that his needs can be catered to by an average practitioner (medical doctor, accountant, lawyer, psychiatrist), that he and his motives are transparent and can be easily gauged, that he will do what he is told, that his temper tantrums will not be tolerated, that no special concessions will be made to accommodate his inflated sense of self, that he is subject to court procedures, etc. – and the narcissist will lose control.

The narcissist believes that he is the cleverest, far above the madding crowd. If contradicted, exposed, humiliated, berated ('You are not as intelligent as you think you are', 'Who is really behind all this? It takes sophistication which you don't seem to have', 'So, you have no formal education', 'You are (mistake his age, make him much older) ... sorry, you are ... old', 'What did you do in your life? Did you study? Do you have a degree? Did you ever establish or run a business? Would you define yourself as a success?', 'Would your children share your view that you are a good father?', 'You were last seen with a Ms. ... who is (suppressed grin) a DOMESTIC (in demeaning disbelief)'.

I know that many of these questions cannot be asked outright in a court of law. But you can hurl these sentences at him during the breaks, inadvertently during the examination or deposition phase, etc."

Return

The Energy of Self

The personality is not a static structure which immutably permeates our being. It is a dynamic, on-going, process. It is a series of cognitive and emotional interactions compounded by extraneous input and endogenous feedback. It is ever-evolving, though following our formative years, all subsequent changes are subtle and infinitesimal. This labyrinthine complex of reactions, behaviour patterns, beliefs, and defence mechanisms consumes a lot of psychic energy. The more primitive the personality, the less organised, the more disordered – the greater the amount of energy required to maintain it in a semblance of balance, however precarious.

The predicament of the narcissist, the histrionic, and the borderline is even more multifarious. People suffering from these all-pervasive and pernicious personality disorders externalise most of the available energy in an effort to secure Narcissistic Supply and, thus, regulate a vicissitudinal sense of self-worth.

Normally, one's energy is expended on the proper functioning of one's personality. The personality disordered devote any shred of vitality to the projection and maintenance of a False Self, whose sole purpose is to elicit attention, admiration, approval, acknowledgement, fear, or adulation from others. The Narcissistic Supply thus obtained helps these unfortunates to calibrate a wildly fluctuating self-esteem and, thus, fulfils critical ego functions.

Yet, the constant pursuit of this drug, the need to stay permanently attuned to one's human environment and to manipulate it ceaselessly – inevitably depletes the narcissist's vigour. His emotional exoskeleton – derived and Sisyphically constructed from the outside – is far more demanding than the normal endoskeletons that healthy people possess. To borrow from Freud, we can say that the narcissist sublimates his Libido. He is an artist with himself as his sole creation. His entire energy is committed to the theatre production that is his False Self.

Hence the narcissist's constant fatigue and ennui, his short attention span, his tendency to devalue Sources of Supply, even his transformed aggression.

The narcissist can afford to dedicate resources only to the most promising founts of Narcissistic Supply. The "path of least investment" – criminal shortcuts, violence, cheating, con-artistry, lies and confabulations – is always preferred by the narcissist because his élan is so run down, his vitality so drenched, and his verve so exhausted by the unusual need to secure from the outside what most people effortlessly produce internally and take for granted.

Return

Whistling in the Dark

The narcissist often strikes people are "laid back" – or, less charitably: lazy, parasitic, spoiled, and self-indulgent. But, as usual with narcissists, appearances deceive. Narcissists are either compulsively driven over-achievers – or chronic under-achieving wastrels. Most of them fail to make full and productive use of their potential and capacities. Many avoid even the now standard path of an academic degree, a career, or family life.

The disparity between the accomplishments of the narcissist and his grandiose fantasies and inflated self-image – the Grandiosity Gap – is staggering and, in the long run, insupportable. It imposes onerous exigencies on the narcissist's grasp of reality and social skills. It pushes him either to seclusion or to a frenzy of "acquisitions" – cars, women, wealth, power.

Yet, no matter how successful the narcissist is – many of them end up being abject failures – the Grandiosity Gap can never be bridged. The narcissist's False Self is so unrealistic and his Superego so sadistic that there is nothing the narcissist can do to extricate himself from the Kafkaesque trial that is his life.

The narcissist is a slave to his own inertia. Some narcissists are forever accelerating on the way to ever higher peaks and ever greener pastures.

Others succumb to numbing routines, the expenditure of minimal energy, and to preying on the vulnerable. But either way, the narcissist's life is out of control, at the mercy of merciless inner voices and internal forces.

Narcissists are one-state machines, programmed to extract Narcissistic Supply from others. To do so, they develop early on a set of immutable routines. This propensity for repetition, this inability to change and rigidity confine the narcissist, stunt his development, and limit his horizons. Add to this his overpowering sense of entitlement, his visceral fear of failure, and his invariable need to both feel unique and be perceived as such – and one often ends up with a recipe for inaction.

The under-achieving narcissist dodges challenges, eludes tests, shirks competition, sidesteps expectations, ducks responsibilities, evades authority – because he is afraid to fail and because doing something everyone else does endangers his sense of uniqueness. Hence the narcissist's apparent "laziness" and "parasitism". His sense of entitlement – with no commensurate accomplishments or investment – aggravates his milieu. People tend to regard such narcissists as "spoiled brats".

In specious contrast, the over-achieving narcissist seeks challenges and risks, provokes competition, embellishes expectations, aggressively bids for responsibilities and authority and seems to be possessed with an eerie self-confidence. People tend to regard such specimen as "entrepreneurial", "daring", "visionary", or "tyrannical". Yet, these narcissists too are mortified by potential failure, driven by a strong conviction of entitlement, and strive to be unique and be perceived as such.

Their hyperactivity is merely the flip side of the under-achiever's inactivity: it is as fallacious and as empty and as doomed to miscarriage and disgrace. It is often sterile or illusory, all smoke and mirrors rather than substance. The precarious "achievements" of such narcissists invariably unravel. They often act outside the law or social norms. Their industriousness, workaholism, ambition, and commitment are intended to disguise their essential inability to produce and build. Theirs is a whistle in the dark, a pretension, a Potemkin life, all make-belief and thunder.

Return

The Embarrassing Narcissist

I was convinced that I possess an unerring sense of rhythm until my wife told me I had none. I thought that my comments, observations, and insights are original and pithy – until I discovered that I am numbingly verbose, repetitive, and coarse. I attributed to myself a great sense of humour until I re-read some of my writings and found how convoluted and dull my pitiful efforts at being witty were. To my mind, my prose was arabesque but lucid and incisive. I have since learned that it is no such thing.

This utter lack of self-awareness is typical of the narcissist. He is intimate only with his False Self, constructed meticulously from years of lying and deceit. The narcissist's True Self is stashed, dilapidated and dysfunctional, in the furthest recesses of his mind. The False Self is omnipotent, omniscient, omnipresent, creative, ingenious, irresistible, and glowing. The narcissist often isn't.

Add combustible paranoia to the narcissist's divorce from himself – and his constant and recurrent failure to assess reality fairly is more understandable. The narcissist overpowering sense of entitlement is rarely commensurate with his accomplishments in his real life or with his traits.

When the world fails to comply with his demands and to support his grandiose fantasies, the narcissist suspects a plot against him by his inferiors.

The narcissist rarely admits to a weakness, ignorance, or deficiency. He filters out information to the contrary – a cognitive impairment with serious consequences. Narcissists are likely to unflinchingly make inflated and inane claims about their sexual prowess, wealth, connections, history, or achievements.

All this is mighty embarrassing to the narcissist's nearest, dearest, colleagues, friends, neighbours, even on-lookers. The narcissist's tales are so patently absurd that he often catches people off-guard. Unbeknownst to him, the narcissist is derided and mockingly imitated. He fast makes a nuisance and an imposition of himself in every company.

But the narcissist's failure of the reality test can have more serious and irreversible consequences. Narcissists, academically unqualified to make life-and-death decisions often insist on rendering them. I "treated" my father for muscular pain for five days at home. All that time, he was enduring a massive heart attack. My vanity wouldn't let me admit my diagnostic error. He survived. Many others don't.

Narcissists pretend to be economists, engineers, or medical doctors – when they are not. But they are not con-artists in the classic, premeditated sense. They firmly believe that, though self-taught at best, they are more qualified than even the properly accredited sort. Narcissists believe in magic and in fantasy. They are no longer with us.

Return

Grandiosity and Intimacy
The Roots of Paranoia

Paranoid ideation – the narcissist's deep-rooted conviction that he is being persecuted by his inferiors, detractors, or powerful ill-wishers – serves two psychodynamic purposes. It upholds the narcissist's grandiosity and it fends off intimacy.

Grandiosity Enhancing Paranoia

Being the target of relentless, ubiquitous, and unjust persecution proves to the paranoid narcissist how important and feared he is. Being hounded by the mighty and the privileged validates his pivotal role in the scheme of things. Only vital, weighty, crucial, essential principals are thus bullied and intimidated, followed and harassed, stalked and intruded upon – goes his unconscious inner dialog. The narcissist consistently baits authority figures into punishing him and thus into upholding his delusional self-image as worthy of their attention. This provocative behaviour is called Projective Identification.

The paranoid delusions of the narcissist are always grandiose, "cosmic", or "historical". His pursuers are influential and formidable. They are after his unique possessions, out to exploit his expertise and special traits, or to force him to abstain and refrain from certain actions. The narcissist feels that he is at the centre of intrigues and conspiracies of colossal magnitudes.

Alternatively, the narcissist feels victimised by mediocre bureaucrats and intellectual dwarves who consistently fail to appreciate his outstanding – really, unparalleled – talents, skills, and accomplishments. Being haunted by his challenged inferiors substantiates the narcissist's comparative superiority. Driven by pathological envy, these pygmies collude to defraud him, badger him, deny him his due, denigrate, isolate, and ignore him.

The narcissist projects onto this second class of lesser persecutors his own deleterious emotions and transformed aggression: hatred, rage, and seething jealousy.

The narcissist's paranoid streak is likeliest to erupt when he lacks Narcissistic Supply. The regulation of his labile sense of self-worth is dependent upon external stimuli – adoration, adulation, affirmation, applause, notoriety, fame, infamy, and, in general, attention of any kind.

When such attention is deficient, the narcissist compensates by confabulating. He constructs ungrounded narratives in which he is the protagonist and uses them to force his human environment into complicity.

Put simply, he provokes people to pay attention to him by misbehaving or behaving oddly.

Intimacy Retarding Paranoia

Paranoia is use by the narcissist to ward off or reverse intimacy. The narcissist is threatened by intimacy because it reduces him to ordinariness by exposing his weaknesses and shortcomings and by causing him to act "normally". The narcissist also dreads the encounter with his deep buried emotions – hurt, envy, anger, aggression – likely to be foisted on him in an intimate relationship.

The paranoid narrative legitimises intimacy repelling behaviours such as keeping one's distance, secrecy, aloofness, reclusion, aggression, intrusion on privacy, lying, desultoriness, itinerancy, unpredictability, and idiosyncratic or eccentric reactions. Gradually, the narcissist succeeds to alienate and wear down all his friends, colleagues, well-wishers, and mates.

Even his closest, nearest, and dearest, his family – feel emotionally detached and "burnt out".

The paranoid narcissist ends life as an oddball recluse – derided, feared, and loathed in equal measures. His paranoia – exacerbated by repeated rejections and ageing – pervades his entire life and diminishes his creativity, adaptability, and functioning. The narcissist personality, buffeted by paranoia, turns ossified and brittle. Finally, atomised and useless, it succumbs and gives way to a great void. The narcissist is consumed.

[See: "The Delusional Way Out"]

Return

Losing for Granted

The narcissist is goal-orientated. Like a sophisticated cruise missile it homes in on Sources of Narcissistic Supply, "conquers" them, conditions and moulds them and proceeds to extract from them attention, adulation, admiration and affirmation. This process demands the persistent investment of inordinate amounts of energy and time. The narcissist appears to be hell-bent, obsessed, smitten and addicted to the pursuit of his Sources of Supply.

Yet, a curious transformation occurs once he has secured and "chained" them.

The narcissist – often abruptly – loses all interest. It is as though, having acquired them, the narcissist takes his sources for granted. He treats them as he would inanimate objects, devoid of will and unable to free themselves from his mesmerising mental grip.

Many Sources of Supply, weighed down by the attiring relationship with the narcissist, break loose and escape his venomous influence. The delusion that he is in total control crumbles as the narcissist is abandoned time and again by spouses, mates, friends and colleagues.

It is then – when loss is tangible – that the narcissist regains his former zeal and erstwhile fervour. He courts a long neglected wife, invests himself in a hated job, befriends spurned colleagues, engulfs with unnatural warmth and empathy offended friends.

It is very common, for instance, for a narcissist to rediscover the joy of sex with an adulterous partner. It is as though being cheated by his wife (or husband) rekindles in the narcissist a competitive urge, a possessive streak, and a perverted carnal pleasure.

The narcissist professes to being shocked by the untoward behaviour of a hitherto faithful spouse, loyal friend, or patient neighbour. "Whatever happened to them?" – he wonders – "What brought this on?" Why did his wife cheat on him? Why did his colleagues demand his resignation? Why did his neighbour turn violent all of a sudden? The narcissist is genuinely puzzled, very much as you would if your personal computer refused to obey your instructions for no good reason.

Aware of impending loss and doom, the narcissist embarks on a charm offensive, parading the most irresistible, brilliant, captivating, titillating, promising and thrilling aspects of his False Self. The aim is to reacquire that which has been forfeited to neglect and indifference, to rebuild relationships ruined by contempt and abuse – and, thus, to regain the mislaid fount of Narcissistic Supply.

Needless to add that once these targets are achieved, the narcissist reverts to old form and goes back to being impatient, negligent, emotionally absent, indifferent and abusive. Until another round of losses looms and reanimates the narcissist – a sad, repetitive automaton, forever imprisoned by his own non-existence.

Return

Facilitating Narcissism

"The new narcissist is haunted not by guilt but by anxiety. He seeks not to inflict his own certainties on others but to find a meaning in life. Liberated from the superstitions of the past, he doubts even the reality of his own existence. Superficially relaxed and tolerant, he finds little use for dogmas of racial and ethnic purity but at the same time forfeits the security of group loyalties and regards everyone as a rival for the favours conferred by a paternalistic state. His sexual attitudes are permissive rather than puritanical, even though his emancipation from ancient taboos brings him no sexual peace. Fiercely competitive in his demand for approval and acclaim, he distrusts competition because he associates it unconsciously with an unbridled urge to destroy. Hence he repudiates the competitive ideologies that flourished at an earlier stage of capitalist development and distrusts even their limited expression in sports and games. He extols cooperation and teamwork while harbouring deeply antisocial impulses. He praises respect for rules and regulations in the secret belief that they do not apply to himself. Acquisitive in the sense that his cravings have no limits, he does not accumulate goods and provisions against the future, in the manner of the acquisitive individualist of nineteenth-century political economy, but demands immediate gratification and lives in a state of restless, perpetually unsatisfied desire."
[Christopher Lasch – The Culture of Narcissism: American Life in an Age of Diminishing Expectations, 1979]

"A characteristic of our times is the predominance, even in groups traditionally selective, of the mass and the vulgar. Thus, in intellectual life, which of its essence requires and presupposes qualification, one can note the progressive triumph of the pseudo-intellectual, unqualified, unqualifiable..."
[Jose Ortega y Gasset – The Revolt of the Masses, 1932]

We are surrounded by malignant narcissists. How come this disorder has hitherto been largely ignored? How come there is such a dearth of research and literature regarding this crucial family of pathologies? Even mental health practitioners are woefully unaware of it and unprepared to assist its victims.

The sad answer is that narcissism meshes well with our culture [see: Lasch – The Cultural Narcissist].

It is kind of a "background cosmic radiation", permeating every social and cultural interaction. It is hard to distinguish pathological narcissists from self-assertive, self-confident, self-promoting, eccentric, or highly individualistic persons. Hard sell, greed, envy, self-centredness, exploitativeness, diminished empathy – are all socially condoned features of Western civilisation.

Our society is atomised, the outcome of individualism gone awry. It encourages narcissistic leadership and role models.

Its sub-structures – institutionalised religion, political parties, civic organisations, the media, corporations – are all suffused with narcissism and pervaded by its pernicious outcomes. [See: Collective Narcissism]

The very ethos of materialism and capitalism upholds certain narcissistic traits, such as reduced empathy, exploitation, a sense of entitlement, or grandiose fantasies ("vision"). [More about this in It is My World]

Narcissists are aided, abetted and facilitated by four types of people and institutions: the adulators, the blissfully ignorant, the self-deceiving and those deceived by the narcissist.

The adulators are fully aware of the nefarious and damaging aspects of the narcissist's behaviour but believe that they are more than balanced by the benefits – to themselves, to their collective, or to society at large. They engage in an explicit trade-off between some of their principles and values – and their personal profit, or the greater good.

They seek to help the narcissist, promote his agenda, shield him from harm, connect him with like-minded people, do his chores for him and, in general, create the conditions and the environment for his success. This kind of alliance is especially prevalent in political parties, the government, multinational, religious organisations and other hierarchical collectives.

The blissfully ignorant are simply unaware of the "bad sides" of the narcissist – and make sure they remain so. They look the other way, or pretend that the narcissist's behaviour is normative, or turn a blind eye to his egregious misbehaviour. They are classic deniers of reality. Some of them maintain a generally rosy outlook premised on the inbred benevolence of Mankind. Others simply cannot tolerate dissonance and discord. They prefer to live in a fantastic world where everything is harmonious and smooth and evil is banished. They react with rage to any information to the contrary and block it out instantly. This type of denial is well evidenced in dysfunctional families.

The self-deceivers are fully aware of the narcissist's transgressions and malice, his indifference, exploitativeness, lack of empathy, and rampant grandiosity – but they prefer to displace the causes, or the effects of such misconduct. They attribute it to externalities ("a rough patch"), or judge it to be temporary. They even go as far as accusing the victim for the narcissist's lapses, or for defending themselves ("she provoked him").

In a feat of cognitive dissonance, they deny any connection between the acts of the narcissist and their consequences ("His wife abandoned him because she was promiscuous, not because of anything he did to her"). They are swayed by the narcissist's undeniable charm, intelligence, or attractiveness. But the narcissist needs not invest resources in converting them to his cause – he does not deceive them. They are self-propelled into the abyss that is narcissism. The Inverted Narcissist, for instance, is a self-deceiver.

The deceived are people – or institutions, or collectives – deliberately taken for a premeditated ride by the narcissist. He feeds them false information, manipulates their judgement, proffers plausible scenarios to account for his indiscretions, soils the opposition, charms them, appeals to their reason, or to their emotions, and promises the Moon.

Again, the narcissist's incontrovertible powers of persuasion and his impressive personality play a part in this predatory ritual. The deceived are especially hard to deprogram. They are often themselves encumbered with narcissistic traits and find it impossible to admit a mistake, or to atone.

They are likely to stay on with the narcissist to his – and their – bitter end.

Regrettably, the narcissist rarely pays the price for his offences. His victims pick up the tab. But even here the malignant optimism of the abused never ceases to amaze.

Return

Telling Them Apart

Narcissists are an elusive breed, hard to spot, harder to pinpoint, impossible to capture. Even an experienced mental health diagnostician with unmitigated access to the record and to the person examined would find it fiendishly difficult to determine with any degree of certainty whether someone suffers from an impairment, i.e., a mental health disorder – or merely possesses narcissistic traits, a narcissistic personality structure ("character"), or a narcissistic "overlay" superimposed on another mental health problem.

Moreover, it is important to distinguish between the traits and behaviour patterns that are independent of the patient's cultural-social context (i.e., inherent, or idiosyncratic) – and reactive patterns, or conformity to cultural and social mores and edicts. Reactions to severe life crises are often characterised by transient pathological narcissism, for instance (Ronningstam and Gunderson, 1996). But such reactions do not a narcissist make.

When a person lives in a society and culture that has often been described as narcissistic by the leading lights of scholarly research (e.g., Theodore Millon) and social thinking (e.g., Christopher Lasch) – how much of his behaviour can be attributed to his milieu – and which of his traits are really his?

Moreover, there is a qualitative difference between having narcissistic traits, a narcissistic personality, or the Narcissistic Personality Disorder. The latter is rigorously defined in the DSM-IV-TR and includes strict criteria and differential diagnoses [for more, see The Primer on Narcissism].

Narcissism is regarded by many scholars to be an adaptative strategy ("healthy narcissism"). It is considered pathological in the clinical sense only when it becomes a rigid personality structure replete with a series of primitive defence mechanisms (such as splitting, projection, Projective Identification, intellectualisation) – and when it leads to dysfunctions in one or more areas of life.

Pathological narcissism is the art of deception. The narcissist projects a False Self and manages all his social interactions through this concocted fictional construct. People often find themselves involved with a narcissist (emotionally, in business, or otherwise) before they have a chance to discover his true nature.

When the narcissist reveals his true colours, it is usually far too late. His victims are unable to separate from him. They are frustrated by this acquired helplessness and angry that they failed to see through the narcissist earlier on.

But the narcissist does emit subtle, almost subliminal, signals ("presenting symptoms") even in a first or casual encounter.

Based on "How to Recognise a Narcissist":

'*Haughty' body language* – *The narcissist adopts a physical posture which implies and exudes an air of superiority, seniority, hidden powers, mysteriousness, amused indifference, etc. Though the narcissist usually maintains sustained and piercing eye contact, he often refrains from physical proximity (he is 'territorial').*

The narcissist takes part in social interactions – even mere banter – condescendingly, from a position of supremacy and faux 'magnanimity and largesse'. But he rarely mingles socially and prefers to remain the 'observer', or the 'lone wolf'.

Entitlement markers – *The narcissist immediately asks for 'special treatment' of some kind. Not to wait his turn, to have a longer or a shorter therapeutic session, to talk directly to authority figures (and not to their assistants or secretaries), to be granted special payment terms, to enjoy custom tailored arrangements.*

The narcissist is the one who – vocally and demonstratively – demands the undivided attention of the head waiter in a restaurant, or monopolises the hostess, or latches on to celebrities in a party. The narcissist reacts with rage and indignantly when denied his wishes and if treated equally with others whom he deems inferior.

Idealisation or devaluation – *The narcissist instantly idealises or devalues his interlocutor. This depends on how the narcissist appraises the potential one has as a Narcissistic Supply Source. The narcissist flatters, adores, admires and applauds the 'target' in an embarrassingly exaggerated and profuse manner – or sulks, abuses, and humiliates her.*

Narcissists are polite only in the presence of a potential Supply Source. But they are unable to sustain even perfunctory civility and fast deteriorate to barbs and thinly-veiled hostility, to verbal or other violent displays of abuse, rage attacks, or cold detachment.

The 'membership' posture – The narcissist always tries to 'belong'. Yet, at the very same time, he maintains his stance as an outsider. The narcissist seeks to be admired for his ability to integrate and ingratiate himself without investing the efforts commensurate with such an undertaking.

For instance: if the narcissist talks to a psychologist, the narcissist first states emphatically that he never studied psychology. He then proceeds to make seemingly effortless use of obscure professional terms, thus demonstrating that he mastered the discipline all the same – which proves that he is exceptionally intelligent or introspective.

In general, the narcissist always prefers show-off to substance. One of the most effective methods of exposing a narcissist is by trying to delve deeper. The narcissist is shallow, a pond pretending to be an ocean. He likes to think of himself as a Renaissance Man, a Jack of all trades. A narcissist never admits to ignorance in any field – yet, typically, he is ignorant of them all. It is surprisingly easy to penetrate the gloss and the veneer of the narcissist's self-proclaimed omniscience.

Bragging and false autobiography – The narcissist brags incessantly. His speech is peppered with 'I', 'my', 'myself', and 'mine'. He describes himself as intelligent, or rich, or modest, or intuitive, or creative – but always excessively, implausibly, and extraordinarily so.

The narcissist's biography sounds unusually rich and complex. His achievements – incommensurate with his age, education, or renown. Yet, his actual condition is evidently and demonstrably incompatible with his claims. Very often, the narcissist lies or fantasies are easily discernible. He always name-drops and appropriates other people's experiences and accomplishments.

Emotion-free language – The narcissist likes to talk about himself and only about himself. He is not interested in others or what they have to say, unless it is a potential Source of Supply and in order to obtain said supply. He acts bored, disdainful, even angry, if he feels an intrusion on and abuse of his precious time.

In general, the narcissist is very impatient, easily bored, with strong attention deficits – unless and until he is the topic of discussion. One can dissect all aspects of the intimate life of a narcissist, providing the discourse is not 'emotionally tinted'. If asked to relate directly to his emotions, the narcissist intellectualises, rationalises, speaks about himself in the third person and in a detached 'scientific' tone or composes a narrative with a fictitious character in it, suspiciously autobiographical.

Seriousness and sense of intrusion and coercion – The narcissist is dead serious about himself. He may possess a fabulous sense of humour, scathing and cynical, but rarely is he self-deprecating. The narcissist regards himself as being on a constant mission, whose importance is cosmic and whose consequences are global. If a scientist – he is always in the throes of revolutionising science. If a journalist – he is in the middle of the greatest story ever.

This self-misperception is not amenable to light-headedness or self-effacement. The narcissist is easily hurt and insulted (narcissistic injury). Even the most innocuous remarks or acts are interpreted by him as belittling, intruding, or coercive. His time is more valuable than others' – therefore, it cannot be wasted on unimportant matters such as social intercourse.

Any suggested help, advice, or concerned inquiry are immediately cast by the narcissist as intentional humiliation, implying that the narcissist is in need of help and counsel and, thus, imperfect. Any attempt to set an agenda is, to the narcissist, an intimidating act of enslavement. In this sense, the narcissist is both schizoid and paranoid and often entertains ideas of reference.

These – the lack of empathy, the aloofness, the disdain, the sense of entitlement, the restricted application of humour, the unequal treatment and the paranoia – make the narcissist a social misfit. The narcissist is able to provoke in his milieu, in his casual acquaintances, even in his psychotherapist, the strongest, most avid and furious hatred and revulsion. To his shock, indignation and consternation, he invariably induces in others unbridled aggression.

He is perceived to be asocial at best and, often, antisocial. This, perhaps, is the strongest presenting symptom. One feels ill at ease in the presence of a narcissist for no apparent reason. No matter how charming, intelligent, thought provoking, outgoing, easy going and social the narcissist is – he fails to secure the sympathy of his fellow humans, a sympathy he is never ready, willing, or able to grant them in the first place."

Return

The Adrenaline Junkie

Narcissistic Supply is exciting. When it is available, the narcissist feels elated, omnipotent, omniscient, handsome, sexy, adventurous, invincible, and irresistible. When it is missing, the narcissist first enters a manic phase of trying to replenish his supply and, if he fails, the narcissist shrivels, withdraws and is reduced to a zombie-like state of numbness.

Some people – and all narcissists – are addicted to excitement, to the adrenaline rush, to the danger inevitably and invariably involved. They are the adrenaline junkies. All narcissists are adrenaline junkies – but not all adrenaline junkies are narcissists.

Narcissistic Supply is the narcissist's particular sort of thrill. Deficient Narcissistic Supply is tantamount to the absence of excitement and thrills in non-narcissistic adrenaline junkies.

Originally, in early childhood, Narcissistic Supply is meant to help the narcissist regulate his volatile sense of self-worth and self-esteem. But Narcissistic Supply, regardless of its psychodynamic functions, also simply feels good. The narcissist grows addicted to the gratifying effects of Narcissistic Supply. He reacts with anxiety when constant, reliable provision is absent or threatened.

Thus, Narcissistic Supply always comes with excitement, on the one hand and with anxiety on the other hand.

When unable to secure "normal" Narcissistic Supply – adulation, recognition, fame, celebrity, notoriety, infamy, affirmation, or mere attention – the narcissist resorts to "abnormal" Narcissistic Supply. He tries to obtain his drug – the thrills, the good feeling that comes with Narcissistic Supply – by behaving recklessly, by succumbing to substance abuse, or by living dangerously.

Such narcissists – faced with a chronic state of deficient Narcissistic Supply – become criminals, or race drivers, or gamblers, or soldiers, or investigative journalists. They defy authority. They avoid safety, routine and boredom – no safe sex, no financial prudence, no stable marriage or career. They become peripatetic, change jobs, or lovers, or vocations, or avocations, or residences, or friendships often.

But sometimes even these extreme and demonstrative steps are not enough. When confronted with a boring, routine existence – with a chronic and permanent inability to secure Narcissistic Supply and excitement – these people compensate by inventing thrills where there are none.

They become paranoid, full of delusional persecutory notions and ideas of reference. Or they develop phobias – fear of flying, of heights, of enclosed or open spaces, of cats or spiders. Fear is a good substitute to the excitement they so crave and that eludes them.

Anxiety leads to the frenetic search for Narcissistic Supply. Obtaining the supply causes a general – albeit transient – sense of wellbeing, relief and release as the anxiety is alleviated. This cycle is addictive.

But what generates the anxiety in the first place? Are people born adrenaline junkies or do they become ones?

No one knows for sure. It may be genetically determined. We may discover one day that adrenaline junkies, conditioned by defective genes, develop special neural and biochemical paths, an unusual sensitivity to adrenaline. Or, it may indeed be the sad outcome of abuse and trauma during the formative years. The brain is plastic and easily influenced by recurrent bouts of capricious and malicious treatment.

Also Read:

The Delusional Way Out

Grandiosity and Intimacy – The Roots of Paranoia

Deficient Narcissistic Supply – FAQ #28

Narcissists – Stable or Unstable? – FAQ #32

(I wish to thank my wife and publisher, Lidija Rangelovska, for many of the ideas in this article.)

Return

Narcissism and Evil

In his bestselling "People of the Lie", Scott Peck claims that narcissists are evil. Are they?

The concept of "evil" in this age of moral relativism is slippery and ambiguous. The "Oxford Companion to Philosophy" [Oxford University Press, 1995] defines it thus: *"The suffering which results from morally wrong human choices."*

To qualify as evil a person (Moral Agent) must meet these requirements:

a. That he can and does consciously choose between the (morally) right and wrong and constantly and consistently prefers the latter;
b. That he acts on his choice irrespective of the consequences to himself and to others.

Clearly, evil must be premeditated. Francis Hutcheson and Joseph Butler argued that evil is a by-product of the pursuit of one's interest or cause at the expense of other people's interests or causes. But this ignores the critical element of conscious choice among equally efficacious alternatives. Moreover, people often pursue evil even when it jeopardises their well-being and obstructs their interests. Sadomasochists even relish this orgy of mutual assured destruction.

Narcissists satisfy both conditions only partly. Their evil is utilitarian. They are evil only when being malevolent secures a certain outcome. Sometimes, they consciously choose the morally wrong – but not invariably so. They act on their choice even if it inflicts misery and pain on others. But they never opt for evil if they are to bear the consequences. They act maliciously because it is expedient to do so – not because it is "in their nature".

The narcissist is able to tell right from wrong and to distinguish between good and evil. In the pursuit of his interests and causes, he sometimes chooses to act wickedly. Lacking empathy, the narcissist is rarely remorseful. Because he feels entitled, exploiting others is second nature. The narcissist abuses others absent-mindedly, off-handedly, as a matter of fact.

The narcissist objectifies people and treats them as expendable commodities to be discarded after use. Admittedly, that, in itself, is evil. Yet, it is the mechanical, thoughtless, heartless face of narcissistic abuse – devoid of human passions and of familiar emotions – that renders it so alien, so frightful and so repellent.

We are often shocked less by the actions of narcissist than by the way he acts. In the absence of a vocabulary rich enough to capture the subtle hues and gradations of the spectrum of narcissistic depravity, we default to habitual adjectives such as "good" and "evil". Such intellectual laziness does this pernicious phenomenon and its victims little justice.

Read Ann's response here: http://www.narcissisticabuse.com/evil.html.

Return

Narcissism, Substance Abuse, And Reckless Behaviours

Pathological narcissism is an addiction to Narcissistic Supply, the narcissist's drug of choice. It is, therefore, not surprising that other addictive and reckless behaviours – workaholism, alcoholism, drug abuse, pathological gambling, compulsory shopping, or reckless driving – piggyback on this primary dependence.

The narcissist – like other types of addicts – derives pleasure from these exploits. But they also sustain and enhance his grandiose fantasies as "unique", "superior", "entitled", and "chosen". They place him above the laws and pressures of the mundane and away from the humiliating and sobering demands of reality. They render him the centre of attention – but also place him in "splendid isolation" from the madding and inferior crowd.

Such compulsory and wild pursuits provide a psychological exoskeleton. They are a substitute to quotidian existence. They afford the narcissist with an agenda, with timetables, goals, and faux achievements. The narcissist – the adrenaline junkie – feels that he is in control, alert, excited, and vital. He does not regard his condition as dependence. The narcissist firmly believes that he is in charge of his addiction, that he can quit at will and on short notice.

The narcissist denies his cravings for fear of "losing face" and subverting the flawless, perfect, immaculate, and omnipotent image he projects. When caught red handed, the narcissist underestimates, rationalises, or intellectualises his addictive and reckless behaviours – converting them into an integral part of his grandiose and fantastic False Self.

Thus, a drug abusing narcissist may claim to be conducting first hand research for the benefit of humanity – or that his substance abuse results in enhanced creativity and productivity. The dependence of some narcissists becomes a way of life: busy corporate executives, race car drivers, or professional gamblers come to mind.

The narcissist's addictive behaviours take his mind off his inherent limitations, inevitable failures, painful and much-feared rejections, and the Grandiosity Gap – the abyss between the image he projects (the False Self) and the injurious truth. They relieve his anxiety and resolve the tension between his unrealistic expectations and inflated self-image – and his incommensurate achievements, position, status, recognition, intelligence, wealth, and physique.

Thus, there is no point in treating the dependence and recklessness of the narcissist without first treating the underlying personality disorder. The narcissist's addictions serve deeply ingrained emotional needs. They intermesh seamlessly with the pathological structure of his disorganised personality, with his character faults, and primitive defence mechanisms.

Techniques such as "12 steps" may prove more efficacious in treating the narcissist's grandiosity, rigidity, sense of entitlement, exploitativeness, and lack of empathy. This is because – as opposed to traditional treatment modalities – the emphasis is on tackling the narcissist's psychological makeup, rather than on behaviour modification.

The narcissist's overwhelming need to feel omnipotent and superior can be co-opted in the therapeutic process. Overcoming an addictive behaviour can be – truthfully – presented by the therapist as a rare and impressive feat, worthy of the narcissist's unique mettle.

Narcissists fall for these transparent pitches surprisingly often. But this approach can backfire. Should the narcissist relapse – an almost certain occurrence – he will feel ashamed to admit his fallibility, need for emotional sustenance, and impotence. He is likely to avoid treatment altogether and convince himself that now, having succeeded once to get rid of his addiction, he is self-sufficient and omniscient.

Return

The Cyber Narcissist

To the narcissist, the Internet is an alluring and irresistible combination of playground and hunting grounds, the gathering place of numerous potential Sources of Narcissistic Supply, a world where false identities are the norm and mind games the bon ton. And it is beyond the reach of the law, the pale of social norms, the strictures of civilised conduct.

The somatic finds cyber-sex and cyber-relationships aplenty. The cerebral claims false accomplishments, fake skills, erudition and talents. Both, if minimally communicative, end up at the instantly gratifying epicentre of a cult of fans, followers, stalkers, erotomaniacs, denigrators, and plain nuts. The constant attention and attendant quasi-celebrity feed and sustain their grandiose fantasies and inflated self-image.

The Internet is an extension of the real-life Narcissistic Pathological Space but without its risks, injuries, and disappointments. In the virtual universe of the Web, the narcissist vanishes and reappears with ease, often adopting a myriad aliases and nicknames. He (or she) can thus fend off criticism, abuse, disagreement, and disapproval effectively and in real time – and, simultaneously, preserve the precarious balance of his infantile personality. Narcissists are, therefore, prone to Internet addiction.

The positive characteristics of the Net are largely lost on the narcissist. He is not keen on expanding his horizons, fostering true relationships, or getting in real contact with other people. The narcissist is forever the provincial because he filters everything through the narrow lens of his addiction. He measures others – and idealises or devalues them – according to one criterion only: how useful they might be as Sources of Narcissistic Supply.

The Internet is an egalitarian medium where people are judged by the consistency and quality of their contributions rather than by the content or bombast of their claims. But the narcissist is driven to distracting discomfiture by a lack of clear and commonly accepted hierarchy (with himself at the pinnacle). He fervently and aggressively tries to impose the "natural order" – either by monopolising the interaction or, if that fails, by becoming a major disruptive influence.

But the Internet may also be the closest many narcissists get to psychodynamic therapy. Because it is still largely text-based, the Web is populated by disembodied entities. By interacting with these intermittent, unpredictable, ultimately unknowable, ephemeral, and ethereal voices – the narcissist is compelled to project unto them his own experiences, fears, hopes, and prejudices.

Transference (and counter-transference) are quite common on the Net and the narcissist's defence mechanisms – notably projection and Projective Identification – are frequently aroused. The therapeutic process is set in motion by the – unbridled, uncensored, and brutally honest – reactions to the narcissist's repertory of antics, pretensions, delusions, and fantasies.

The narcissist – ever the intimidating bully – is not accustomed to such resistance. Initially, it may heighten and sharpen his paranoia and lead him to compensate by extending and deepening his grandiosity. Some narcissists withdraw altogether, reverting to the schizoid posture. Others become openly antisocial and seek to subvert, sabotage, and destroy the online sources of their frustration. A few retreat and confine themselves to the company of adoring sycophants and unquestioning groupies.

But a long exposure to the culture of the Net – irreverent, sceptical, and populist – usually exerts a beneficial effect even on the staunchest and most rigid narcissist. Far less convinced of his own superiority and infallibility, the online narcissist mellows and begins – hesitantly – to listen to others and to collaborate with them.

Return

Abusing the Gullible Narcissist

"Such a one (the narcissist - SV) is encased, is he not, in an armour - such an armour! The armour of the crusaders was nothing to it - an armour of arrogance, of pride, of complete self-esteem. This armour, it is in some ways a protection, the arrows, the everyday arrows of life glance off it. But there is this danger; Sometimes a man in armour might not even know he was being attacked. He will be slow to see, slow to hear - slower still to feel."
["Dead Man's Mirror" by Agatha Christie in "Hercule Poirot - The Complete Short Stories", Great Britain, HarperCollins Publishers, 1999]

The irony is that narcissists, who consider themselves worldly, discerning, knowledgeable, shrewd, erudite, and astute - are actually more gullible than the average person. This is because they are fake. Their Self is False, their life a confabulation, their reality test gone. They live in a fantasy land all their own in which they are the centre of the universe, admired, feared, held in awe, and respected for their omnipotence and omniscience.

Narcissists are prone to magical thinking. They hold themselves immune to the consequences of their actions (or inaction) and, therefore, beyond punishment and the laws of Man. Narcissists are easily persuaded to assume unreasonable risks and expect miracles to happen. They often find themselves on the receiving end of investment scams, for instance.

Narcissists feel entitled to money, power, and honours incommensurate with their accomplishments or toil. The world, or God, or the nation, or society, or their families, co-workers, employers, even neighbours owe them a trouble-free, exalted, and luxurious existence. They are rudely shocked when they are penalised for their misconduct or when their fantasies remain just that.

The narcissist believes that he is destined to greatness - or at least the easy life. He wakes up every morning fully ready for a fortuitous stroke of luck. That explains the narcissist's reckless behaviours and his lazed lack of self-discipline. It also explains why is so easily duped.

By playing on the narcissist's grandiosity and paranoia, it is possible to deceive and manipulate him effortlessly. Just offer him [Narcissistic Supply](#) – admiration, affirmation, adulation – and he is yours. Harp on his insecurities and his persecutory delusions – and he is likely to trust only you and cling to you for dear life.

Narcissists attract abuse. Haughty, exploitative, demanding, insensitive, and quarrelsome – they tend to draw opprobrium and provoke anger and even hatred. Sorely lacking in interpersonal skills, devoid of empathy, and steeped in irksome grandiose fantasies – they invariably fail to mitigate the irritation and revolt that they induce in others.

Successful narcissists are frequently targeted by stalkers and erotomaniacs – usually mentally ill people who develop a fixation of a sexual and emotional nature on the narcissist. When inevitably rebuffed, they become vindictive and even violent.

Less prominent narcissists end up sharing life with co-dependents and [inverted narcissists](#).

The narcissist's situation is exacerbated by the fact that, often, the narcissist himself is an abuser. Like the boy who cried "wolf", people do not believe that the perpetrator of egregious deeds can himself fall prey to maltreatment. They tend to ignore and discard the narcissist's cries for help and disbelieve his protestations.

The narcissist reacts to abuse as would any other victim. Traumatised, he goes through the phases of denial, helplessness, rage, depression, and acceptance. But, the narcissist's reactions are amplified by his shattered sense of omnipotence. Abuse breeds humiliation. To the narcissist, helplessness is a novel experience.

The narcissistic defence mechanisms and their behavioural manifestations – diffuse rage, idealisation and devaluation, exploitation – are useless when confronted with a determined, vindictive, or delusional stalker. That the narcissist is flattered by the attention he receives from the abuser, renders him more vulnerable to the former's manipulation.

Nor can the narcissist come to terms with his need for help or acknowledge that wrongful behaviour on his part may have contributed somehow to the situation. His self-image as an infallible, mighty, all-knowing person, far superior to others, won't let him admit to shortfalls or mistakes.

As the abuse progresses, the narcissist feels increasingly cornered. His conflicting emotional needs – to preserve the integrity of his grandiose False Self even as he seeks much needed support – place an unbearable strain on the precarious balance of his immature personality. Decompensation (the disintegration of the narcissist's defence mechanisms) leads to acting out and, if the abuse is protracted, to withdrawal and even to psychotic micro-episodes.

Abusive acts in themselves are rarely dangerous. Not so the reactions to abuse – above all, the overwhelming sense of violation and humiliation. When asked how is the narcissist likely to react to continued mistreatment, I wrote this in one of my [Pathological Narcissism FAQs](#):

"*The initial reaction of the narcissist to a perceived humiliation is a conscious rejection of the humiliating input. The narcissist tries to ignore it, talk it out of existence, or belittle its importance. If this crude mechanism of cognitive dissonance fails, the narcissist resorts to denial and repression of the humiliating material. He 'forgets' all about it, gets it out of his mind and, when reminded of it, denies it.*

But these are usually merely stopgap measures. The disturbing data is bound to impinge on the narcissist's tormented consciousness. Once aware of its re-emergence, the narcissist uses fantasy to counteract and counterbalance it. He imagines all the horrible things that he would have done (or will do) to the sources of his frustration.

It is through fantasy that the narcissist seeks to redeem his pride and dignity and to re-establish his damaged sense of uniqueness and grandiosity. Paradoxically, the narcissist does not mind being humiliated if this were to make him more unique or to draw more attention to his person.

For instance: if the injustice involved in the process of humiliation is unprecedented, or if the humiliating acts or words place the narcissist in a unique position, or if they transform him into a public figure – the narcissist tries to encourage such behaviours and to elicit them from others.

In this case, he fantasises how he defiantly demeans and debases his opponents by forcing them to behave even more barbarously than before, so that their unjust conduct is universally recognised as such and condemned and the narcissist is publicly vindicated and his self-respect restored. In short: martyrdom is as good a method of obtaining [Narcissist Supply](#) as any.

Fantasy, though, has its limits and once reached, the narcissist is likely to experience waves of self-hatred and self-loathing, the outcomes of helplessness and of realising the depths of his dependence on Narcissistic Supply. These feelings culminate in severe self-directed aggression: depression, destructive, self-defeating behaviours or suicidal ideation.

These self-negating reactions, inevitably and naturally, terrify the narcissist. He tries to project them on to his environment. He may decompensate by developing obsessive-compulsive traits or by going through a psychotic microepisode.

At this stage, the narcissist is suddenly besieged by disturbing, uncontrollable violent thoughts. He develops ritualistic reactions to them: a sequence of motions, an act, or obsessive counter-thoughts. Or he might visualise his aggression, or experience auditory hallucinations. Humiliation affects the narcissist this deeply.

Luckily, the process is entirely reversible once Narcissistic Supply is resumed. Almost immediately, the narcissist swings from one pole to another, from being humiliated to being elated, from being put down to being reinstated, from being at the bottom of his own, imagined, pit to occupying the top of his own, imagined, hill."

Return

The Two Loves of the Narcissist

Narcissists "love" their spouses or other significant others - as long as they continue to reliably provide them with Narcissistic Supply (in one word, with attention). Inevitably, they regard others as mere "sources", objects, or functions. Lacking empathy and emotional maturity, the narcissist's love is pathological. But the precise locus of the pathology depends on the narcissist's stability or instability in different parts of his life.

From "The Unstable Narcissist":

[I have omitted below large sections. For a more elaborate treatment, please read the FAQ itself.]

"Narcissists belong to two broad categories: the 'compensatory stability' and the 'enhancing instability' types.

I. Compensatory Stability ('Classic') Narcissists

These narcissists isolate one or more (but never most) aspects of their lives and 'make these aspect/s stable'. They do not really invest themselves in it. The stability is maintained by artificial means: money, celebrity, power, fear. A typical example is a narcissist who changes numerous workplaces, a few careers, a myriad of hobbies, value systems or faiths. At the same time, he maintains (preserves) a relationship with a single woman (and even remains faithful to her). She is his 'island of stability'. To fulfil this role, she just needs to be there physically.

The narcissist is dependent upon 'his' woman to maintain the stability lacking in all other areas of his life (to compensate for his instability). Yet, emotional closeness is bound to threaten the narcissist. Thus, he is likely to distance himself from her and to remain detached and indifferent to most of her needs. Despite this cruel emotional treatment, the narcissist considers her to be a point of exit, a form of sustenance, a fountain of empowerment. This mismatch between what he wishes to receive and what he is able to give, the narcissist prefers to deny, repress and bury deep in his unconscious. This is why he is always shocked and devastated to learn of his wife's estrangement, infidelity, or divorce intentions. Possessed of no emotional depth, being completely one track minded – he cannot fathom the needs of others. In other words, he cannot empathise.

II. Enhancing Instability ('Borderline') Narcissist

The other kind of narcissist enhances instability in one aspect or dimension of his life – by introducing instability in others. Thus, if such a narcissist resigns (or, more likely, is made redundant) – he also relocates to another city or country. If he divorces, he is also likely to resign his job. This added instability gives these narcissists the feeling that all the dimensions of their life are changing simultaneously, that they are being 'unshackled', that a transformation is in progress. This, of course, is an illusion. Those who know the narcissist, no longer trust his frequent 'conversions', 'decisions', 'crises', 'transformations', 'developments' and 'periods'. They see through his pretensions and declarations into the core of his instability. They know that he is not to be relied upon. They know that with narcissists, temporariness is the only permanence."

We are, therefore, faced with two pathological forms of narcissistic "love".

One type of narcissist "loves" others as one would attach to objects. He "loves" his spouse, for instance, simply because she exists and is available to provide him with Narcissistic Supply. He "loves" his children because they are part of his self-image as a successful husband and father. He "loves" his "friends" because – and only as long as – he can exploit them.

Such a narcissist reacts with alarm and rage to any sign of independence and autonomy in his "charges". He tries to "freeze" everyone around him in their "allocated" positions and "assigned roles". His world is rigid and immovable, predictable and static, fully under his control. He punishes for "transgressions" against this ordained order. He thus stifles life as a dynamic process of compromising and growing – rendering it instead a mere theatre, a tableau vivant.

The other type of narcissist abhors monotony and constancy, equating them, in his mind, with death. He seeks upheaval, drama, and change – but only when they conform to his plans, designs, and views of the world and of himself. Thus, he does not encourage growth in his nearest and dearest. By monopolising their lives, he, like the other kind of narcissist, also reduces them to mere objects, props in the exciting drama of his life.

This narcissist likewise rages at any sign of rebellion and disagreement. But, as opposed to the first sub-species, he seeks to animate others with his demented energy, grandiose plans, and megalomaniacal self-perception. An adrenaline junkie, his world is a whirlwind of comings and goings, reunions and separations, loves and hates, vocations adopted and discarded, schemes erected and dismantled, enemies turned friends and vice versa. His Universe is equally a theatre, but a more ferocious and chaotic one.

Where is love in all this? Where is the commitment to the loved one's welfare, the discipline, the extension of oneself to incorporate the beloved, the mutual growth?

Nowhere to be seen. The narcissist's "love" is hate and fear disguised – fear of losing control and hatred of the very people his precariously balanced personality so depends on. The narcissist is egotistically committed only to his own well-being. To him, the objects of his "love" are interchangeable and inferior.

He idealises his nearest and dearest not because he is smitten by emotion – but because he needs to captivate them and to convince himself that they are worthy Sources of Supply, despite their flaws and mediocrity. Once he deems them useless, he discards and devalues them similarly cold-bloodedly. A predator, always on the lookout, he debases the coin of "love" as he corrupts everything else in himself and around him.

Return

The Professions of the Narcissist

The narcissist naturally gravitates towards those professions which guarantee the abundant and uninterrupted provision of Narcissistic Supply. He seeks to interact with people from a position of authority, advantage, or superiority. He thus elicits their automatic admiration, adulation, and affirmation – or, failing that, their fear and obedience.

Several vocations meet these requirements: teaching, the priesthood, show business, corporate management, the medical professions, politics, and sports. It is safe to predict that narcissists would be over-represented in these occupations.

The cerebral narcissist is likely to emphasise his intellectual prowess and accomplishments (real and imaginary) in an attempt to solicit supply from awe-struck students, devoted parishioners, admiring voters, obsequious subordinates, or dependent patients. His somatic counterpart derives his sense of self-worth from body building, athletic achievements, tests of resilience or endurance, and sexual conquests.

The narcissistic medical doctor or mental health professional and his patients, the narcissistic guide, teacher, or mentor and his students, the narcissistic leader, guru, pundit, or psychic and his followers or admirers, and the narcissistic business tycoon, boss, or employer and his underlings – all are instances of Pathological Narcissistic Spaces.

This is a worrisome state of affairs. Narcissists are liars. They misrepresent their credentials, knowledge, talents, skills, and achievements. A narcissist medical doctor would rather let patients die than expose his ignorance. A narcissistic therapist often traumatises his clients with his acting out, rage, exploitativeness, and lack of empathy. Narcissistic businessmen bring ruin on their firms and employees.

Moreover, even when all is "well", the narcissist's relationship with his sycophants is abusive. He perceives others as objects, mere instruments of gratification, dispensable and interchangeable. An addict, the narcissist tends to pursue an ever-larger dose of adoration, and an ever-bigger fix of attention, while gradually losing what's left of his moral constraints.

When his sources become weary, rebellious, tired, bored, disgusted, repelled, or plainly amused by the narcissist's incessant dependence, his childish craving for attention, his exaggerated or even paranoid fears which lead to obsessive-compulsive behaviours, and his "drama queen" temper tantrums – he resorts to emotional extortion, straight blackmail, abuse, or misuse of his authority, and criminal or antisocial conduct. If these fail, the narcissist devalues and discards the very people he so idealised and cherished only a short while before.

As opposed to their "normal" colleagues or peers, narcissists in authority lack empathy and ethical standards. Thus, they are prone to immorally, cynically, callously and consistently abuse their position. Their socialisation process – usually the product of problematic early relationships with Primary Objects (parents, or caregivers) – is often perturbed and results in social dysfunctioning.

Nor is the narcissist deterred by possible punishment or regards himself subject to Man-made laws. His sense of entitlement coupled with the conviction of his own superiority lead him to believe in his invincibility, invulnerability, immunity, and divinity. The narcissist holds human edicts, rules, and regulations in disdain and human penalties in disdain. He regards human needs and emotions as weaknesses to be predatorily exploited.

Return

Misdiagnosing Narcissism

The Bipolar I Disorder

The use of gender pronouns in this article reflects the clinical facts: most narcissists are men.

The manic phase of Bipolar I Disorder is often misdiagnosed as Narcissistic Personality Disorder (NPD).
    Bipolar patients in the manic phase exhibit many of the signs and symptoms of pathological narcissism – hyperactivity, self-centredness, lack of empathy, and control freakery. During this recurring chapter of the disease, the patient is euphoric, has grandiose fantasies, spins unrealistic schemes, and has frequent rage attacks (is irritable) if her or his wishes and plans are (inevitably) frustrated.
    The manic phases of the bipolar disorder, however, are limited in time – NPD is not. Furthermore, the mania is followed by – usually protracted – depressive episodes. The narcissist is also frequently dysphoric. But whereas the bipolar sinks into deep self-deprecation, self-devaluation, unbounded pessimism, all-pervasive guilt and anhedonia – the narcissist, even when depressed, never forgoes his narcissism: his grandiosity, sense of entitlement, haughtiness, and lack of empathy.
    Narcissistic dysphorias are much shorter and reactive – they constitute a response to the Grandiosity Gap. In plain words, the narcissist is dejected when confronted with the abyss between his inflated self-image and grandiose fantasies – and the drab reality of his life: his failures, lack of accomplishments, disintegrating interpersonal relationships, and low status. Yet, one dose of Narcissistic Supply is enough to elevate the narcissists from the depth of misery to the heights of manic euphoria.
    Not so with the bipolar. The source of her or his mood swings is assumed to be brain biochemistry – not the availability of Narcissistic Supply. Whereas the narcissist is in full control of his

faculties, even when maximally agitated, the bipolar often feels that s/he has lost control of his/her brain ("flight of ideas"), his/her speech, his/her attention span (distractibility), and his/her motor functions.

The bipolar is prone to reckless behaviours and substance abuse only during the manic phase. The narcissist does drugs, drinks, gambles, shops on credit, indulges in unsafe sex or in other compulsive behaviours both when elated and when deflated.

As a rule, the bipolar's manic phase interferes with his/her social and occupational functioning. Many narcissists, in contrast, reach the highest rungs of their community, church, firm, or voluntary organisation. Most of the time, they function flawlessly – though the inevitable blowups and the grating extortion of Narcissistic Supply usually put an end to the narcissist's career and social liaisons.

The manic phase of bipolar sometimes requires hospitalisation and – more frequently than admitted – involves psychotic features. Narcissists are never hospitalised as the risk for self-harm is minute. Moreover, psychotic microepisodes in narcissism are decompensatory in nature and appear only under unendurable stress (e.g., in intensive therapy).

The bipolar's mania provokes discomfort in both strangers and in the patient's nearest and dearest. His/her constant cheer and compulsive insistence on interpersonal, sexual, and occupational, or professional interactions engenders unease and repulsion. Her/his lability of mood – rapid shifts between uncontrollable rage and unnatural good spirits – is downright intimidating. The narcissist's gregariousness, by comparison, is calculated, "cold", controlled, and goal-orientated (the extraction of Narcissistic Supply). His cycles of mood and affect are far less pronounced and less rapid.

The bipolar's swollen self-esteem, overstated self-confidence, obvious grandiosity, and delusional fantasies are akin to the narcissist's and are the source of the diagnostic confusion. Both types of patients purport to give advice, carry out an assignment, accomplish a mission, or embark on an enterprise for which they are uniquely unqualified and lack the talents, skills, knowledge, or experience required.

But the bipolar's bombast is far more delusional than the narcissist's. Ideas of reference and magical thinking are common and, in this sense, the bipolar is closer to the schizotypal than to the narcissistic.

There are other differentiating symptoms:

Sleep disorders – notably acute insomnia – are common in the manic phase of bipolar and uncommon in narcissism. So is "manic speech" – pressured, uninterruptible, loud, rapid, dramatic (includes singing and humorous asides), sometimes incomprehensible, incoherent, chaotic, and lasts for hours. It reflects the bipolar's inner turmoil and his/her inability to control his/her racing and kaleidoscopic thoughts.

As opposed to narcissists, bipolar in the manic phase are often distracted by the slightest stimuli, are unable to focus on relevant data, or to maintain the thread of conversation. They are "all over the place" – simultaneously initiating numerous business ventures, joining a myriad organisation, writing umpteen letters, contacting hundreds of friends and perfect strangers, acting in a domineering, demanding, and intrusive manner, totally disregarding the needs and emotions of the unfortunate recipients of their unwanted attentions. They rarely follow up on their projects.

The transformation is so marked that the bipolar is often described by his/her closest as "not himself/herself". Indeed, some bipolars relocate, change name and appearance, and lose contact with their "former life". Antisocial or even criminal behaviour is not uncommon and aggression is marked, directed at both others (assault) and oneself (suicide). Some biploars describe an acuteness of the senses, akin to experiences recounted by drug users: smells, sounds, and sights are accentuated and attain an unearthly quality.

As opposed to narcissists, bipolars regret their misdeeds following the manic phase and try to atone for their actions. They realise and accept that "something is wrong with them" and seek help. During the depressive phase they are ego-dystonic and their defences are autoplastic (they blame themselves for their defeats, failures, and mishaps).

Finally, pathological narcissism is already discernible in early adolescence. The full-fledged bipolar disorder – including a manic phase – rarely occurs before the age of 20. The narcissist is consistent in his pathology – not so the bipolar. The onset of the manic episode is fast and furious and results in a conspicuous metamorphosis of the patient.

More about this topic here:

Stormberg, D., Roningstam, E., Gunderson, J., & Tohen, M. [1998] Pathological Narcissism in Bipolar Disorder Patients. Journal of Personality Disorders, 12, 179-185

Roningstam, E. [1996], Pathological Narcissism and Narcissistic Personality Disorder in Axis I Disorders. Harvard Review of Psychiatry, 3, 326-340

Also Read:

Narcissism with Other Mental Health Disorders - FAQ #82
Narcissists, Inverted Narcissists and Schizoids - FAQ #67
The Inverted Narcissist - FAQ #66
Narcissism, Substance Abuse, and Reckless Behaviours

Return

Misdiagnosing Narcissism

Asperger's Disorder

The use of gender pronouns in this article reflects the clinical facts: most narcissists and most Asperger's patients are male.

Asperger's Disorder is often misdiagnosed as Narcissistic Personality Disorder (NPD), though evident as early as age 3 (while pathological narcissism cannot be safely diagnosed prior to early adolescence).

In both cases, the patient is self-centred and engrossed in a narrow range of interests and activities. Social and occupational interactions are severely hampered and conversational skills (the give and take of verbal intercourse) are primitive. The Asperger's patient body language – eye to eye gaze, body posture, facial expressions – is constricted and artificial, akin to the narcissist's. Nonverbal cues are virtually absent and their interpretation in others lacking.

Yet, the gulf between Asperger's and pathological narcissism is vast.

The narcissist switches between social agility and social impairment voluntarily. His social dysfunctioning is the outcome of conscious haughtiness and the reluctance to invest scarce mental energy in cultivating relationships with inferior and unworthy others. When confronted with potential Sources of Narcissistic Supply, however, the narcissist easily regains his social skills, his charm, and his gregariousness.

Many narcissists reach the highest rungs of their community, church, firm, or voluntary organisation. Most of the time, they function flawlessly – though the inevitable blowups and the grating extortion of Narcissistic Supply usually put an end to the narcissist's career and social liaisons.

The Asperger's patient often wants to be accepted socially, to have friends, to marry, to be sexually active, and to sire offspring.

He just doesn't have a clue how to go about it. His affect is limited. His initiative – for instance, to share his experiences with nearest and dearest or to engage in foreplay – is thwarted. His ability to divulge his emotions stilted. He is incapable or reciprocating and is largely unaware of the wishes, needs, and feelings of his interlocutors or counterparties.

Inevitably, Asperger's patients are perceived by others to be cold, eccentric, insensitive, indifferent, repulsive, exploitative or emotionally-absent. To avoid the pain of rejection, they confine themselves to solitary activities – but, unlike the schizoid, not by choice. They limit their world to a single topic, hobby, or person and dive in with the greatest, all-consuming intensity, excluding all other matters and everyone else. It is a form of hurt-control and pain regulation.

Thus, while the narcissist avoids pain by excluding, devaluing, and discarding others – the Asperger's patient achieves the same result by withdrawing and by passionately incorporating in his universe only one or two people and one or two subjects of interest. Both narcissists and Asperger's patients are prone to react with depression to perceived slights and injuries – but Asperger's patients are far more at risk of self-harm and suicide.

The use of language is another differentiating factor.

The narcissist is a skilled communicator. He uses language as an instrument to obtain Narcissistic Supply or as a weapon to obliterate his "enemies" and discarded sources with. Cerebral narcissists derive Narcissistic Supply from the consummate use they make of their innate verbosity.

Not so the Asperger's patient. He is equally verbose at times (and taciturn on other occasions) but his topics are few and, thus, tediously repetitive. He is unlikely to obey conversational rules and etiquette (for instance, to let others speak in turn). Nor is the Asperger's patient able to decipher nonverbal cues and gestures or to monitor his own misbehaviour on such occasions. Narcissists are similarly inconsiderate – but only towards those who cannot possibly serve as Sources of Narcissistic Supply.

More about Autism Spectrum Disorders here:

McDowell, Maxson J. [2002] The Image of the Mother's Eye: Autism and Early Narcissistic Injury, Behavioural and Brain Sciences (Submitted)

Benis, Anthony – "Toward Self & Sanity: On the Genetic Origins of the Human Character" – Narcissistic-Perfectionist Personality Type (NP) with special reference to infantile autism

Stringer, Kathi [2003] An Object Relations Approach to Understanding Unusual Behaviours and Disturbances

James Robert Brasic, MD, MPH [2003] Pervasive Developmental Disorder: Asperger Syndrome

Also Read:

Narcissism with Other Mental Health Disorders - FAQ #82
Narcissists, Inverted Narcissists and Schizoids - FAQ #67
The Inverted Narcissist - FAQ #66
Narcissism, Substance Abuse, and Reckless Behaviours

Return

Misdiagnosing Narcissism

Generalised Anxiety Disorder (GAD)

The use of gender pronouns in this article reflects the clinical facts: most narcissists are men.

Anxiety Disorders – and especially Generalised Anxiety Disorder (GAD) – are often misdiagnosed as Narcissistic Personality Disorder (NPD).

Anxiety is uncontrollable and excessive apprehension. Anxiety disorders usually come replete with obsessive thoughts, compulsive and ritualistic acts, restlessness, fatigue, irritability, difficulty concentrating, and somatic manifestations (such as an increased heart rate, sweating, or, in Panic Attacks, chest pains).

By definition, narcissists are anxious for social approval or attention (Narcissistic Supply). The narcissist cannot control this need and the attendant anxiety because he requires external feedback to regulate his labile sense of self-worth. This dependence makes most narcissists irritable. They fly into rages and have a very low threshold of frustration.

Like patients who suffer from Panic Attacks and Social Phobia (another anxiety disorder), narcissists are terrified of being embarrassed or criticised in public. Consequently, most narcissists fail to function well in various settings (social, occupational, romantic, etc.).

Many narcissists develop obsessions and compulsions. Like sufferers of GAD, narcissists are perfectionists and preoccupied with the quality of their performance and the level of their competence. As the Diagnostic and Statistical Manual (DSM-IV-TR, p. 473) puts it, GAD patients (especially children):

"... (A)re typically overzealous in seeking approval and require excessive reassurance about their performance and their other worries."

This could apply equally well to narcissists. Both classes of patients are paralysed by the fear of being judged as imperfect or lacking. Narcissists as well as patients with anxiety disorders constantly fail to measure up to an inner, harsh, and sadistic critic and a grandiose, inflated self-image.

The narcissistic solution is to avoid comparison and competition altogether and to demand special treatment. The narcissist's sense of entitlement is incommensurate with the narcissist's true accomplishments. He withdraws from the rat race because he does not deem his opponents, colleagues, or peers worthy of his efforts.

As opposed to narcissists, patients with Anxiety Disorders are invested in their work and their profession. To be exact, they are over-invested. Their preoccupation with perfection is counter-productive and, ironically, renders them underachievers.

It is easy to mistake the presenting symptoms of certain anxiety disorders with pathological narcissism. Both types of patients are worried about social approbation and seek it actively. Both present a haughty or impervious facade to the world. Both are dysfunctional and weighed down by a history of personal failure on the job and in the family. But the narcissist is ego-dystonic: he is proud and happy of who he is. The anxious patient is distressed and is looking for help and a way out of his or her predicament. Hence the differential diagnosis.

Bibliography

Goldman, Howard G. – Review of General Psychiatry, 4th ed. – London, Prentice-Hall International, 1995 – pp. 279-282

Gelder, Michael et al., eds. – Oxford Textbook of Psychiatry, 3rd ed. – London, Oxford University Press, 2000 – pp. 160-169

Klein, Melanie – The Writings of Melanie Klein – Ed. Roger Money-Kyrle – 4 vols. – New York, Free Press – 1964-75

Kernberg O. – Borderline Conditions and Pathological Narcissism – New York, Jason Aronson, 1975

Millon, Theodore (and Roger D. Davis, contributor) – Disorders of Personality: DSM IV and Beyond – 2nd ed. – New York, John Wiley and Sons, 1995

Millon, Theodore – Personality Disorders in Modern Life – New York, John Wiley and Sons, 2000

Schwartz, Lester – Narcissistic Personality Disorders – A Clinical Discussion – Journal of Am. Psychoanalytic Association – 22 (1974): 292-305

Vaknin, Sam – Malignant Self Love – Narcissism Revisited, 6th revised impression – Skopje and Prague, Narcissus Publications, 2005

Return

Acquired Situational Narcissism

The Narcissistic Personality Disorder (NPD) is a systemic, all-pervasive condition, very much like pregnancy: either you have it or you don't. Once you have it, you have it day and night, it is an inseparable part of the personality, a recurrent set of behaviour patterns.

Recent research [1996] by Roningstam and others, however, shows that there is a condition which might be called "Transient or Temporary or Short Term Narcissism" as opposed to the full-fledged version. Even prior to their discovery, "Reactive Narcissistic Regression" was well known: people regress to a transient narcissistic phase in response to a major life crisis which threatens their mental composure.

But can narcissism be acquired or learned? Can it be provoked by certain, well-defined, situations?

Robert B. Millman, professor of psychiatry at New York Hospital – Cornell Medical School thinks it can. He proposes to reverse the accepted chronology. According to him, pathological narcissism can be induced in adulthood by celebrity, wealth, and fame.

The "victims" – billionaire tycoons, movie stars, renowned authors, politicians, and other authority figures – develop grandiose fantasies, lose their erstwhile ability to empathise, react with rage to slights, both real and imagined and, in general, act like textbook narcissists.

But is the occurrence of Acquired Situational Narcissism (ASN) inevitable and universal – or are only certain people prone to it?

It is likely that ASN is merely an amplification of earlier narcissistic conduct, traits, style, and tendencies. Celebrities with ASN already had a narcissistic personality and have acquired it long before it "erupted". Being famous, powerful, or rich only "legitimised" and conferred immunity from social sanction on the unbridled manifestation of a pre-existing disorder. Indeed, narcissists tend to gravitate to professions and settings which guarantee fame, celebrity, power, and wealth.

As Millman correctly notes, the celebrity's life is abnormal. The adulation is often justified and plentiful, the feedback biased and filtered, the criticism muted and belated, social control either lacking or excessive and vitriolic. Such vicissitudinal existence is not conducive to mental health even in the most balanced person.

The confluence of a person's narcissistic predisposition and his pathological life circumstances gives rise to ASN. Acquired Situational Narcissism borrows elements from both the classic Narcissistic Personality Disorder – ingrained and all-pervasive – and from Transient or Reactive Narcissism.

Celebrities are, therefore, unlikely to "heal" once their fame or wealth or might are gone. Instead, their basic narcissism merely changes form. It continues unabated, as insidious as ever – but modified by life's ups and downs.

In a way, all narcissistic disturbances are acquired. Patients acquire their pathological narcissism from abusive or overbearing parents, from peers, and from role models. Narcissism is a defence mechanism designed to fend off hurt and danger brought on by circumstances – such as celebrity – beyond the person's control.

Social expectations play a role as well. Celebrities try to conform to the stereotype of a creative but spoiled, self-centred, monomaniacal, and emotive individual. A tacit trade takes place. We offer the famous and the powerful all the Narcissistic Supply they crave – and they, in turn, act the consummate, fascinating albeit repulsive, narcissists.

Return

The Narcissist's Reality Substitutes

Pathological narcissism is a defence mechanism intended to isolate the narcissist from his environment and to shield him from hurt and injury, both real and imagined. Hence the False Self – an all-pervasive psychological construct which gradually displaces the narcissist's True Self. It is a work of fiction intended to elicit praise and deflect criticism.

The unintended consequence of this fictitious existence is a diminishing ability to grasp reality correctly and to cope with it effectively. Narcissistic Supply replaces genuine, veritable, and tested feedback. Analysis, disagreement, and uncomfortable facts are screened out. Layers of bias and prejudice distort the narcissist's experience.

Yet, deep inside, the narcissist is aware that his life is an artefact, a confabulated sham, a vulnerable cocoon. The world inexorably and repeatedly intrudes upon these ramshackle battlements, reminding the narcissist of the fantastic and feeble nature of his grandiosity. This is the much-dreaded Grandiosity Gap.

To avoid the agonising realisation of his failed, defeat-strewn, biography, the narcissist resorts to reality-substitutes. The dynamics are simple: as the narcissist grows older, his Sources of Supply become scarcer, and his Grandiosity Gap yawns wider. Mortified by the prospect of facing his actuality, the narcissist withdraws ever deeper into a dreamland of concocted accomplishments, feigned omnipotence and omniscience, and brattish entitlement.

The narcissist's reality substitutes fulfil two functions. They help him "rationally" ignore painful realities with impunity – and they proffer an alternative universe in which he reigns supreme and emerges triumphant.

The most common form of denial involves persecutory delusions. I described these in The Delusional Way Out.

The narcissist's paranoid narrative serves as an organising principle. It structures his here and now and gives meaning to his life. It aggrandises him as worthy of being persecuted. The mere battle with his demons is an achievement not to be sniggered at. By overcoming his "enemies", the narcissist emerges victorious and powerful.

The narcissist's self-inflicted paranoia – projections of threatening internal objects and processes – legitimises, justifies, and "explains" his abrupt, comprehensive, and rude withdrawal from an ominous and unappreciative world. The narcissist's pronounced misanthropy – fortified by these oppressive thoughts – renders him a schizoid, devoid of all social contact, except the most necessary.

But even as the narcissist divorces his environment, he remains aggressive, or even violent. The final phase of narcissism involves verbal, psychological, situational (and, mercifully, more rarely, physical) abuse directed at his "foes" and "inferiors". It is the culmination of a creeping mode of psychosis, the sad and unavoidable outcome of a choice made long ago to forego the real in favour of the surreal.

Return

The Narcissist's Confabulated Life

Confabulations are an important part of life. They serve to heal emotional wounds or to prevent ones from being inflicted in the first place. They prop-up the confabulator's self-esteem, regulate his (or her) sense of self-worth, and buttress his (or her) self-image. They serve as organising principles in social interactions.

Father's wartime heroism, mother's youthful good looks, one's oft-recounted exploits, erstwhile alleged brilliance, and past purported sexual irresistibility - are typical examples of white, fuzzy, heart-warming lies wrapped around a shrivelled kernel of truth.

But the distinction between reality and fantasy is rarely completely lost. Deep inside, the healthy confabulator knows where facts end and wishful thinking takes over. Father acknowledges he was no war hero, though he did his share of fighting. Mother understands she was no ravishing beauty, though she may have been attractive. The confabulator realises that his recounted exploits are overblown, his brilliance exaggerated, and his sexual irresistibility a myth.

Such distinctions never rise to the surface because everyone - the confabulator and his audience alike - have a common interest to maintain the confabulation. To challenge the integrity of the confabulator or the veracity of his confabulations is to threaten the very fabric of family and society. Human intercourse is built around such entertaining deviations from the truth.

This is where the narcissist differs from others (from "normal" people).

His very self is a piece of fiction concocted to fend off hurt and to nurture the narcissist's grandiosity. He fails in his "reality test" - the ability to distinguish the actual from the imagined. The narcissist fervently believes in his own infallibility, brilliance, omnipotence, heroism, and perfection. He doesn't dare confront the truth and admit it even to himself.

Moreover, he imposes his personal mythology on his nearest and dearest. Spouse, children, colleagues, friends, neighbours – sometimes even perfect strangers – must abide by the narcissist's narrative or face his wrath. The narcissist countenances no disagreement, alternative points of view, or criticism. To him, confabulation IS reality.

The coherence of the narcissist's dysfunctional and precariously-balanced personality depends on the plausibility of his stories and on their acceptance by his Sources of Narcissistic Supply. The narcissist invests an inordinate time in substantiating his tales, collecting "evidence", defending his version of events, and in re-interpreting reality to fit his scenario. As a result, most narcissists are self-delusional, obstinate, opinionated, and argumentative.

The narcissist's lies are not goal-orientated. This is what makes his constant dishonesty both disconcerting and incomprehensible. The narcissist lies at the drop of a hat, needlessly, and almost ceaselessly. He lies in order to avoid the Grandiosity Gap – when the abyss between fact and (narcissistic) fiction becomes too gaping to ignore.

The narcissist lies in order to preserve appearances, uphold fantasies, support the tall (and impossible) tales of his False Self and extract Narcissistic Supply from unsuspecting sources, who are not yet on to him. To the narcissist, confabulation is not merely a way of life – but life itself.

We are all conditioned to let other indulge in pet delusions and get away with white, not too egregious, lies. The narcissist makes use of our socialisation. We dare not confront or expose him, despite the outlandishness of his claims, the improbability of his stories, the implausibility of his alleged accomplishments and conquests. We simply turn the other cheek, or meekly avert our eyes, often embarrassed.

Moreover, the narcissist makes clear, from the very beginning, that it is his way or the highway. His aggression – even violent streak – are close to the surface. He may be charming in a first encounter – but even then there are telltale signs of pent-up abuse. His interlocutors sense this impending threat and avoid conflict by acquiescing with the narcissist's fairy tales. Thus he imposes his private universe and virtual reality on his milieu – sometimes with disastrous consequences.

Return

The Narcissist
From Abuse to Suicide

"Suicide – suicide! It is all wrong, I tell you. It is wrong psychologically. How did (the narcissist in the story) think of himself? As a Colossus, as an immensely important person, as the centre of the universe! Does such a man destroy himself? Surely not. He is far more likely to destroy someone else – some miserable crawling ant of a human being who had dared to cause him annoyance... Such an act may be regarded as necessary – as sanctified! But self-destruction? The destruction of such a Self? ... From the first I could not consider it likely that (the narcissist) had committed suicide. He had pronounced egomania, and such a man does not kill himself."

["Dead Man's Mirror" by Agatha Christie in "Hercule Poirot – The Complete Short Stories", Great Britain, HarperCollins Publishers, 1999]

There is one place in which one's privacy, intimacy, integrity and inviolability are guaranteed – one's body and mind, a unique temple and a familiar territory of sensa and personal history. The abuser invades, defiles and desecrates this shrine. He does so publicly, deliberately, repeatedly and, often, sadistically and sexually, with undisguised pleasure. Hence the all-pervasive, long-lasting, and, frequently, irreversible effects and outcomes of abuse.

In a way, the abuse victim's own body and mind are rendered his worse enemies. It is mental and corporeal agony that compels the sufferer to mutate, his identity to fragment, his ideals and principles to crumble. The body, one's very brain, become accomplices of the bully or tormentor, an uninterruptible channel of communication, a treasonous, poisoned territory. This fosters a humiliating dependency of the abused on the perpetrator. Bodily needs denied – touch, light, sleep, toilet, food, water, safety – and nagging reactions of guilt and humiliation are wrongly perceived by the victim as the direct causes of his degradation and dehumanisation. As he sees it, he is rendered bestial not by the sadistic bullies around him but by his own flesh and consciousness.

The concepts of "body" or "psyche" can easily be extended to "family", or "home". Abuse – especially in familial settings – is often applied to kin and kith, compatriots, or colleagues. This intends to disrupt the continuity of "surroundings, habits, appearance, relations with others", as the CIA put it in one of its torture training manuals. A sense of cohesive self-identity depends crucially on the familiar and the continuous. By attacking both one's biological-mental body and one's "social body", the victim's mind is strained to the point of dissociation.

Abuse robs the victim of the most basic modes of relating to reality and, thus, is the equivalent of cognitive death. Space and time are warped by sleep deprivation – the frequent outcome of anxiety and stress. The self ("I") is shattered. When the abuser is a family member, or a group of peers, or an adult role model (for instance, a teacher), the abused have nothing familiar to hold on to: family, home, personal belongings, loved ones, language, one's own name – all seem to evaporate in the turmoil of abuse. Gradually, the victim loses his mental resilience and sense of freedom. He feels alien and objectified – unable to communicate, relate, attach, or empathise with others.

Abuse splinters early childhood grandiose narcissistic fantasies of uniqueness, omnipotence, invulnerability, and impenetrability. But it enhances the fantasy of merger with an idealised and omnipotent (though not benign) other – the inflicter of agony. The twin processes of individuation and separation are reversed.

Abuse is the ultimate act of perverted intimacy. The abuser invades the victim's body, pervades his psyche, and possesses his mind. Deprived of contact with others and starved for human interactions, the prey bonds with the predator. "Traumatic bonding", akin to the Stockholm syndrome, is about hope and the search for meaning in the brutal and indifferent and nightmarish universe of the abusive relationship. The abuser becomes the black hole at the centre of the victim's surrealistic galaxy, sucking in the sufferer's universal need for solace. The victim tries to "control" his tormentor by becoming one with him (introjecting him) and by appealing to the monster's presumably dormant humanity and empathy.

This bonding is especially strong when the abuser and the abused form a dyad and "collaborate" in the rituals and acts of abuse (for instance, when the victim is coerced into selecting the abuse implements and the types of torment to be inflicted, or to choose between two evils).

Obsessed by endless ruminations, demented by pain and the reactions to maltreatment – sleeplessness, malnutrition, and substance abuse – the victim regresses, shedding all but the most primitive defence mechanisms: splitting, narcissism, dissociation, Projective Identification, introjection, and cognitive dissonance. The victim constructs an alternative world, often suffering from depersonalisation and derealisation, hallucinations, ideas of reference, delusions, and psychotic episodes. Sometimes the victim comes to crave pain – very much as self-mutilators do – because it is a proof and a reminder of his individuated existence otherwise blurred by the incessant abuse. Pain shields the sufferer from disintegration and capitulation. It preserves the veracity of his unthinkable and unspeakable experiences. It reminds him that he can still feel and, therefore, that he is still human.

These dual processes of the victim's alienation and addiction to anguish complement the perpetrator's view of his quarry as "inhuman", or "subhuman". The abuser assumes the position of the sole authority, the exclusive fount of meaning and interpretation, the source of both evil and good.

Abuse is about reprogramming the victim to succumb to an alternative exegesis of the world, proffered by the abuser. It is an act of deep, indelible, traumatic indoctrination. The abused also swallows whole and assimilates the abuser's negative view of him and often, as a result, is rendered suicidal, self-destructive, or self-defeating.

Thus, abuse has no cut-off date. The sounds, the voices, the smells, the sensations reverberate long after the episode has ended – both in nightmares and in waking moments. The victim's ability to trust other people – i.e., to assume that their motives are at least rational, if not necessarily benign – has been irrevocably undermined. Social institutions – even the family itself – are perceived as precariously poised on the verge of an ominous, Kafkaesque mutation. Nothing is either safe, or credible anymore.

Victims typically react by undulating between emotional numbing and increased arousal: insomnia, irritability, restlessness, and attention deficits. Recollections of the traumatic events intrude in the form of dreams, night terrors, flashbacks, and distressing associations.

The abused develop compulsive rituals to fend off obsessive thoughts. Other psychological sequelae reported include cognitive impairment, reduced capacity to learn, memory disorders, sexual dysfunction, social withdrawal, inability to maintain long-term relationships, or even mere intimacy, phobias, ideas of reference and superstitions, delusions, hallucinations, psychotic microepisodes, and emotional flatness. Depression and anxiety are very common. These are forms and manifestations of self-directed aggression. The sufferer rages at his own victimhood and resulting multiple dysfunctions.

He feels shamed by his new disabilities and responsible, or even guilty, somehow, for his predicament and the dire consequences borne by his nearest and dearest. His sense of self-worth and self-esteem are crippled. Suicide is perceived as both a relief and a solution.

In a nutshell, abuse victims suffer from a Post Traumatic Stress Disorder (PTSD). Their strong feelings of anxiety, guilt, and shame are also typical of victims of childhood abuse, domestic violence, and rape. They feel anxious because the perpetrator's behaviour is seemingly arbitrary and unpredictable – or mechanically and inhumanly regular.

They feel guilty and disgraced because, to restore a semblance of order to their shattered world and a modicum of dominion over their chaotic life, they need to transform themselves into the cause of their own degradation and the accomplices of their tormentors.

Inevitably, in the aftermath of abuse, its victims feel helpless and powerless. This loss of control over one's life and body is manifested physically in impotence, attention deficits, and insomnia. This is often exacerbated by the disbelief many abuse victims encounter, especially if they are unable to produce scars, or other "objective" proof of their ordeal. Language cannot communicate such an intensely private experience as pain.

Bystanders resent the abused because they make them feel guilty and ashamed for having done nothing to prevent the atrocity. The victims threaten their sense of security and their much-needed belief in predictability, justice, and rule of law. The victims, on their part, do not believe that it is possible to effectively communicate to "outsiders" what they have been through. The abuse seems to have occurred on "another galaxy". This is how Auschwitz was described by the author K. Zetnik in his testimony in the Eichmann trial in Jerusalem in 1961.

Often, continued attempts to repress fearful memories result in psychosomatic illnesses (conversion). The victim wishes to forget the abuse, to avoid re-experiencing the often life threatening torment and to shield his human environment from the horrors. In conjunction with the victim's pervasive distrust, this is frequently interpreted as hypervigilance, or even paranoia. It seems that the victims can't win. Abuse is forever.

When the victim realises that the abuse he suffered is now an integral part of his very being, a determinant of his self-identity, and that he is doomed to bear his pains and fears, shackled to his trauma, and tortured by it – suicide often appears to be a benign alternative.

Return

The Narcissist's Object Constancy

Narcissists often carry on talking (rather, lecturing) long after their interlocutors - bored stiff and resentful - have physically departed or mentally switched off. They are shocked to discover that they have been conversing with thin air for awhile. They are equally astounded when they are abandoned or shunned by spouses, friends, colleagues, the media, their fans, or audiences.

The root of this recurrent astonishment is the narcissist's perverse object constancy.

According to the great developmental psychologist, Margaret Mahler, between the ages of 24 and 36 months of life, the infant is finally able to cope with the mother's absence (by finding appropriate substitutes to her presence). It knows that she will return and trusts her to do so time and again.

The psychic image of the mother is internalised as a stable, reliable, and predictable object. As the infant's sense of time and verbal skills evolve, it becomes more immune to delayed gratification and tolerant of inevitable separation.

Piaget, the renowned child psychologist, concurred with Mahler and coined the term "object constancy" to describe the dynamics she observed.

As opposed to Mahler, Daniel Stern, another prominent psychoanalyst, proposes that the child is born with a sense of Self:

"Infants begin to experience a sense of an emergent self from birth. They are pre-designed to be aware of self - organising processes. They never experience a period of total self / other undifferentiation. There is no confusion of self and other in the beginning or at any point during infancy.

They are pre-designed to be selectively responsive to external social events and never experience an autistic like phase.

During the period of 2-6 months the infant consolidates the core sense of self as a separate, cohesive, bounded, physical unit with a sense of their own agency, affectivity and continuity in time. There is no symbiotic like phase. In fact the subjective experiences of union with another can occur only after a core self and a core other exists."

But even Stern accepts the existence of a distinct and separate "other" versus the nascent "self".

Pathological narcissism is a reaction to deficient bonding and dysfunctional attachment (Bowlby). Object relations in narcissists are infantile and chaotic (Winnicott, Guntrip). Many narcissists have no psychological-object constancy at all. In other words, many of them do not feel that other people are benign, reliable, helpful, constant, predictable, and trustworthy.

To compensate for this lack in ability (or willingness) to relate to real, live people, the narcissist invents and moulds substitute-objects or surrogate-objects.

These are mental representations of meaningful or significant others (Sources of Narcissistic Supply). They have little or nothing to do with reality. These imagoes – images – are confabulations, works of fiction. They respond to the narcissist's needs and fears – and do not correspond to the persons they purport to stand for.

The narcissist internalises these pliable representations, manipulates them, and interacts with them – not with the originals. The narcissist is entirely immersed in his world, talking to these "figurines", arguing with these substitutes, contracting with these surrogates, being admired by them.

Hence his dismay when confronted with real people, their needs, feelings, preferences, and choices.

Thus, the typical narcissist refrains from any meaningful discourse with his spouse and children, friends and colleagues. Instead, he spins a narrative in which these people – represented by mental avatars – admire him, find him fascinating, fervently wish to oblige him, love him, or fear him.

These "avatars" have little or nothing to do with the way his kin and kith REALLY feel about him. The protagonists in the narcissist's yarns do not incorporate veritable data about his wife, or offspring, or colleagues, or friends. They are mere projections of the narcissist's inner world. Thus, when the narcissist faces the real thing – he refuses to believe and accept the facts:

"My wife has always been so cooperative – whatever happened to her lately?"

(She was never cooperative – she was subservient or frightened into submission. But the narcissist didn't notice because he never actually "saw her".)

"My son always wanted to follow in my footsteps – I don't know what possesses him!"

(The narcissist's poor son never wanted to be a lawyer or a doctor. He always dreamed of being an actor or an artist. But the narcissist was not aware of it.)

"My friends used to listen to my stories enraptured – I have no idea why they no longer do so!"

(At first, his friends politely listened to the narcissist's interminable rants and ravings. Finally, they dropped from his social circle, one by one.)

"I was admired by the media – now I am constantly ignored!"

(At first, an object of derision and morbid fascination, the novelty wore off and the media moved on to other narcissists.)

Puzzled, hurt, and clueless – the narcissist withdraws further and further with every narcissistic injury. Finally, he is forced into choosing the delusional way out.

Return

Back to La-la Land

Relationships with narcissists peter out slowly and tortuously. Narcissists do not provide closure. They stalk. They cajole, beg, promise, persuade, and, ultimately, succeed in doing the impossible yet again: sweep you off your feet, though you know better than to succumb to their spurious and superficial charms.

So, you go back to your "relationship" and hope for a better ending. You walk on eggshells. You become the epitome of submissiveness, a perfect Source of Narcissistic Supply, the ideal mate or spouse or partner or colleague. You keep your fingers crossed.

But how does the narcissist react to the resurrection of the bond?

It depends on whether you have re-entered the liaison from a position or strength – or of vulnerability and weakness.

The narcissist casts all interactions with other people in terms of conflicts or competitions to be won. He does not regard you as a partner – but as an adversary to be subjugated and defeated. Thus, as far as he is concerned, your return to the fold is a triumph, proof of his superiority and irresistibility.

If he perceives you as autonomous, dangerously independent, and capable of bailing out and abandoning him – the narcissist acts the part of the sensitive, loving, compassionate, and empathic counterpart. Narcissists respect strength, they are awed by it. As long as you maintain a "no nonsense" attitude, placing the narcissist on probation, he is likely to behave himself.

If, on the other hand, you have resumed contact because you have capitulated to his threats or because you are manifestly dependent on him financially or emotionally – the narcissist will pounce on your frailty and exploit your fragility to the maximum. Following a perfunctory honeymoon, he will immediately seek to control and abuse you.

In both cases, the narcissist's thespian reserves are exhausted and his true nature and feelings emerge. The facade crumbles and beneath it lurks the same old heartless falsity that is the narcissist. His gleeful smugness at having bent you to his wishes and rules, his all-consuming sense of entitlement, his sexual depravity, his aggression, pathological envy, and rage – all erupt uncontrollably.

The prognosis for the renewed affair is far worse if it follows a lengthy separation in which you have made a life for yourself with your own interests, pursuits, set of friends, needs, wishes, plans, and obligations, independent of your narcissistic ex and unrelated to him.

The narcissist cannot countenance your separateness. To him, you are a mere instrument of gratification or an extension of his bloated False Self. He resents your pecuniary wherewithal, is insanely jealous of your friends, refuses to accept your preferences or compromise his own, in envious and dismissive of your accomplishments.

Ultimately, the very fact that you have survived without his constant presence seems to deny him his much-needed Narcissistic Supply. He rides the inevitable cycle of idealisation and devaluation. He berates you, humiliates you publicly, threatens you, destabilises you by behaving unpredictably, fosters [ambient abuse](), and uses others to intimidate and humble you ("[abuse by proxy]()").

You are then faced with a tough choice:

To leave again and give up all the emotional and financial investments that went into your attempt to resurrect the relationship – or to go on trying, subject to daily abuse and worse?

It is a well-known landscape. You have been here before. But this familiarity doesn't make it less nightmarish.

[Return]()

The Cult of the Narcissist

The narcissist is the guru at the centre of a cult. Like other gurus, he demands complete obedience from his flock: his spouse, his offspring, other family members, friends, and colleagues. He feels entitled to adulation and special treatment by his followers. He punishes the wayward and the straying lambs. He enforces discipline, adherence to his teachings, and common goals. The less accomplished he is in reality – the more stringent his mastery and the more pervasive the brainwashing.

The – often involuntary – members of the narcissist's mini-cult inhabit a twilight zone of his own construction. He imposes on them a shared psychosis, replete with persecutory delusions, "enemies", mythical narratives, and apocalyptic scenarios if he is flouted.

The narcissist's control is based on ambiguity, unpredictability, fuzziness, and [ambient abuse](). His ever-shifting whims exclusively define right versus wrong, desirable and unwanted, what is to be pursued and what to be avoided. He alone determines the rights and obligations of his disciples and alters them at will.

The narcissist is a micro-manager. He exerts control over the minutest details and behaviours. He punishes severely and abuses withholders of information and those who fail to conform to his wishes and goals.

The narcissist does not respect the boundaries and privacy of his reluctant adherents. He ignores their wishes and treats them as objects or instruments of gratification. He seeks to control both situations and people compulsively.

He strongly disapproves of others' personal autonomy and independence. Even innocuous activities, such as meeting a friend or visiting one's family require his permission. Gradually, he isolates his nearest and dearest until they are fully dependent on him emotionally, sexually, financially, and socially.

He acts in a patronising and condescending manner and criticises often. He alternates between emphasising the minutest faults (devalues) and exaggerating the talents, traits, and skills (idealises) of the members of his cult. He is wildly unrealistic in his expectations – which legitimises his subsequent abusive conduct.

The narcissist claims to be infallible, superior, talented, skilful, omnipotent, and omniscient. He often lies and confabulates to support these unfounded claims. Within his cult, he expects awe, admiration, adulation, and constant attention commensurate with his outlandish stories and assertions. He reinterprets reality to fit his fantasies.

His thinking is dogmatic, rigid, and doctrinaire. He does not countenance free thought, pluralism, or free speech and doesn't brook criticism and disagreement. He demands – and often gets – complete trust and the relegation to his capable hands of all decision-making.

He forces the participants in his cult to be hostile to critics, the authorities, institutions, his personal enemies, or the media – if they try to uncover his actions and reveal the truth. He closely monitors and censors information from the outside, exposing his captive audience only to selective data and analyses.

The narcissist's cult is "missionary" and "imperialistic". He is always on the lookout for new recruits – his spouse's friends, his daughter's girlfriends, his neighbours, new colleagues at work. He immediately attempts to "convert" them to his "creed" – to convince them how wonderful and admirable he is. In other words, he tries to render them Sources of Narcissistic Supply.

Often, his behaviour on these "recruiting missions" is different to his conduct within the "cult". In the first phases of wooing new admirers and proselytising to potential "conscripts" – the narcissist is attentive, compassionate, empathic, flexible, self-effacing, and helpful. At home, among the "veterans" he is tyrannical, demanding, wilful, opinionated, aggressive, and exploitative.

As the leader of his congregation, the narcissist feels entitled to special amenities and benefits not accorded the "rank and file". He expects to be waited on hand and foot, to make free use of everyone's money and dispose of their assets liberally, and to be cynically exempt from the rules that he himself established (if such violation is pleasurable or gainful).

In extreme cases, the narcissist feels above the law – any kind of law. This grandiose and haughty conviction leads to criminal acts, incestuous or polygamous relationships, and recurrent friction with the authorities.

Hence the narcissist's panicky and sometimes violent reactions to "dropouts" from his cult. There's a lot going on that the narcissist wants kept under wraps. Moreover, the narcissist stabilises his fluctuating sense of self-worth by deriving Narcissistic Supply from his victims. Abandonment threatens the narcissist's precariously balanced personality.

Add to that the narcissist's paranoid and schizoid tendencies, his lack of introspective self-awareness, and his stunted sense of humour (lack of self-deprecation) and the risks to the grudging members of his cult are clear.

The narcissist sees enemies and conspiracies everywhere. He often casts himself as the heroic victim (martyr) of dark and stupendous forces. In every deviation from his tenets he espies malevolent and ominous subversion. He, therefore, is bent on disempowering his devotees. By any and all means.

The narcissist is dangerous.

Return

The Pathological Charmer

The narcissist is confident that people find him irresistible. His unfailing charm is part of his self-imputed omnipotence. This inane conviction is what makes the narcissist a "pathological charmer". The somatic narcissist and the histrionic flaunt their sex appeal, virility or femininity, sexual prowess, musculature, physique, training, or athletic achievements.

The cerebral narcissist seeks to enchant and entrance his audience with intellectual pyrotechnics. Many narcissists brag about their wealth, health, possessions, collections, spouses, children, personal history, family tree - in short: anything that garners them attention and renders them alluring.

Both types of narcissists firmly believe that being unique, they are entitled to special treatment by others. They deploy their "charm offensives" to manipulate their nearest and dearest (or even complete strangers) and use them as instruments of gratification. Exerting personal magnetism and charisma become ways of asserting control and obviating other people's personal boundaries.

The pathological charmer feels superior to the person he captivates and fascinates. To him, charming someone means having power over her, controlling her, or even subjugating her. It is all a mind game intertwined with a power play. The person to be thus enthralled is an object, a mere prop, and of dehumanised utility.

In some cases, pathological charm involves more than a grain of sadism. It provokes in the narcissist sexual arousal by inflicting the "pain" of subjugation on the beguiled who "cannot help" but be enchanted. Conversely, the pathological charmer engages in infantile magical thinking. He uses charm to help maintain object constancy and fend off abandonment - in other words, to ensure that the person he "bewitched" won't disappear on him.

Pathological charmers react with rage and aggression when their intended targets prove to be impervious and resistant to their lure. This kind of narcissistic injury – being spurned and rebuffed – makes them feel threatened, rejected, and denuded. Being ignored amounts to a challenge to their uniqueness, entitlement, control, and superiority. Narcissists wither without constant Narcissistic Supply. When their charm fails to elicit it – they feel annulled, non-existent, and "dead".

Expectedly, they go to great lengths to secure said supply. It is only when their efforts are frustrated that the mask of civility and congeniality drops and reveals the true face of the narcissist – a predator on the prowl.

Return

The Misanthropic Altruist

Some narcissists are ostentatiously generous – they donate to charity, lavish gifts on their closest, abundantly provide for their nearest and dearest, and, in general, are open-handed and unstintingly benevolent. How can this be reconciled with the pronounced lack of empathy and with the pernicious self-preoccupation that is so typical of narcissists?

The act of giving enhances the narcissist's sense of omnipotence, his fantastic grandiosity, and the contempt he holds for others. It is easy to feel superior to the supplicating recipients of one's largesse. Narcissistic altruism is about exerting control and maintaining it by fostering dependence in the beneficiaries.

But narcissists give for other reasons as well.

The narcissist flaunts his charitable nature as a bait. He impresses others with his selflessness and kindness and thus lures them into his lair, entraps them, and manipulates and brainwashes them into subservient compliance and obsequious collaboration. People are attracted to the narcissist's larger than life posture – only to discover his true personality traits when it is far too late. "Give a little to take a lot" – is the narcissist's creed.

This does not prevent the narcissist from assuming the role of the exploited victim. Narcissists always complain that life and people are unfair to them and that they invest far more than their "share of the profit". The narcissist feels that he is the sacrificial lamb, the scapegoat, and that his relationships are asymmetric and imbalanced. "She gets out of our marriage far more than I do" – is a common refrain. Or: "I do all the work around here – and they get all the perks and benefits!"

Faced with such (mis)perceived injustice – and once the relationship is clinched and the victim is "hooked" – the narcissist tries to minimise his contributions. He regards his input as a contractual maintenance chore and the unpleasant and inevitable price he has to pay for his Narcissistic Supply.

After many years of feeling deprived and wronged, some narcissists lapse into "sadistic generosity" or "sadistic altruism". They use their giving as a weapon to taunt and torment the needy and to humiliate them. In the distorted thinking of the narcissist, donating money gives him the right and license to hurt, chastise, criticise, and berate the recipient. His generosity, feels the narcissist, elevates him to a higher moral ground.

Most narcissists confine their giving to money and material goods. Their munificence is an abusive defence mechanism, intended to avoid real intimacy. Their "big-hearted" charity renders all their relationships – even with their spouses and children – "business-like", structured, limited, minimal, non-emotional, unambiguous, and non-ambivalent. By doling out bounteously, the narcissist "knows where he stands" and does not feel threatened by demands for commitment, emotional investment, empathy, or intimacy.

In the narcissist's wasteland of a life, even his benevolence is spiteful, sadistic, punitive, and distancing.

Return

Grandiosity Bubbles

As one Source of Narcissistic Supply dwindles, the narcissist finds himself trapped in a frantic (though, at times, unconscious) effort to secure alternatives. As one Pathological Narcissistic Space (the narcissist's stomping grounds) is rendered "uninhabitable" (too many people "see through" the narcissist's manipulation and machinations) – the narcissist wanders off to find another.

These hysterical endeavours sometimes lead to boom-bust cycles which involve, in the first stage, the formation of a Grandiosity Bubble.

A Grandiosity Bubble is an imagined, self-aggrandising, narrative involving the narcissist and elements from his real life – people around him, places he frequents, or conversations he is having. The narcissist weaves a story incorporating these facts, inflating them in the process and endowing them with bogus internal meaning and consistency. In other words: he confabulates – but, this time, his confabulation is loosely based on reality.

In the process, the narcissist re-invents himself and his life to fit the new-fangled tale. He re-casts himself in newly adopted roles. He suddenly fancies himself an actor, a guru, a political activist, an entrepreneur, or an irresistible hunk. He modifies his behaviour to conform to these new functions. He gradually morphs into the fabricated character and "becomes" the fictitious protagonist he has created.

All the mechanisms of pathological narcissism are at work during the bubble phase. The narcissist idealises the situation, the other "actors", and the environment. He tries to control and manipulate his milieu into buttressing his false notions and perceptions. Faced with an inevitable Grandiosity Gap, he becomes disillusioned and bitter and devalues and discards the people, places, and circumstances involved in the bubble.

Still, Grandiosity Bubbles are not part of the normal narcissistic mini-cycle. They are rare events, much like trying on a new outfit for size and comfort. They fizzle out rapidly and the narcissist reverts to his regular pattern: idealising new Sources of Supply, devaluing and discarding them, pursuing the next victims to be drained.

Actually, the deflation of a Grandiosity Bubble is met with relief by the narcissist. It does not involve a narcissistic injury. The narcissist views the bubble as merely an experiment at being someone else for a while. It is a safety valve, allowing the narcissist to effectively cope with negative emotions and frustration. Thus cleansed, the narcissist can go back to doing what he does best – projecting a False Self and garnering attention from others.

Return

The Depressive Narcissist

Many scholars consider pathological narcissism to be a form of depressive illness. This is the position of the authoritative magazine "Psychology Today". The life of the typical narcissist is, indeed, punctuated with recurrent bouts of dysphoria (ubiquitous sadness and hopelessness), anhedonia (loss of the ability to feel pleasure), and clinical forms of depression (cyclothymic, dysthymic, or other). This picture is further obfuscated by the frequent presence of mood disorders, such as Bipolar I (co-morbidity).

While the distinction between reactive (exogenous) and endogenous depression is obsolete, it is still useful in the context of narcissism. Narcissists react with depression not only to life crises but to fluctuations in Narcissistic Supply.

The narcissist's personality is disorganised and precariously balanced. He regulates his sense of self-worth by consuming Narcissistic Supply from others. Any threat to the uninterrupted flow of said supply compromises his psychological integrity and his ability to function. It is perceived by the narcissist as life threatening.

Loss Induced Dysphoria

This is the narcissist's depressive reaction to the loss of one or more Sources of Narcissistic Supply - or to the disintegration of a Pathological Narcissistic Space (PN Space, his stalking or hunting grounds, the social unit whose members lavish him with attention).

Deficiency Induced Dysphoria

Deep and acute depression which follows the aforementioned losses of Supply Sources or a PN Space. Having mourned these losses, the narcissist now grieves their inevitable outcome - the absence or deficiency of Narcissistic Supply. Paradoxically, this dysphoria energises the narcissist and moves him to find new

Sources of Supply to replenish his dilapidated stock (thus initiating a Narcissistic Cycle).

Self-Worth Dysregulation Dysphoria

The narcissist reacts with depression to criticism or disagreement, especially from a trusted and long-term Source of Narcissistic Supply. He fears the imminent loss of the source and the damage to his own, fragile, mental balance. The narcissist also resents his vulnerability and his extreme dependence on feedback from others. This type of depressive reaction is, therefore, a mutation of self-directed aggression.

Grandiosity Gap Dysphoria

The narcissist's firmly, though counterfactually, perceives himself as omnipotent, omniscient, omnipresent, brilliant, accomplished, irresistible, immune, and invincible. Any data to the contrary is usually filtered, altered, or discarded altogether. Still, sometimes reality intrudes and creates a Grandiosity Gap. The narcissist is forced to face his mortality, limitations, ignorance, and relative inferiority. He sulks and sinks into an incapacitating but short-lived dysphoria.

Self-Punishing Dysphoria

Deep inside, the narcissist hates himself and doubts his own worth. He deplores his desperate addiction to Narcissistic Supply. He judges his actions and intentions harshly and sadistically. He may be unaware of these dynamics – but they are at the heart of the narcissistic disorder and the reason the narcissist had to resort to narcissism as a defence mechanism in the first place.

This inexhaustible well of ill will, self-chastisement, self-doubt, and self-directed aggression yields numerous self-defeating and self-destructive behaviours – from reckless driving and substance abuse to suicidal ideation and constant depression.

It is the narcissist's ability to confabulate that saves him from himself. His grandiose fantasies remove him from reality and prevent recurrent narcissistic injuries. Many narcissists end up delusional, schizoid, or paranoid. To avoid agonising and gnawing depression, they give up on life itself.

Return

The Narcissist and His Friends

"Who's the fairest of them all?" – asks the Bad Queen in the fairy tale. Having provided the wrong answer, the mirror is smashed to smithereens. Not a bad allegory for how the narcissist treats his "friends".

Literature helps us grasp the intricate interactions between the narcissist and members of his social circle.

Both Sherlock Holmes and Hercules Poirot, the world's most renowned fiction detectives, are quintessential narcissists. Both are also schizoids – they have few friends and are largely confined to their homes, engaged in solitary activities. Both have fatuous, sluggish, and anodyne sidekicks who slavishly cater to their whims and needs and provide them with an adulating gallery – Holmes' Dr. Watson and Poirot's poor Hastings.

Both Holmes and Poirot assiduously avoid the "competition" – equally sharp minds who seek their company for a fertilising intellectual exchange among equals. They feel threatened by the potential need to admit to ignorance and confess to error. Both gumshoes are self-sufficient and consider themselves peerless.

The Watsons and Hastings of this world provide the narcissist with an obsequious, unthreatening, audience and with the kind of unconditional and unthinking obedience that confirms to him his omnipotence. They are sufficiently vacuous to make the narcissist look sharp and omniscient – but not so asinine as to be instantly discernible as such. They are the perfect backdrop, never likely to attain centre stage and overshadow their master.

Moreover, both Holmes and Poirot sadistically – and often publicly – taunt and humiliate their Sancho Panzas, explicitly chastising them for being dim-witted. Narcissism and sadism are psychodynamic cousins and both Watson and Hastings are perfect victims of abuse: docile, understanding, malignantly optimistic, self-deluding, and idolising.

Narcissists can't empathise or love and, therefore, have no friends. The narcissist is one track minded. He is interested in securing Narcissistic Supply from Narcissistic Supply Sources. He is not interested in people as such. He is incapable of empathising, is a solipsist, and recognises only himself as human. To the narcissist, all others are three dimensional cartoons, tools and instruments in the tedious and Sisyphean task of generating and consuming Narcissistic Supply.

The narcissist over-values people (when they are judged to be potential sources of such supply), uses them, devalues them (when no longer able to supply him) and discards them nonchalantly. This behaviour pattern tends to alienate and to distance people from him.

Gradually, the social circle of the narcissist dwindles (and ultimately vanishes). People around him who are not turned off by the ugly succession of his acts and attitudes – are rendered desperate and fatigued by the turbulent nature of the narcissist's life.

Those few still loyal to him, gradually abandon him because they can no longer withstand and tolerate the ups and downs of his career, his moods, his confrontations and conflicts with authority, his chaotic financial state and the dissolution of his emotional affairs. The narcissist is a human roller coaster – fun for a limited time, nauseating in the long run.

This is the process of narcissistic confinement.

Anything which might – however remotely – endanger the availability, or the quantity of the narcissist's Narcissistic Supply is excised. The narcissist avoids certain situations (for instance: where he is likely to encounter opposition, or criticism, or competition). He refrains from certain activities and actions (which are incompatible with his projected False Self). And he steers clear of people he deems insufficiently amenable to his charms.

To avoid narcissistic injury, the narcissist employs a host of Emotional Involvement Prevention Measures (EIPMs). He becomes rigid, repetitive, predictable, boring, limits himself to "safe subjects" (such as, endlessly, himself) and to "safe conduct", and often rages hysterically (when confronted with unexpected situations or with the slightest resistance to his preconceived course of action).

The narcissist's rage is not so much a reaction to offended grandiosity as it is the outcome of panic. The narcissist maintains a precarious balance, a mental house of cards, poised on a precipice. His equilibrium is so delicate that anything and anyone can upset it: a casual remark, a disagreement, a slight criticism, a hint, or a fear.

The narcissist magnifies it all into monstrous, ominous, proportions. To avoid these (not so imagined) threats – the narcissist prefers to "stay at home". He limits his social intercourse. He abstains from daring, trying, or venturing out. He is crippled. This, indeed, is the very essence of the malignancy that is at the heart of narcissism: the fear of flying.

Return

The Enigma of Normal People

I can't understand "normal" people. I don't know what makes them tick. To me, they are an enigma, wrapped in mystery. I try hard not to offend them, to act civil, to be helpful and forthcoming. I give so much in my relationships that I often feel exploited. I make it a point not to strain my contacts, not to demand too much, not to impose.

But it's not working. Folks I consider friends vanish suddenly without as much as a "goodbye". The more I help someone – the less grateful he or she seems to be and the more repelled by me.

I find jobs for people, lend a hand with various chores, make valuable introductions, give advice, and charge nothing for my services (which, in some cases, are rendered over many years, day in and day out). Yet, it seems that I can do nothing right. They accept my aid and succour grudgingly and then disengage – until the next time I am needed.

I am not the victim of a group of callous and ruthless people. Some of these ingrates are otherwise most warm and empathic. It just seems that they cannot find in them warmth and empathy enough for me, no matter how much I try to make myself both useful and agreeable.

Perhaps I try too hard? Maybe my efforts show? Am I transparent?

Of course I am. What comes to "normal" people naturally – social interaction – to me is an excruciating effort that involves analyses, pretence and thespian skills. I misread the ubiquitous language of social cues. I am awkward and unpleasant. But I rarely ask for anything in return for my favours, except to be somewhat tolerated. Maybe the recipients of my recurrent magnanimity feel humiliated and inferior and hate me for it, I don't know what to think anymore.

My social milieu resembles bubbles in a stream. People pop up, make my acquaintance, avail themselves of anything I have to offer them, and disappear discourteously. Inevitably, I trust no one and avoid hurt by remaining emotionally aloof. But this only exacerbates the situation.

When I try to press the point, when I ask "Is anything wrong with me, how can I improve?" – my interlocutors impatiently detach, seldom to reappear. When I try to balance the equation by (very rarely) asking for a commensurate service or a favour in return – I am utterly ignored or my request is curtly and monosyllabically declined.

It's like people are saying:

"You are such a loathsome being that merely keeping your company is a sacrifice. You should bribe us to associate with you, however coolly. You should buy our icy friendship and our limited willingness to listen. You deserve no better than these concessions that we are granting you reluctantly. You should feel grateful that we agree to take that which you have to give us. Expect nothing in return but our truncated attention."

And I, the mental leper, endorse these terms of dubious endearment. I dole out gifts: my knowledge, my contacts, my political influence, my writing skills (such as they are). All I ask in return is not to be abandoned hastily, a few moments of make-believe, of feigned grace. I acquiesce in the asymmetry of my relationships, for I deserve no better and have known no differently since my early tortured childhood.

Return

The Intermittent Explosive Narcissist

Narcissists invariably react with *narcissistic rage* to *narcissistic injury*.

These two terms bear clarification:

Narcissistic Injury

Any threat (real or imagined) to the narcissist's grandiose and fantastic self-perception (False Self) as perfect, omnipotent, omniscient, and entitled to special treatment and recognition, regardless of his actual accomplishments (or lack thereof).

The narcissist actively solicits Narcissistic Supply - adulation, compliments, admiration, subservience, attention, being feared - from others in order to sustain his fragile and dysfunctional Ego. Thus, he constantly courts possible rejection, criticism, disagreement, and even mockery.

The narcissist is, therefore, dependent on other people. He is aware of the risks associated with such all-pervasive and essential dependence. He resents his weakness and dreads possible disruptions in the flow of his drug - Narcissistic Supply. He is caught between the rock of his habit and the hard place of his frustration. No wonder he is prone to raging, lashing and acting out, and to pathological, all-consuming envy (all expressions of pent-up aggression).

The narcissist is constantly on the lookout for slights. He is hypervigilant. He perceives every disagreement as criticism and every critical remark as complete and humiliating rejection - nothing short of a threat. Gradually, his mind turns into a chaotic battlefield of paranoia and ideas of reference.

Most narcissists react defensively. They become conspicuously indignant, aggressive, and cold. They detach emotionally for fear of yet another (narcissistic) injury. They devalue the person who made the disparaging remark, the critical comment, the unflattering observation, the innocuous joke at the narcissist's expense.

By holding the critic in contempt, by diminishing the stature of the discordant conversant – the narcissist minimises the impact of the disagreement or criticism on himself. This is a defence mechanism known as cognitive dissonance.

Narcissistic Rage

Narcissists can be imperturbable, resilient to stress, and sangfroid. Narcissistic rage is not a reaction to stress – it is a reaction to a perceived slight, insult, criticism, or disagreement (in other words, to narcissistic injury). It is intense and disproportional to the "offence".

Raging narcissists usually perceive their reaction to have been triggered by an intentional provocation with a hostile purpose. Their targets, on the other hand, invariably regard raging narcissists as incoherent, unjust, and arbitrary.

Narcissistic rage should not be confused with anger, though they have many things in common.

It is not clear whether action diminishes anger or anger is used up in action – but anger in healthy persons is diminished through action and expression. It is an aversive, unpleasant emotion. It is intended to generate action in order to reduce frustration. Anger is coupled with physiological arousal.

Another enigma is:

Do we become angry because we say that we are angry, thus identifying the anger and capturing it – or do we say that we are angry because we are angry to begin with?

Anger is provoked by adverse treatment, deliberately or unintentionally inflicted. Such treatment must violate either prevailing conventions regarding social interactions or some otherwise a deeply ingrained sense of what is fair and what is just. The judgement of fairness or justice is a cognitive function impaired in the narcissist.

Anger is induced by numerous factors. It is almost a universal reaction. Any threat to one's welfare (physical, emotional, social, financial, or mental) is met with anger. So are threats to one's affiliates, nearest, dearest, nation, favourite football club, pet and so on. The territory of anger includes not only the angry person himself, but also his real and perceived environment and social milieu.

Threats are not the only situations to incite anger. Anger is also the reaction to injustice (perceived or real), to disagreements, and to inconvenience (discomfort) caused by dysfunction.

Still, all manner of angry people – narcissists or not – suffer from a cognitive deficit and are worried and anxious. They are unable to conceptualise, to design effective strategies, and to execute them. They dedicate all their attention to the here and now and ignore the future consequences of their actions. Recent events are judged more relevant and weighted more heavily than any earlier ones. Anger impairs cognition, including the proper perception of time and space.

In all people, narcissists and normal, anger is associated with a suspension of empathy. Irritated people cannot empathise. Actually, "counter-empathy" develops in a state of aggravated anger. The faculties of judgement and risk evaluation are also altered by anger. Later provocative acts are judged to be more serious than earlier ones – just by "virtue" of their chronological position.

Yet, normal anger results in taking some action regarding the source of frustration (or, at the very least, the planning or contemplation of such action). In contrast, pathological rage is mostly directed at oneself, displaced, or even lacks a target altogether.

Narcissists often vent their anger at "insignificant" people. They yell at a waitress, berate a taxi driver, or publicly chide an underling. Alternatively, they sulk, feel anhedonic or pathologically bored, drink, or do drugs – all forms of self-directed aggression.

From time to time, no longer able to pretend and to suppress their rage, they have it out with the real source of their anger. Then they lose all vestiges of self-control and rave like lunatics. They shout incoherently, make absurd accusations, distort facts, and air long-suppressed grievances, allegations and suspicions.

These episodes are followed by periods of saccharine sentimentality and excessive flattering and submissiveness towards the victim of the latest rage attack. Driven by the mortal fear of being abandoned or ignored, the narcissist repulsively debases and demeans himself.

Most narcissists are prone to be angry. Their anger is always sudden, raging, frightening and without an apparent provocation by an outside agent. It would seem that narcissists are in a CONSTANT state of rage, which is effectively controlled most of the time. It manifests itself only when the narcissist's defences are down, incapacitated, or adversely affected by circumstances, inner or external.

Pathological anger is neither coherent, not externally induced. It emanates from the inside and it is diffuse, directed at the "world" and at "injustice" in general. The narcissist is capable of identifying the IMMEDIATE cause of his fury. Still, upon closer scrutiny, the cause is likely to be found lacking and the anger excessive, disproportionate, and incoherent.

It might be more accurate to say that the narcissist is expressing (and experiencing) TWO layers of anger, simultaneously and always. The first layer, of superficial ire, is indeed directed at an identified target, the alleged cause of the eruption. The second layer, however, incorporates the narcissist's self-aimed wrath.

Narcissistic rage has two forms:

1. *Explosive* – The narcissist flares up, attacks everyone in his immediate vicinity, causes damage to objects or people, and is verbally and psychologically abusive.
2. *Pernicious or Passive-Aggressive (P/A)* – The narcissist sulks, gives the silent treatment, and is plotting how to punish the transgressor and put her in her proper place. These narcissists are vindictive and often become stalkers. They harass and haunt the objects of their frustration. They sabotage and damage the work and possessions of people whom they regard to be the sources of their mounting wrath.

Return

The Narcissism of Differences Big and Small

Freud coined the phrase "*narcissism of small differences*" in a paper titled "The Taboo of Virginity" that he published in 1917. Referring to earlier work by British anthropologist Ernest Crawley, he said that we reserve our most virulent emotions – aggression, hatred, envy – towards those who resemble us the most. We feel threatened not by the Other with whom we have little in common – but by the "nearly-we", who mirror and reflect us.

The "nearly-he" imperils the narcissist's selfhood and challenges his uniqueness, perfection, and superiority – the fundaments of the narcissist's sense of self-worth. It provokes in him primitive narcissistic defences and leads him to adopt desperate measures to protect, preserve, and restore his balance. I call it the Gulliver Array of Defence Mechanisms.

The very existence of the "nearly-he" constitutes a narcissistic injury. The narcissist feels humiliated, shamed, and embarrassed not to be special after all – and he reacts with envy and aggression towards this source of frustration.

In doing so, he resorts to splitting, projection, and Projective Identification. He attributes to other people personal traits that he dislikes in himself and he forces them to behave in conformity with his expectations. In other words, the narcissist sees in others those parts of himself that he cannot countenance and deny. He forces people around him to become him and to reflect his shameful behaviours, hidden fears, and forbidden wishes.

But how does the narcissist avoid the realisation that what he loudly decries and derides is actually part of him? By exaggerating, or even dreaming up and creatively inventing, differences between his qualities and conduct and other people's. The more hostile he becomes towards the "nearly-he", the easier it is to distinguish himself from "the Other".

To maintain this self-differentiating aggression, the narcissist stokes the fires of hostility by obsessively and vengefully nurturing grudges and hurts (some of them imagined). He dwells on injustice and pain inflicted on him by these stereotypically "bad or unworthy" people. He devalues and dehumanises them and plots revenge to achieve closure. In the process, he indulges in grandiose fantasies, aimed to boost his feelings of omnipotence and magical immunity.

In the process of acquiring an adversary, the narcissist blocks out information that threatens to undermine his emerging self-perception as righteous and offended. He begins to base his whole identity on the brewing conflict which is by now a major preoccupation and a defining or even all-pervasive dimension of his existence.

Very much the same dynamic applies to coping with major differences between the narcissist and others. He emphasises the large disparities while transforming even the most minor ones into decisive and unbridgeable.

Deep inside, the narcissist is continuously subject to a gnawing suspicion that his self-perception as omnipotent, omniscient, and irresistible is flawed, confabulated, and unrealistic. When criticised, the narcissist actually agrees with the critic. In other words, there are only minor differences between the narcissist and his detractors. But this threatens the narcissist's internal cohesion. Hence the wild rage at any hint of disagreement, resistance, or debate.

Similarly, intimacy brings people closer together – it makes them more similar. There are only minor differences between intimate partners. The narcissist perceives this as a threat to his sense of uniqueness. He reacts by devaluing the source of his fears: the mate, spouse, lover, or partner. He re-establishes the boundaries and the distinctions that were removed by intimacy. Thus restored, he is emotionally ready to embark on another round of idealisation (the Approach-Avoidance Repetition Complex).

Return

Inner Dialog, Cognitive Deficits, And Introjects in Narcissism

"Man can will nothing unless he has first understood that he must count no one but himself; that he is alone, abandoned on earth in the midst of his infinite responsibilities, without help, with no other aim than the one he sets himself, with no other destiny than the one he forges for himself on this earth."
[Jean Paul Sartre, Being and Nothingness, 1943]

The narcissist lacks empathy. He is, therefore, unable to meaningfully relate to other people and to truly appreciate what it is to be human. Instead, he withdraws inside, into a universe populated by avatars – simple or complex representations of parents, peers, role models, authority figures, and other members of his social milieu. There, in this twilight zone of simulacra, he develops "relationships" and maintains an on-going internal dialog with them.

All of us generate such representations of meaningful others and internalise these objects. In a process called introjection, we adopt, assimilate, and, later, manifest their traits and attitudes (the introjects).

But the narcissist is different. He is incapable of holding an external dialog. Even when he seems to be interacting with someone else – the narcissist is actually engaged in a self-referential discourse. To the narcissist, all other people are cardboard cut-outs, two dimensional animated cartoon characters, or symbols. They exist only in his mind. He is startled when they deviate from the script and prove to be complex and autonomous.

But this is not the narcissist's sole cognitive deficit.

The narcissist attributes his failures and mistakes to circumstances and external causes. This propensity to blame the world for one's mishaps and misfortunes is called "alloplastic defence". At the same time, the narcissist regards his successes and achievements (some of which are imaginary) as proofs of his omnipotence and omniscience. This is known in attribution theory as "defensive attribution".

Conversely, the narcissist traces other people's errors and defeats to their inherent inferiority, stupidity, and weakness. Their successes he dismisses as "being in the right place at the right time" - i.e., the outcome of luck and circumstance.

Thus, the narcissist falls prey to an exaggerated form of what is known in attribution theory as the "fundamental attribution error". Moreover, these fallacies and the narcissist's magical thinking are not dependent on objective data and tests of distinctiveness, consistency, and consensus.

The narcissist never questions his reflexive judgements and never stops to ask himself: are these events distinct or are they typical? Do they repeat themselves consistently or are they unprecedented? And what do others have to say about them?

The narcissist learns nothing because he regards himself as born perfect. Even when he fails a thousand times, the narcissist still feels the victim of happenstance. And someone else's repeated outstanding accomplishments are never proof of mettle or merit. People who disagree with the narcissist and try to teach him differently are, to his mind, biased or morons or both.

But the narcissist pays a dear price for these distortions of perception. Unable to gauge his environment with accuracy, he develops paranoid ideation and fails the reality test. Finally, he lifts the drawbridges and vanishes into a state of mind that can best be described as borderline psychosis.

Return

The Prodigy as Narcissistic Injury

The prodigy – the precocious "genius" – feels <u>entitled to special treatment</u>. Yet, he rarely gets it. This frustrates him and renders him even more <u>aggressive</u>, driven, and <u>overachieving</u> than he is by nature.

As Horney pointed out, the child-prodigy is dehumanised and instrumentalised. His parents love him not for what he really is – but for what they wish and imagine him to be: the fulfilment of their dreams and frustrated wishes. The child becomes the vessel of his parents' discontented lives, a tool, the magic brush with which they can transform their failures into successes, their humiliation into victory, their frustrations into happiness.

The child is taught to ignore reality and to occupy the parental fantastic space. Such an unfortunate child feels omnipotent and omniscient, perfect and brilliant, worthy of adoration and entitled to special treatment. The faculties that are honed by constantly brushing against bruising reality – empathy, compassion, a realistic assessment of one's abilities and limitations, realistic expectations of oneself and of others, personal boundaries, team work, social skills, perseverance and goal-orientation, not to mention the ability to postpone gratification and to work hard to achieve it – are all lacking or missing altogether.

The child turned adult sees no reason to invest in his skills and education, convinced that his inherent genius should suffice. He feels entitled for merely being, rather than for actually doing (rather as the nobility in days gone by felt entitled not by virtue of its merit but as the inevitable, foreordained outcome of its birth right). In other words, he is not meritocratic – but aristocratic. In short: a narcissist is born.

Not all precocious prodigies end up under-accomplished and petulant. Many of them go on to attain great stature in their communities and great standing in their <u>professions</u>. But, even then, the gap between the kind of treatment they believe that they deserve and the one they are getting is unbridgeable.

This is because narcissistic prodigies often misjudge the extent and importance of their accomplishments and, as a result, erroneously consider themselves to be indispensable and worthy of special rights, perks, and privileges. When they find out otherwise, they are devastated and furious.

Moreover, people are envious of the prodigy. The genius serves as a constant reminder to others of their mediocrity, lack of creativity, and mundane existence. Naturally, they try to "bring him down to their level" and "cut him down to size". The gifted person's haughtiness and high-handedness only exacerbate his strained relationships.

In a way, merely by existing, the prodigy inflicts constant and repeated narcissistic injuries on the less endowed and the pedestrian. This creates a vicious cycle. People try to hurt and harm the overweening and arrogant genius and he becomes defensive, aggressive, and aloof. This renders him even more obnoxious than before and others resent him more deeply and more thoroughly. Hurt and wounded, he retreats into fantasies of grandeur and revenge. And the cycle re-commences.

Mistreating Celebrities - An Interview

Granted to Superinteressante Magazine in Brazil March 2005

Q: Fame and TV shows about celebrities usually have a huge audience. This is understandable: people like to see other successful people. But why people like to see celebrities being humiliated?

A: As far as their fans are concerned, celebrities fulfil two emotional functions: they provide a mythical narrative (a story that the fan can follow and identify with) and they function as blank screens onto which the fans project their dreams, hopes, fears, plans, values, and desires (wish fulfilment). The slightest deviation from these prescribed roles provokes enormous rage and makes us want to punish (humiliate) the "deviant" celebrities.

Q: But why?

A: When the human foibles, vulnerabilities, and frailties of a celebrity are revealed, the fan feels humiliated, "cheated", hopeless, and "empty". To reassert his self-worth, the fan must establish his or her moral superiority over the erring and "sinful" celebrity. The fan must "teach the celebrity a lesson" and show the celebrity "who's boss". It is a primitive defence mechanism – narcissistic grandiosity. It puts the fan on equal footing with the exposed and "naked" celebrity.

Q: This taste for watching a person being humiliated has something to do with the attraction to catastrophes and tragedies?

A: There is always a sadistic pleasure and a morbid fascination in vicarious suffering. Being spared the pains and tribulations others go through makes the observer feel "chosen", secure, and virtuous. The higher celebrities rise, the harder they fall. There is something gratifying in hubris defied and punished.

Q: Do you believe the audience put themselves in the place of the reporter (when he asks something embarrassing to a celebrity) and become in some way revenged?

A: The reporter "represents" the "bloodthirsty" public. Belittling celebrities or watching their comeuppance is the modern equivalent of the gladiator rink. Gossip used to fulfil the same function and now the mass media broadcast live the slaughtering of fallen gods. There is no question of revenge here – just Schadenfreude, the guilty joy of witnessing your superiors penalised and "cut down to size".

Q: In your country, who are the celebrities people love to hate?

A: Israelis like to watch politicians and wealthy businessmen reduced, demeaned, and slighted. In Macedonia, where I live, all famous people, regardless of their vocation, are subject to intense, proactive, and destructive envy. This love-hate relationship with their idols, this ambivalence, is attributed by psychodynamic theories of personal development to the child's emotions towards his parents. Indeed, we transfer and displace many negative emotions we harbour onto celebrities.

Q: I would never dare asking some questions the reporters from Panico ask the celebrities. What are the characteristics of people like these reporters?

A: Sadistic, ambitious, narcissistic, lacking empathy, self-righteous, pathologically and destructively envious, with a fluctuating sense of self-worth (possibly an inferiority complex).

Q: Do you believe the actors and reporters want themselves to be as famous as the celebrities they tease? Because I think this is almost happening...

A: The line is very thin. Newsmakers and newsmen and women are celebrities merely because they are public figures and regardless of their true accomplishments. A celebrity is famous for being famous. Of course, such journalists will likely to fall prey to up and coming colleagues in an endless and self-perpetuating food chain...

Q: I think that the fan-celebrity relationship gratifies both sides. What are the advantages the fans get and what are the advantages the celebrities get?

A: There is an implicit contract between a celebrity and his fans. The celebrity is obliged to "act the part", to fulfil the expectations of his admirers, not to deviate from the roles that they impose and he or she accepts. In return the fans shower the celebrity with adulation. They idolise him or her and make him or her feel omnipotent, immortal, "larger than life", omniscient, superior, and sui generis (unique).

Q: What are the fans getting for their trouble?

A: Above all, the ability to vicariously share the celebrity's fabulous (and, usually, partly confabulated) existence. The celebrity becomes their "representative" in fantasyland, their extension and proxy, the reification and embodiment of their deepest desires and most secret and guilty dreams. Many celebrities are also role models or father/mother figures. Celebrities are proof that there is more to life than drab and routine. That beautiful – nay, perfect – people do exist and that they do lead charmed lives. There's hope yet – this is the celebrity's message to his fans.

The celebrity's inevitable downfall and corruption is the modern-day equivalent of the medieval morality play. This trajectory – from rags to riches and fame and back to rags or worse – proves that order and justice do prevail, that hubris invariably gets punished, and that the celebrity is no better, neither is he superior, to his fans.

Q: Why are celebrities narcissists? How is this disorder born?

A: No one knows if pathological narcissism is the outcome of inherited traits, the sad result of abusive and traumatising upbringing, or the confluence of both. Often, in the same family, with the same set of parents and an identical emotional environment – some siblings grow to be malignant narcissists, while others are perfectly "normal". Surely, this indicates a genetic predisposition of some people to develop narcissism.

It would seem reasonable to assume – though, at this stage, there is not a shred of proof – that the narcissist is born with a propensity to develop narcissistic defences. These are triggered by abuse or trauma during the formative years in infancy or during early adolescence. By "abuse" I am referring to a spectrum of behaviours which objectify the child and treat it as an extension of the caregiver (parent) or as a mere instrument of gratification. Dotting and smothering are as abusive as beating and starving. And abuse can be dished out by peers as well as by parents, or by adult role models.

Not all celebrities are narcissists. Still, some of them surely are.

We all search for positive cues from people around us. These cues reinforce in us certain behaviour patterns. There is nothing special in the fact that the narcissist-celebrity does the same. However there are two major differences between the narcissistic and the normal personality.

The first is quantitative. The normal person is likely to welcome a moderate amount of attention – verbal and non-verbal – in the form of affirmation, approval, or admiration. Too much attention, though, is perceived as onerous and is avoided. Destructive and negative criticism is avoided altogether.

The narcissist, in contrast, is the mental equivalent of an alcoholic. He is insatiable. He directs his whole behaviour, in fact his life, to obtain these pleasurable titbits of attention. He embeds them in a coherent, completely biased, picture of himself. He uses them to regulates his labile (fluctuating) sense of self-worth and self-esteem.

To elicit constant interest, the narcissist projects on to others a [confabulated](), fictitious version of himself, known as the [False Self](). The False Self is everything the narcissist is not: omniscient, omnipotent, charming, intelligent, rich, or well-connected.

The narcissist then proceeds to harvest reactions to this projected image from family members, friends, co-workers, neighbours, business partners and from colleagues. If these – the adulation, admiration, attention, fear, respect, applause, affirmation – are not forthcoming, the narcissist demands them, or extorts them. Money, compliments, a favourable critique, an appearance in the media, a sexual conquest are all converted into the same currency in the narcissist's mind, into Narcissistic Supply.

So, the narcissist is not really interested in publicity per se or in being famous. Truly he is concerned with the REACTIONS to his fame: how people watch him, notice him, talk about him, debate his actions. It "proves" to him that he exists.

The narcissist goes around "hunting and collecting" the way the expressions on people's faces change when they notice him. He places himself at the centre of attention, or even as a figure of controversy. He constantly and recurrently pesters those nearest and dearest to him in a bid to reassure himself that he is not losing his fame, his magic touch, the attention of his social milieu.

[Return]()

Indifference and Decompensation in Pathological Narcissism

The narcissist lacks empathy. Consequently, he is not really interested in the lives, emotions, needs, preferences, and hopes of people around him. Even his nearest and dearest are, to him, mere [instruments of gratification](). They require his undivided attention only when they "malfunction" – when they become disobedient, independent, or [critical](). He loses all interest in them if they cannot be "fixed" (for instance, when they are terminally ill or develop a modicum of personal autonomy and independence).

Once he gives up on his erstwhile Sources of Supply, the narcissist proceeds to promptly and peremptorily [devalue and discard]() them. This is often done by simply ignoring them – a facade of indifference that is known as the "silent treatment" and is, at heart, hostile and aggressive. Indifference is, therefore, a form of devaluation. People find the narcissist "cold", "inhuman", "heartless", "clueless", "[robotic or machine-like]()".

Early on in life, the narcissist learns to disguise his socially-unacceptable indifference as benevolence, equanimity, cool-headedness, composure, or superiority. "It is not that I don't care about others" – he shrugs off his critics – "I am simply more level-headed, more resilient, more composed under pressure... They mistake my equanimity for apathy."

The narcissist tries to convince people that he is compassionate. His profound lack of interest in his spouse's life, vocation, interests, hobbies, and whereabouts he cloaks as [benevolent altruism](). "I give her all the freedom she can wish for!" – he protests – "I don't spy on her, follow her, or nag her with endless questions. I don't bother her. I let her lead her life the way she sees fit and don't interfere in her affairs!" He makes a virtue out of his emotional truancy.

All very commendable but when taken to extremes such benign neglect turns malignant and signifies the voidance of true love and attachment. The narcissist's emotional (and, often, physical) absence from all his relationships is a form of aggression and a defence against his own thoroughly repressed feelings.

In rare moments of self-awareness, the narcissist realises that without his input – even in the form of feigned emotions – people will abandon him. He then swings from cruel aloofness to maudlin and grandiose gestures intended to demonstrate the "larger than life" nature of his sentiments. This bizarre pendulum only proves the narcissist's inadequacy at maintaining adult relationships. It convinces no one and repels many.

The narcissist's guarded detachment is a sad reaction to his unfortunate formative years. Pathological narcissism is thought to be the result of a prolonged period of severe abuse by primary caregivers, peers, or authority figures. In this sense, pathological narcissism is, therefore, a reaction to trauma. Narcissism IS a form of Post Traumatic Stress Disorder that got ossified and fixated and mutated into a personality disorder.

All narcissists are traumatised and all of them suffer from a variety of post-traumatic symptoms: abandonment anxiety, reckless behaviours, anxiety and mood disorders, somatoform disorders, and so on. But the presenting signs of narcissism rarely indicate post-trauma. This is because pathological narcissism is an EFFICIENT coping (defence) mechanism. The narcissist presents to the world a facade of invincibility, equanimity, superiority, skilfulness, cool-headedness, invulnerability, and, in short: indifference.

This front is penetrated only in times of great crises that threaten the narcissist's ability to obtain Narcissistic Supply. The narcissist then "falls apart" in a process of disintegration known as decompensation. The dynamic forces which render him paralysed and fake – his vulnerabilities, weaknesses, and fears – are starkly exposed as his defences crumble and become dysfunctional. The narcissist's extreme dependence on his social milieu for the regulation of his sense of self-worth are painfully and pitifully evident as he is reduced to begging and cajoling.

At such times, the narcissist acts out self-destructively and anti-socially. His mask of superior equanimity is pierced by displays of impotent rage, self-loathing, self-pity, and crass attempts at manipulation of his friends, family, and colleagues. His ostensible benevolence and caring evaporate. He feels caged and threatened and he reacts as any animal would do – by striking back at his perceived tormentors, at his hitherto "nearest" and "dearest".

Return

Pathological Narcissism, Psychosis, And Delusions

One of the most important symptoms of pathological narcissism (the Narcissistic Personality Disorder) is grandiosity. Grandiose fantasies (megalomaniac delusions of grandeur) permeate every aspect of the narcissist's personality. They are the reason that the narcissist feels entitled to special treatment which is typically incommensurate with his real accomplishments. The Grandiosity Gap is the abyss between the narcissist's self-image (as reified by his False Self) and reality.

When Narcissistic Supply is deficient, the narcissist decompensates and acts out in a variety of ways. Narcissists often experience psychotic micro-episodes during therapy and when they suffer narcissistic injuries in a life crisis. But can the narcissist "go over the edge"? Do narcissists ever become psychotic?

Some terminology first:

The narrowest definition of *psychosis*, according to the DSM-IV-TR, is "restricted to delusions or prominent hallucinations, with the hallucinations occurring in the absence of insight into their pathological nature".

And what are delusions and hallucinations?

A *delusion* is "a false belief based on incorrect inference about external reality that is firmly sustained despite what almost everyone else believes and despite what constitutes incontrovertible and obvious proof or evidence to the contrary".

A *hallucination* is a "sensory perception that has the compelling sense of reality of a true perception but that occurs without external stimulation of the relevant sensory organ".

Granted, the narcissist's hold on reality is tenuous (narcissists sometimes fail the reality test). Admittedly, narcissists often seem to believe in their own confabulations. They are unaware of the pathological nature and origin of their self-delusions and are, thus, technically delusional (though they rarely suffer from hallucinations, disorganised speech, or disorganised or catatonic behaviour). In the strictest sense of the word, narcissists appear to be psychotic.

But, actually, they are not. There is a qualitative difference between benign (though well-entrenched) self-deception or even malignant con-artistry – and "losing it".

Pathological narcissism should not be construed as a form of psychosis because:

1. The narcissists is usually fully aware of the difference between true and false, real and make-belief, the invented and the extant, right and wrong. The narcissist consciously chooses to adopt one version of the events, an aggrandising narrative, a fairy-tale existence, a "what-if" counterfactual life. He is emotionally invested in his personal myth. The narcissist feels better as fiction than as fact – but he never loses sight of the fact that it is all just fiction.
2. Throughout, the narcissist is in full control of his faculties, cognisant of his choices, and goal-orientated. His behaviour is intentional and directional. He is a manipulator and his delusions are in the service of his stratagems. Hence his chameleon-like ability to change guises, his conduct, and his convictions on a dime.
3. Narcissistic delusions rarely persist in the face of blanket opposition and reams of evidence to the contrary. The narcissist usually tries to convert his social milieu to his point of view. He attempts to condition his nearest and dearest to positively reinforce his delusional False Self. But, if he fails, he modifies his profile on the fly. He "plays it by ear". His False Self is extemporaneous – a perpetual work of art, permanently reconstructed in a reiterative process designed around intricate and complex feedback loops.

Though the narcissistic personality is rigid – its content is always in flux. Narcissists forever re-invent themselves, adapt their consumption of Narcissistic Supply to the "marketplace", attuned to the needs of their "suppliers". Like the performers that they are, they resonate with their "audience", giving it what it expects and wants. They are efficient instruments for the extraction and consumption of human reactions.

As a result of this interminable process of fine tuning, narcissists have no loyalties, no values, no doctrines, no beliefs, no affiliations, and no convictions. Their only constraint is their addiction to human attention, positive or negative.

Psychotics, by comparison, are fixated on a certain view of the world and of their place in it. They ignore any and all information that might challenge their delusions. Gradually, they retreat into the inner recesses of their tormented mind and become dysfunctional.

Narcissists can't afford to shut out the world because they so heavily depend on it for the regulation of their labile sense of self-worth. Owing to this dependence, they are hypersensitive and hypervigilant, alert to every bit of new data. They are continuously busy rearranging their self-delusions to incorporate new information in an ego-syntonic manner.

This is why the Narcissistic Personality Disorder is insufficient grounds for claiming a "diminished capacity" (insanity) defence. Narcissists are never divorced from reality – they crave it, and need it, and consume it in order to maintain the precarious balance of their disorganised, borderline-psychotic personality. All narcissists, even the freakiest ones, can tell right from wrong, act with intent, and are in full control of their faculties and actions.

Return

The Narcissist as Eternal Child

"Puer Aeternus" – the eternal adolescent, the semipternal Peter pan – is a phenomenon often associated with pathological narcissism. People who refuse to grow up strike others as self-centred and aloof, petulant and brattish, haughty and demanding – in short: as childish or infantile.

The narcissist is a partial adult. He seeks to avoid adulthood. Infantilisation – the discrepancy between one's advanced chronological age and one's retarded behaviour, cognition, and emotional development – is the narcissist's preferred art form. Some narcissists even use a childish tone of voice occasionally and adopt a toddler's body language.

But most narcissist resort to more subtle means.

They reject or avoid adult chores and functions. They refrain from acquiring adult skills (such as driving) or an adult's formal education. They evade adult responsibilities towards others, including and especially towards their nearest and dearest. They hold no steady jobs, never get married, raise no family, cultivate no roots, maintain no real friendships or meaningful relationships.

Many a narcissist remains attached to his (or her) family of origin. By clinging to his parents, the narcissist continues to act in the role of a child. He thus avoids the need to make adult decisions and (potentially painful) choices. He transfers all adult chores and responsibilities – from laundry to baby-sitting – to his parents, siblings, spouse, or other relatives. He feels unshackled, a free spirit, ready to take on the world (in other words omnipotent and omnipresent).

Such "delayed adulthood" is very common in many poor and developing countries, especially those with patriarchal societies. I wrote in "The Last Family":

"To the alienated and schizoid ears of Westerners, the survival of family and community in Central and Eastern Europe (CEE) sounds like an attractive proposition. A dual purpose safety net, both emotional and economic, the family in countries in

transition provides its members with unemployment benefits, accommodation, food and psychological advice to boot.

Divorced daughters, saddled with little (and not so little) ones, the prodigal sons incapable of finding a job befitting their qualifications, the sick, the unhappy – all are absorbed by the compassionate bosom of the family and, by extension the community. The family, the neighbourhood, the community, the village, the tribe – are units of subversion as well as useful safety valves, releasing and regulating the pressures of contemporary life in the modern, materialistic, crime ridden state.

The ancient blood feud laws of the kanoon were handed over through familial lineages in northern Albania, in defiance of the paranoiac Enver Hoxha regime. Criminals hide among their kin in the Balkans, thus effectively evading the long arm of the law (state). Jobs are granted, contracts signed and tenders won on an open and strict nepotistic basis and no one finds it odd or wrong. There is something atavistically heart-warming in all this.

Historically, the rural units of socialisation and social organisation were the family and the village. As villagers migrated to the cities, these structural and functional patterns were imported by them, en masse. The shortage of urban apartments and the communist invention of the communal apartment (its tiny rooms allocated one per family with kitchen and bathroom common to all) only served to perpetuate these ancient modes of multi-generational huddling. At best, the few available apartments were shared by three generations: parents, married off-spring and their children. In many cases, the living space was also shared by sickly or no-good relatives and even by unrelated families.

These living arrangements – more adapted to rustic open spaces than to high rises – led to severe social and psychological dysfunctions. To this very day, Balkan males are spoiled by the subservience and servitude of their in-house parents and incessantly and compulsively catered to by their submissive wives. Occupying someone else's home, they are not well acquainted with adult responsibilities.

Stunted growth and stagnant immaturity are the hallmarks of an entire generation, stifled by the ominous proximity of suffocating, invasive love. Unable to lead a healthy sex life behind paper thin walls, unable to raise their children and as many children as they see fit, unable to develop emotionally under the anxiously watchful eye of their parents – this greenhouse generation is doomed to a zombie-like existence in *the twilight nether land of their parents' caves. Many ever more eagerly await the demise of their caring captors and the promised land of their inherited apartments, free of their parents' presence.*

The daily pressures and exigencies of co-existence are enormous. The prying, the gossip, the criticism, the chastising, the small agitating mannerisms, the smells, the incompatible personal habits and preferences, the pusillanimous bookkeeping – all serve to erode the individual and to reduce him or her to the most primitive mode of survival. This is further exacerbated by the need to share expenses, to allocate labour and tasks, to plan ahead for contingencies, to see off threats, to hide information, to pretend and to fend off emotionally injurious behaviour. It is a sweltering tropic of affective cancer."

Alternatively, by acting as surrogate caregiver to his siblings or parents, the narcissist displaces his adulthood into a fuzzier and less demanding territory. The social expectations from a husband and a father are clear-cut. Not so from a substitute, mock, or ersatz parent. By investing his efforts, resources, and emotions in his family of origin, the narcissist avoids having to establish a new family and face the world as an adult. His is an "adulthood by proxy", a vicarious imitation of the real thing.

The ultimate in dodging adulthood is finding God (long recognised as a father-substitute), or some other "higher cause". The believer allows the doctrine and the social institutions that enforce it to make decisions for him and thus relieve him of responsibility. He succumbs to the paternal power of the collective and surrenders his personal autonomy. In other words, he is a child once more. Hence the allure of faith and the lure of dogmas such as nationalism or Communism or liberal democracy.

But why does the narcissist refuse to grow up? Why does he postpone the inevitable and regards adulthood as a painful experience to be avoided at a great cost to personal growth and self-realisation? Because remaining essentially a toddler caters to all his narcissistic needs and defences and nicely tallies with the narcissist's inner psychodynamic landscape.

Pathological narcissism is an infantile defence against abuse and trauma, usually occurring in early childhood or early adolescence. Thus, narcissism is inextricably entwined with the abused child's or adolescent's emotional make-up, cognitive deficits, and worldview. To say "narcissist" is to say "thwarted, tortured child".

It is important to remember that overweening, smothering, spoiling, overvaluing, and idolising the child – are all forms of parental abuse. There is nothing more narcissistically-gratifying than the admiration and adulation (Narcissistic Supply) garnered by precocious child-prodigies (Wunderkinder). Narcissists who are the sad outcomes of excessive pampering and sheltering become addicted to it.

In a paper published in Quadrant in 1980 and titled "Puer Aeternus: The Narcissistic Relation to the Self", Jeffrey Satinover, a Jungian analyst, offers these astute observations:

"The individual narcissistically bound to (the image or archetype of the divine child) for identity can experience satisfaction from a concrete achievement only if it matches the grandeur of this archetypal image. It must have the qualities of greatness, absolute uniqueness, of being the best and ... prodigiously precocious. This latter quality explains the enormous fascination of child prodigies, and also explains why even a great success yields no permanent satisfaction for the puer: being an adult, no accomplishment is precocious unless he stays artificially young or equates his accomplishments with those of old age (hence the premature striving after the wisdom of those who are much older)."

The simple truth is that children get away with narcissistic traits and behaviours. Narcissists know that. They envy children, hate them, try to emulate them and, thus, compete with them for scarce Narcissistic Supply.

Children are forgiven for feeling grandiose and self-important or even encouraged to develop such emotions as part of "building up their self-esteem". Kids frequently exaggerate with impunity accomplishments, talents, skills, contacts, and personality traits – exactly the kind of conduct that narcissists are chastised for!

As part of a normal and healthy development trajectory, young children are as obsessed as narcissists are with fantasies of unlimited success, fame, fearsome power or omnipotence, and unequalled brilliance. Adolescent are expected to be preoccupied with bodily beauty or sexual performance (as is the somatic narcissist), or ideal, everlasting, all-conquering love or passion. What is normal in the first 16 years of life is labelled a pathology later on.

Children are firmly convinced that they are unique and, being special, can only be understood by, should only be treated by, or associate with, other special or unique, or high-status people. In time, through the process of socialisation, young adults learn the benefits of collaboration and acknowledge the innate value of each and every person. Narcissists never do. They remain fixated in the earlier stage.

Preteens and teenagers require excessive admiration, adulation, attention and affirmation. It is a transient phase that gives place to the self-regulation of one's sense of inner worth. Narcissists, however, remain dependent on others for their self-esteem and self-confidence. They are fragile and fragmented and thus very susceptible to criticism, even if it is merely implied or imagined.

Well into pubescence, children feel entitled. As toddlers, they demand automatic and full compliance with their unreasonable expectations for special and favourable priority treatment. They grow out of it as they develop empathy and respect for the boundaries, needs, and wishes of other people. Again, narcissists never mature, in this sense.

Children, like adult narcissists, are "interpersonally exploitative", i.e., use others to achieve their own ends. During the formative years (0-6 years old), children are devoid of empathy. They are unable to identify with, acknowledge, or accept the feelings, needs, preferences, priorities, and choices of others.

Both adult narcissists and young children are envious of others and sometimes seek to hurt or destroy the causes of their frustration. Both groups behave arrogantly and haughtily, feel superior, omnipotent, omniscient, invincible, immune, "above the law", and omnipresent (magical thinking), and rage when frustrated, contradicted, challenged, or confronted.

The narcissist seeks to legitimise his child-like conduct and his infantile mental world by actually remaining a child, by refusing to mature and to grow up, by avoiding the hallmarks of adulthood, and by forcing others to accept him as the Puer Aeternus, the Eternal Youth, a worry-free, unbounded, Peter Pan.

Return

Idealisation, Grandiosity, Cathexis, And Narcissistic Progress

When I re-read articles I have written only a month ago and had deemed, at the time of composing, to be the epitome of incisiveness and proficiency, I invariably find them woefully lacking, verbose, and obscure.

What causes this dramatic shift in judgement within an inordinately short period of time? How could I have so misperceived my own work? What new have I learned and how was I thus enlightened?

The narcissist cathexes (emotionally invests) with grandiosity everything he owns or does: his nearest and dearest, his work, his environment. But, as time passes, this pathologically intense aura fades. The narcissist finds fault with things and people he had first thought impeccable. He energetically berates and denigrates that which he equally zealously exulted and praised only a short while before.

This inexorable and (to the outside world) disconcerting roller-coaster is known as the "Idealisation-Devaluation Cycle". It involves serious cognitive and emotional deficits and a formidable series of triggered defence mechanisms.

The Cycle starts with the narcissist's hunger for Narcissistic Supply - the panoply of reactions to the narcissist's False Self (his feigned facade of omnipotence and omniscience). The narcissist uses these inputs to regulate his fluctuating sense of self-worth.

It is important to distinguish between the various components of the process of Narcissistic Supply:
1. The *Trigger of Supply* is the person or object that provokes the source into yielding Narcissistic Supply by confronting the source with information about the narcissist's False Self;
2. The *Source of Narcissistic Supply* is the person that provides the Narcissistic Supply;
3. *Narcissistic Supply* is the reaction of the source to the trigger.

The narcissist homes in on Triggers and Sources of Narcissistic Supply – people, possessions, creative works, money – and imbues these sources and triggers with attributed uniqueness, perfection, brilliance, and grandiose qualities (omnipotence, omnipresence, omniscience). He filters out any data that contradict these fantastic misperceptions. He rationalises, intellectualises, denies, represses, projects – and, in general, defends against – contrarian information.

Back to my writing:

My articles are triggers. The readers of my articles are my Sources of Narcissistic Supply. The fact that my articles are read and that they influence my readership is Narcissistic Supply to me – as are my readers' written and verbal reactions (both negative and positive).

When I produce an essay, I am proud of it. I am emotionally invested in it. I regard it as reified perfection. Though I try very hard, I can see nothing wrong with my vocabulary, grammar, syntax, turn of phrase, and ideas. In other words, I idealise my creative effort.

Why is it, then, that when I revert to it a mere few weeks later, I find the syntax tortured, the grammar shoddy, the choice of words forced, the whole piece repulsively bloviated, and the ideas hopelessly tangled and dim? In other words, why do I devalue my work?

The narcissist realises and resents his dependence on Narcissistic Supply. Moreover, deep inside, he is aware of the fact that his False Self is an untenable sham. Still, omnipotent as he holds himself to be, the narcissist believes in his ability to make it all come true, to asymptotically approximate his grandiose fantasies. He is firmly convinced that, given enough time and practice, he can and will become his lofty False Self.

Hence the narcissist's idea of progress: the frustrating and masochistic pursuit of an ever-receding mirage of perfection, brilliance, omniscience, omnipresence, and omnipotence. The narcissist dumps old sources and triggers of supply because he is convinced that he is perpetually improving and that he deserves better and that "better" is just around the corner. He is driven by his own impossible Ego Ideal.

An article I write tomorrow is, therefore, bound to be far superior to yesterday's output. Miraculously, my grammar and syntax will have mended, my vocabulary will have expanded, my ideas will have resolved themselves coherently. Last month's essays are bound to be inferior in comparison to later pieces.

I am a work in progress, reaching ever closer to flawless consummation. The chronology of my articles merely reflects my increasingly elevated state of being.

Return

The Narcissist's Inner Judge

The narcissist is besieged and tormented by a sadistic Superego which sits in constant judgement. It is an amalgamation of negative evaluations, criticisms, angry or disappointed voices, and disparagement meted out in the narcissist's formative years and adolescence by parents, peers, role models, and authority figures.

These harsh and repeated comments reverberate throughout the narcissist's inner landscape, berating him for failing to conform to his unattainable ideals, fantastic goals, and grandiose or impractical plans. The narcissist's sense of self-worth is, therefore, catapulted from one pole to another: from an inflated view of himself (incommensurate with real life accomplishments) to utter despair and self-denigration.

Hence the narcissist's need for Narcissistic Supply to regulate this wild pendulum. People's adulation, admiration, affirmation, and attention restore the narcissist's self-esteem and self-confidence.

The narcissist's sadistic and uncompromising Superego affects three facets of his personality:

1. His sense of self-worth and worthiness (the deeply ingrained conviction that one deserves love, compassion, care, and empathy regardless of what one achieves). The narcissist feels worthless without Narcissistic Supply.
2. His self-esteem (self-knowledge, the deeply ingrained and realistic appraisal of one's capacities, skills, limitations, and shortcomings). The narcissist lacks clear boundaries and, therefore, is not sure of his abilities and weaknesses. Hence his grandiose fantasies.
3. His self-confidence (the deeply ingrained belief, based on lifelong experience, that one can set realistic goals and accomplish them). The narcissist knows that he is a fake and a fraud. He, therefore, does not trust his ability to manage his own affairs and to set practical aims and realize them.

By becoming a success (or at least by appearing to have become one) the narcissist hopes to quell the voices inside him that constantly question his veracity and aptitude. The narcissist's whole life is a two-fold attempt to both satisfy the inexorable demands of his inner tribunal and to prove wrong its harsh and merciless criticism.

It is this dual and self-contradictory mission, to conform to the edicts of his internal enemies and to prove their very judgement wrong, that is at the root of the narcissist's unresolved conflicts.

On the one hand, the narcissist accepts the authority of his introjected (internalised) critics and disregards the fact that they hate him and wish him dead. He sacrifices his life to them, hoping that his successes and accomplishments (real or perceived) will ameliorate their rage.

On the other hand, he confronts these very gods with proofs of their fallibility. "You claim that I am worthless and incapable" - he cries - "Well, guess what? You are dead wrong! Look how famous I am, look how rich, how revered, and accomplished!"

But then much rehearsed self-doubt sets in and the narcissist feels yet again compelled to falsify the claims of his trenchant and indefatigable detractors by conquering another woman, giving one more interview, taking over yet another firm, making an extra million, or getting re-elected one more time.

To no avail. The narcissist is his own worst foe. Ironically, it is only when incapacitated that the narcissist gains a modicum of peace of mind. When terminally ill, incarcerated, or inebriated the narcissist can shift the blame for his failures and predicaments to outside agents and objective forces over which he has no control. "It's not my fault" - he gleefully informs his mental tormentors - "There was nothing I could do about it! Now, go away and leave me be."

And then - with the narcissist defeated and broken - they do and he is free at last.

Return

THE AUTHOR

Shmuel (Sam) Vaknin

Curriculum Vitae

Born in 1961 in Qiryat-Yam, Israel

Served in the Israeli Defence Force (1979-1982) in training and education units

Full proficiency in Hebrew and in English

Education

1970 to 1978

Completed nine semesters in the Technion – Israel Institute of Technology, Haifa

1982 to 1983

Ph.D. in Philosophy (dissertation: "Time Asymmetry Revisited") – California Miramar University, California, USA
(formerly: Pacific Western University)

1982 to 1985

Graduate of numerous courses in Finance Theory and International Trading in the UK and USA.

Certified in Psychological Counselling Techniques by Brainbench

Certified E-Commerce Concepts Analyst by Brainbench

Certified Financial Analyst by Brainbench

Business Experience

1980 to 1983

Founder and co-owner of a chain of computerized information kiosks in Tel-Aviv, Israel

1982 to 1985

Senior positions with the Nessim D. Gaon Group of Companies in Geneva, Paris and New-York (NOGA and APROFIM SA):
- Chief Analyst of Edible Commodities in the Group's Headquarters in Switzerland
- Manager of the Research and Analysis Division
- Manager of the Data Processing Division
- Project Manager of the Nigerian Computerized Census
- Vice President in charge of RND and Advanced Technologies
- Vice President in charge of Sovereign Debt Financing

1985 to 1986

Represented Canadian Venture Capital Funds in Israel

1986 to 1987

General Manager of IPE Ltd. in London. The firm financed international multi-lateral countertrade and leasing transactions.

1988 to 1990

Co-founder and Director of "Mikbats-Tesuah", a portfolio management firm based in Tel-Aviv

Activities included large-scale portfolio management, underwriting, forex trading and general financial advisory services.

1990 to Present

Freelance consultant to many of Israel's Blue-Chip firms, mainly on issues related to the capital markets in Israel, Canada, the UK and the USA.

Consultant to foreign RND ventures and to Governments on macro-economic matters

Freelance journalist in various media in the United States

1990 to 1995

President of the Israel chapter of the Professors World Peace Academy (PWPA) and (briefly) Israel representative of the "Washington Times"

1993 to 1994

Co-owner and Director of many business enterprises:
- The Omega and Energy Air-conditioning Concern
- AVP Financial Consultants
- Handiman Legal Services - Total annual turnover of the group: 10 million USD.

Co-owner, Director and Finance Manager of COSTI Ltd. - Israel's largest computerized information vendor and developer. Raised funds through a series of private placements locally in the USA, Canada and London.

1993 to 1996

Publisher and Editor of a Capital Markets Newsletter distributed by subscription only to dozens of subscribers countrywide

Tried and incarcerated for 11 months for his role in an attempted takeover of Israel's Agriculture Bank involving securities fraud.

Managed the Internet and International News Department of an Israeli mass media group, "Ha-Tikshoret and Namer"

Assistant in the Law Faculty in Tel-Aviv University (to Prof. S.G. Shoham)

1996 to 1999

Financial consultant to leading businesses in Macedonia, Russia and the Czech Republic

Economic commentator in "Nova Makedonija", "Dnevnik", "Makedonija Denes", "Izvestia", "Argumenti i Fakti", "The Middle East Times", "The New Presence", "Central Europe Review", and other periodicals, and in the economic programs on various channels of Macedonian Television.

Chief Lecturer in courses in Macedonia organized by the Agency of Privatization, by the Stock Exchange, and by the Ministry of Trade

1999 to 2002

Economic Advisor to the Government of the Republic of Macedonia and to the Ministry of Finance

2001 to 2003

Senior Business Correspondent for United Press International (UPI)

2005 to Present

Associate Editor and columnist, Global Politician

Founding Analyst, The Analyst Network

Contributing Writer, The American Chronicle Media Group

Expert, Self-growth and Bizymoms and contributor to Mental Health Matters

2007 to 2008

Columnist and analyst in "Nova Makedonija", "Fokus", and "Kapital" (Macedonian papers and newsweeklies)

2008 to 2011

Member of the Steering Committee for the Advancement of Healthcare in the Republic of Macedonia

Advisor to the Minister of Health of Macedonia

Seminars and lectures on economic issues in various forums in Macedonia

Contributor to CommentVision

2011 to Present

Editor in Chief of Global Politician

Columnist in Dnevnik and Publika (Macedonia)

Columnist in InfoPlus

Member CFACT Board of Advisors

Contributor to Recovering the Self

Web and Journalistic Activities

Author of extensive Web sites in:
- Psychology ("Malignant Self-love: Narcissism Revisited") – an Open Directory Cool Site for 8 years
- Philosophy ("Philosophical Musings")
- Economics and Geopolitics ("World in Conflict and Transition")

Owner of the Narcissistic Abuse Study List, the Toxic Relationships List, and the Abusive Relationships Newsletter (more than 7,000 members)

Owner of the Economies in Conflict and Transition Study List and the Links and Factoid Study List

Editor of mental health disorders and Central and Eastern Europe categories in various Web directories (Open Directory, Search Europe, Mentalhelp.net)

Editor of the Personality Disorders, Narcissistic Personality Disorder, the Verbal and Emotional Abuse, and the Spousal (Domestic) Abuse and Violence topics on Suite 101 and contributing author on Bellaonline.

Columnist and commentator in "The New Presence", United Press International (UPI), InternetContent, eBookWeb, PopMatters, Global Politician, The Analyst Network, Conservative Voice, The American Chronicle Media Group, eBookNet.org, and "Central Europe Review".

Publications and Awards

"Managing Investment Portfolios in States of Uncertainty", Limon Publishers, Tel-Aviv, 1988

"The Gambling Industry", Limon Publishers, Tel-Aviv, 1990

"Requesting My Loved One: Short Stories", Miskal-Yedioth Aharonot, Tel-Aviv, 1997

"The Suffering of Being Kafka" (electronic book of Hebrew and English Short Fiction), Prague, 1998-2004

"The Macedonian Economy at a Crossroads – On the Way to a Healthier Economy" (dialogues with Nikola Gruevski), Skopje, 1998

"The Exporter's Pocketbook" Ministry of Trade, Republic of Macedonia, Skopje, 1999

"Malignant Self-love: Narcissism Revisited", Narcissus Publications, Prague and Skopje, 1999-2013 (Read excerpts - click here)

The Narcissism, Psychopathy, and Abuse in Relationships Series (electronic books regarding relationships with abusive narcissists and psychopaths), Prague, 1999-2013

"After the Rain – How the West Lost the East", Narcissus Publications in association with Central Europe Review/CEENMI, Prague and Skopje, 2000

Personality Disorders Revisited (electronic book about personality disorders), Prague, 2007

More than 30 e-books about psychology, international affairs, business and economics, philosophy, short fiction, and reference (free downloads here)

Winner of numerous awards, among them Israel's Council of Culture and Art Prize for Maiden Prose (1997), The Rotary Club Award for Social Studies (1976), and the Bilateral Relations Studies Award of the American Embassy in Israel (1978).

Hundreds of articles in all fields of finance, political economics, and geopolitics, published in both print and Web periodicals in many countries.

Many appearances in the electronic and print media on subjects in psychology, philosophy, and the sciences, and concerning economic matters.

Write to Me:

samvaknin@gmail.com

narcissisticabuse-owner@yahoogroups.com

My Web Sites:
Economy/Politics:
http://ceeandbalkan.tripod.com/

Psychology:
http://www.narcissistic-abuse.com/

Philosophy:
http://philosophos.tripod.com/

Poetry:
http://samvak.tripod.com/contents.html

Fiction:
http://samvak.tripod.com/sipurim.html

Participate in discussions about Abusive Relationships:
https://plus.google.com/communities/116582645889927140499
http://www.runboard.com/bnarcissisticabuserecovery
http://thepsychopath.freeforums.org/

The Narcissistic Abuse Study List
http://health.groups.yahoo.com/group/narcissisticabuse/

The Toxic Relationships Study List
http://groups.yahoo.com/group/toxicrelationships

Abusive Relationships Newsletter
http://groups.google.com/group/narcissisticabuse/

**Follow my work on NARCISSISTS and PSYCHOPATHS
As well as international affairs and economics**

Be my friend on **Facebook**:
http://www.facebook.com/samvaknin

Subscribe to my **YouTube** channel (280 videos about narcissists and psychopaths and abuse in relationships):
http://www.youtube.com/samvaknin

Subscribe to my other **YouTube** channel (100 videos about international affairs, economics, and philosophy):

http://www.youtube.com/vakninmusings

Subscribe to my **YouTube** channel Vaknin Says:

http://www.youtube.com/vakninsays

You may also with to join Malignant Self-love: Narcissism Revisited on **Facebook** and **Google Plus**:

http://www.facebook.com/pages/Malignant-Self-Love-Narcissism-Revisited/50634038043 or

https://www.facebook.com/NarcissusPublications

http://www.facebook.com/narcissistpsychopathabuse

https://plus.google.com/u/0/111189140058482892878/posts

Follow me on **Twitter**, **MySpace**, **Google Plus**, **Pinterest**, **Tumblr**, **SoCl**, **Linkedin**, or **FriendFeed**:

http://www.twitter.com/samvaknin

http://www.myspace.com/samvaknin

https://plus.google.com/115041965408538110094

http://pinterest.com/samvaknin/the-psychopathic-narcissist-and-his-world/

http://narcissistpsychopath-abuse.tumblr.com/

http://www.so.cl/#/profile/Sam-Vaknin

http://www.linkedin.com/in/samvaknin

http://www.friendfeeed.com/samvaknin

Subscribe to my **Scribd** page: dozens of books for download at no charge to you!

http://www.scribd.com/samvaknin

Return

Abused? Stalked? Harassed? Bullied? Victimized?
Afraid? Confused? Need HELP? DO SOMETHING ABOUT IT!

Brought up by a Narcissistic Parent?
Married to a Narcissist – or Divorcing One?
Afraid your Children will turn out to be the same?
Want to cope with this pernicious, baffling condition?
OR
Are You a Narcissist – or suspect that you are one...
These books and video lectures will teach you how to...
Cope, Survive, and Protect Your Loved Ones!

We offer you three types of products:

I. **"Malignant Self-love: Narcissism Revisited"** (the print edition) via Barnes and Noble or directly from the publisher;

II. **E-books** (electronic files to be read on a computer, laptop, NOOK, or Kindle e-reader devices, or smartphone); and

III. **DVDs** with video lectures.

I. PRINT EDITION

1. From BARNES and NOBLE

You can buy the PRINT edition of "Malignant Self-love: Narcissism Revisited" (May 2013) from Barnes and Noble (the cheapest option, but does not include a bonus pack):

http://search.barnesandnoble.com/bookSearch/isbnInquiry.asp?r=1&ISBN=9788023833843

Or, click on this link - http://www.bn.com - and search for "Sam Vaknin" or "Malignant Self-love".

2. From the PUBLISHER

"Malignant Self-love: Narcissism Revisited" is now available also from the publisher (more expensive, but includes a bonus pack):

More information:

http://www.narcissistic-abuse.com/thebook.html

To purchase - click on this link:

http://www.ccnow.com/cgi-local/cart.cgi?vaksam_MSL

II. ELECTRONIC BOOKS (e-Books)

An electronic book is a computer file, sent to you as an attachment to an e-mail message. Just save it to your hard disk, smartphone, or e-reader (Kindle, NOOK) and click on the file to open, read, and learn!

A library of kindle e-books about narcissists, psychopaths, and abuse in relationships and the workplace – click on this link to purchase the titles:

https://www.amazon.com/author/samvaknin

To purchase the e-books click on these links:

"The Narcissism Series"

Save 63$! Buy SIXTEEN electronic books (e-books) regarding Pathological Narcissism, relationships with abusive narcissists and psychopaths, and Narcissistic Personality Disorder (NPD):

http://www.ccnow.com/cgi-local/cart.cgi?vaksam_SERIES

You can also purchase some of the books comprising the Narcissism Series separately:

1. "The Narcissist and Psychopath in the Workplace"
   http://www.ccnow.com/cgi-local/cart.cgi?vaksam_WORKPLACE
2. "Abusive Relationships WORKBOOK"
   http://www.ccnow.com/cgi-local/cart.cgi?vaksam_WORKBOOK
3. "Toxic Relationships: Abuse and its Aftermath"
   http://www.ccnow.com/cgi-local/cart.cgi?vaksam_ABUSE

4. NEW!!! "The Narcissist and Psychopath in Therapy"
   http://www.ccnow.com/cgi-local/cart.cgi?vaksam_THERAPY

5. "Malignant Self-love: Narcissism Revisited"
   NINTH, Revised Edition - FULL TEXT
   http://www.ccnow.com/cgi-local/cart.cgi?vaksam_MSL-EBOOK

6. "Pathological Narcissism FAQs (Frequently Asked Questions)"
   http://www.ccnow.com/cgi-local/cart.cgi?vaksam_FAQS

7. "The World of the Narcissist"
   http://www.ccnow.com/cgi-local/cart.cgi?vaksam_ESSAY

8. "Excerpts from the Archives of the Narcissism List"
   http://www.ccnow.com/cgi-local/cart.cgi?vaksam_EXCERPTS

9. "Diary of a Narcissist"
   http://www.ccnow.com/cgi-local/cart.cgi?vaksam_JOURNAL

"Personality Disorders Revisited"

450 pages about Borderline, Narcissistic, Antisocial-Psychopathic, Histrionic, Paranoid, Obsessive-Compulsive, Schizoid, Schizotypal, Masochistic, Sadistic, Depressive, Negativistic-Passive-Aggressive, Dependent, and other Personality Disorders!

Click on this link to purchase the ebook:

http://www.ccnow.com/cgi-local/cart.cgi?vaksam_PERSONALITY

NEW!!! How to Divorce a Narcissist or a Psychopath

Divorcing a narcissist or a psychopath is no easy or dangerless task. This book is no substitute for legal aid, though it does provide copious advice on anything from hiring an attorney, to domestic violence shelters, planning your getaway, involving the police, and obtaining restraining orders. Issues from court-mandated evaluation to custody are elaborated upon. The book describes the psychology of psychopathic narcissists, paranoids, bullies and stalkers and guides you through dozens of coping strategies and techniques, especially if you have shared children.

Click on this link now:

http://www.ccnow.com/cgi-local/cart.cgi?vaksam_DIVORCEABUSER

New eBook! How to Cope with Narcissistic and Psychopathic Abusers and Stalkers

How to cope with stalkers, bullies, narcissists, psychopaths, and other abusers in the family, community, and workplace; how to navigate a system, which is often hostile to the victim: the courts, law enforcement (police), psychotherapists, evaluators, and social or welfare services; tips, advice, and information.

Click on this link now:

http://www.ccnow.com/cgi-local/cart.cgi?vaksam_COPING

III. Video Lectures on DVDs

Purchase **3 DVDs** with 16 hours of video lectures on narcissists, psychopaths, and abuse in relationships - click on this link:

http://www.ccnow.com/cgi-local/cart.cgi?vaksam_DVD

Save 73$! Purchase the **3 DVDs** (16 hours of video lectures) + The Narcissism, Psychopathy and Abuse in Relationships Series of **SIXTEEN e-BOOKS** - click on this link:

http://www.ccnow.com/cgi-local/cart.cgi?vaksam_DVDSERIES

Purchase the **3 DVDs** (16 hours of video lectures) + the print book **"Malignant Self-love: Narcissism Revisited"** (ninth print edition) - click on this link:

http://www.ccnow.com/cgi-local/cart.cgi?vaksam_DVDPRINT

Free excerpts from the NINTH, Revised Impression of "Malignant Self-love: Narcissism Revisited" are available as well as a **NEW EDITION of the Narcissism Book of Quotes.**

Click on this link to download the files:

http://www.narcissistic-abuse.com/freebooks.html

Download Free Electronic Books - click on this link:

http://www.narcissistic-abuse.com/freebooks.html

Additional Resources

Testimonials and Additional Resources

You can read Readers' Reviews at the Barnes and Noble Web page dedicated to "Malignant Self-love" – HERE:

http://search.barnesandnoble.com/bookSearch/isbnInquiry.asp?r=1&ISBN=9788023833843

Links to Therapist Directories, Psychological Tests, NPD Resources, Support Groups for Narcissists and Their Victims, and Tutorials

http://health.groups.yahoo.com/group/narcissisticabuse/message/5458

Support Groups for Victims of Narcissists and Narcissists

http://dmoz.org/Health/Mental_Health/Disorders/Personality/Narcissistic

Return

Malignant Self Love
Narcissism Revisited

The Book

"Narcissists live in a state of constant rage, repressed aggression, envy and hatred. They firmly believe that everyone is like them. As a result, they are paranoid, aggressive, haughty and erratic. Narcissists are forever in pursuit of Narcissistic Supply.
They know no past or future, are not constrained by any behavioural consistency, 'rules' of conduct or moral considerations. You signal to a narcissist that you are a willing source – and he is bound to extract his supply from you.
This is a reflex.
He would have reacted absolutely the same to any other source. If what is needed to obtain supply from you is intimations of intimacy – he will supply them liberally."

This book is comprised of two parts.
The first part is an exposition of the various psychodynamic theories regarding pathological narcissism and a proposed new vocabulary.
The second part contains 102 Frequently Asked Questions related to the various aspects of pathological narcissism, relationships with abusive narcissists, and the Narcissistic Personality Disorder (NPD).

The Author

Sam Vaknin was born in Israel in 1961. A financial consultant and columnist, he lived (and published) in 12 countries. He is a published and awarded author of short fiction and reference and an editor of mental health categories in various Web directories. This is his twelfth book.

Made in United States
North Haven, CT
14 October 2021